DOVER
AT WAR
1939–45

Ever since the first Roman invasion of Britain, Dover has been the scene of many conflicts. After the Second World War this part of the country figured more prominently than ever before in the annals of fame

DOVER
AT WAR
1939-45

Roy Humphreys

ALAN SUTTON

First published in the United Kingdom in 1993 by
Alan Sutton Publishing Limited
Phoenix Mill · Far Thrupp · Stroud · Gloucestershire

First published in the United States of America in 1993 by
Alan Sutton Publishing Inc · 83 Washington Street · Dover · NH 03820

British Library Cataloguing in Publication Data
A catalogue record for this book is available from the British Library

Library of Congress Cataloging in Publication Data applied for

Typeset in 11/13 Bembo.
Typesetting and origination by
Alan Sutton Publishing Limited.
Printed in Great Britain by
The Bath Press, Avon.

Contents

*Day by day contemplate your country's power
till you grow full of passionate love for her.
And when you realise her greatness, remember
that it was the dead who won it for you.*

Thucydides

Glossary

AA	Anti-aircraft
AAA	American anti-aircraft
AFS	Auxiliary Fire Service
ARP	Air Raid Precautions
ASR	Air Sea Rescue
CD	Civil Defence
CHL	Chain Home Low (Radar)
CDR	Commander (Royal Navy)
CO	Commanding Officer
DFC	Distinguished Flying Cross
DSM	Distinguished Service Medal
DSO	Distinguished Service Order
ENSA	Entertainments National Services Association
FAP	First Aid Post
FO	Flying Officer
GOC-in-C	General Officer Commanding-in-Chief
HAA	Heavy Anti-aircraft
HE	High Explosive
HMD	Drifter
HMT	Trawler
HMY	Yacht
HQ	Head Quarters
IB	Incendiary Bomb
JG	*Jagdeschwader* (*Luftwaffe* Fighter Squadron)
KG	*Kampfgeschwader* (*Luftwaffe* Bomber Squadron)
LDV	Local Defence Volunteers
Lt.	Lieutenant (British)
Lt.	*Leutnant* (*Luftwaffe* Pilot Officer)

MASB	Motor Anti-submarine Boat
MC	Military Cross
MGB	Motor Gun Boat
ML	Motor Launch
MTB	Motor Torpedo Boat
PAC	Parachute and Cable
NAAFI	Navy, Army, and Air Force Institutes
NCO	Non-commissioned Officer
NFS	National Fire Service
RA	Royal Artillery
RCNVR	Royal Canadian Naval Volunteer Reserve
RNR	Royal Naval Reserve
RNVR	Royal Naval Volunteer Reserve
SS	Steam Ship
Staffel	*Luftwaffe* Squadron
UXB	Unexploded Bomb
WVS	Women's Voluntary Service

Acknowledgements

Nostalgia being a powerful emotion in most people has induced a willingness and generosity in Dovorians, and indeed others, whose invaluable contributions to this work are acknowledged with sincere gratitude.

Winston G. Ramsey, Editor of *After The Battle*; Major General C.A. Ramsey; Major P. Ross; Captain R.H. Clark, MC; John Guy, Chairman, Kent Defence Research Group; Jeremy Wells, Editor, *Dover Express & Folkestone Herald*; Terry Sutton, MBE, *Dover Express*; Bob Hollingsbee, *Folkestone Herald*; J. Lockyer; Reginald Foster; A.E. Whittamore; Ken Flint; David Collyer; Ken Owen; Paul Alexa (USA); Frank Young; Arthur Tolputt; Colin Betts; Roy Hogben; Michael Prior; Jack Hewitt; Finn-Christian M. Stumoen; E.R. Longley; Cyril W.A. Brown, GM; J.G. Harman; O. Ward; Reginald Leppard; W.P. Mills; Christine Waterman, Dover Museum; John Iverson, Dover Museum; Kathleen Harding, BEM; J.E. Dean; Gwendoline Curd; Joan Simmonds; Hannah Menzies; G. Wild; Mary Twyman; John Mellor, *Kent Messenger* Group; Michael Llewellyn; Bernard & Tricia Ashman; P.K. Toynbee; R. Ellis; N.G.A. Sheppard; Kathleen Higgins; Vera Selwood; Kathleen Stanbrook; E.M. Owen; Imperial War Museum; Guy Murchie; A. Doolin; Carla McDonough; Royal Norwegian Navy Museum.

Preface

No town in England had been so much in the world's news, seen through the eyes of visiting journalists. Their colourful stories, full of emphasis, dramatically caught the atmosphere of those traumatic years of 1939 to 1945.

There is little doubt that Dover, with its world-renowned Norman Castle and the white cliffs, became an emphatic symbol of defiance throughout World War II.

Written a generation at least in arrears, this chronicle of events largely depends on source material which has survived. In addition, however, I have set down my own impressions of selected incidents and realizing, none the less, that I have only scratched the surface of it.

While these impressions may be of questionable value when the whole gamut of events are summed up, they may give, on the other hand, some flesh and blood to the skeleton of history. In truth, if it is just a matter of future usefulness, then what matters most, is that the reader may have some regard for Dover and its people.

Maybe it will fall on the shoulders of those who so willingly gave their services to the town – indeed country – for it is to the people of Dover that this book is dedicated.

CHAPTER ONE

1939

Prelude to War

After Neville Chamberlain's radio broadcast at 11.00 on Sunday 3 September 1939, eleven-year-old John Lockyer, a pupil at St Mary's School for Boys, was in his usual place in the church choir, on the decani side, not far from the organ console.

The service had already started by the time a sidesman had handed a slip of paper to the vicar, who nodded in turn towards the organist, George Baggaley, so that he would pause in his playing. Having delivered the dreaded news to the congregation, 'We are now at war with Germany,' the vicar, the Reverend Ritchie, gave an assurance that it was far safer to remain within the church and continue with the service as the air-raid sirens sounded.

'Baggy', the choirmaster, glanced along the stalls to make sure that none of his 'tadpoles' had fled for cover. When the service ended, the vicar told the boys to go on home as soon as possible. John Lockyer recalled:

We left full of expectation. Would our town soon be like those newsreel pictures of the war-torn cities of Spain or China? At home, which was next to the Royal Hippodrome in Snargate Street, my parents were busy making last minute preparations in case of an air raid. All our family necessities were packed ready for a hasty exit to Barwick's Cave about 150 yards away. Everyone in Snargate Street ventured to discuss the topic of shelters with their neighbours, making grim necessity a new dimension of social life.

It was a beautiful sunny day, and as if to defy their fear and uncertainty, large numbers of Dovorians decided to walk along their beloved seafront. Everyone had their gas masks slung over one shoulder, a pale buff-coloured cardboard box hanging from a loop of clean white string. Some, caring little that an air raid might catch them at an awkward stage of dressing or undressing, were enjoying a swim.

With my parents and two younger sisters, I proudly sported my gas mask box and a brand-new pair of long grey flannels. Hoping to see something out of the ordinary – perhaps an enemy aircraft, or even a submarine periscope, I took with me a five-shilling telescope, bought earlier that summer at Brewington's toy shop. The enemy did not appear that day.

When Adolph Hitler and his Nazi Party took control of Germany in January 1933, it was apparent from the onset that the dictator was determined to make war with his neighbours. The subsequent Munich crisis of the early autumn of 1938 really set the seal on Hitler's war-like intentions, and the British Government rose to the occasion by ordering the defences of Great Britain to mobilize.

At Dover, the Kent and Sussex Heavy AA Regiment, RA (TA), were sent immediately to take over the two 6-in guns on the breakwater. There had been little financial support for the coast-defences during the inter-war period and, as a consequence, there had been no significant change in coast-fortifications or the general layout of batteries. Even more disconcerting, no great thought had been given to protecting the coast-batteries against air attack. The breakwater battery stood exposed, not only to gale-force winds and tumultuous seas, but more importantly, was soon vulnerable to low-flying attacking aircraft.

The breakwater battery along with the rest of the Dover defences, stood down at the end of September when the crisis had faded with the signing of the Four-Power Agreement over Czechoslovakia. The Territorials had, by and large, enjoyed their stint on the breakwater, for after all, they had spent ten days there in good summer weather and had received £5 in pay and allowances. The coast-regiments were, on the whole, an enthusiastic bunch, well trained and efficient, despite their ancient equipment.

In March the following year Hitler invaded and took the whole of Czechoslovakia, then, during the summer, he turned his attentions upon Poland. Both Great Britain and France had already pledged their support of Poland and during August the whole situation looked menacing. At once, both at home and abroad, coast-defences were again brought into mobilization. On 1 September 1939, Germany invaded Poland and three days later Great Britain and France declared war on Germany.

Together with their depot ship, the *Sandhurst,* six destroyers of the Reserve Fleet sailed into Dover harbour. As in World War I the harbour became a naval port, headquarters of the Dover Patrol, and under the command of Vice-Admiral Sir Bertram Ramsey.

Town and port were now guarded by six gun batteries. On the shore side there were those of Citadel and Langdon, with four additional sites on the eastern and western arms of the harbour and also the breakwater.

Soldiers watched the final run of the night ferry on 26 August. The last pas-senger sailing on the short sea route took place on 3 September, when the *Canterbury* left Dover for Calais on the final Golden Arrow service before war started. The port was officially closed on 5 September and all civilian cross-Channel traffic was diverted to Folkestone, including the Belgian Marine's Ostend boats. No other vessels from that day onwards were ever allowed to enter Dover harbour without special Admiralty permission.

When the Air-Raid Precautions Act was passed in 1937, the Chief Constable of Dover, Marshall H. Bolt, together with the Mayor, J.R. Cairns, and selected councillors, set about arranging the town's emergency services. The initial response to advertising in the local newspapers and the posters stuck up around the town was encouraging. In the event there was no shortage of suitable volun-teers to join either the ARP, AFS, or any other organization directly associated with what later became known as the Civil Defence Services.

The Chief Constable was in sole charge, for at that time he was also Chief Fire Officer of the Dover Fire Brigade. Within the brief of the Emergency Committee was the provision to acquire suitable basements in the larger store premises, to accommodate townspeople in the event of enemy action. Seven chalk caves already existed and were almost completed and ready for occupation when the Potential Emergency notices were published on 3 August 1939. A fur-ther two were soon ready and the caves were eventually to provide invaluable sheltering, not only for civilians but also for service personnel stationed in the town. Nobody anticipated anything worse than a few desultory bombs falling on the town and most firmly believed that any shelling to come their way would have been fired from enemy warships. How wrong they were.

The Civil Defence structure, incorporating the ARP wardens, got into its stride during the so-called 'phoney war' period, a term which in reality con-cerned only the military in France. But elsewhere there was action enough. The German magnetic mines rapidly became a menace in our home waters because at first there was not the sophisticated defence against them.

The Dover Patrol was, in fact, the Royal Naval Patrol Service, a unique navy within a navy, a fighting fleet of hundreds of coal-burning trawlers, drifters and whalers, commandeered from the fishing grounds and fitted with either a machine gun or a two-pounder. Fish holds became mess-decks, and trawls were quickly replaced by minesweeping gear. Largely manned by fishermen, tugmen and lightermen, their officers were often skippers from the fishing fleets. Some held senior ranks in the RNVR and they, at least, brought some measure of dis-cipline to the service. Later, when asdic equipment was fitted to selected ships for anti-submarine detection, naval communication ratings were seconded.

These weather-beaten craft – 'minor war vessels' the Royal Navy called them

– earned the name of Harry Tate's Navy and, together with an assorted fleet of other light craft, sailed down to Dover from northern ports. Most of them were converted into minesweepers at Dover and were given a white ensign to fly at their mast-head, instead of the red.

Soon to come under attack from enemy aircraft, shell fire and E-boats, theirs was an unenviable existence of minesweeping, convoy escorts, rescuing ships' crews and 'ditched' airmen. Added to this was the spiralling casualties they experienced when they were blown up by the mines they were seeking. The crews required nerves of steel to survive these constant pressures.

In the first few months of the war the trawler *Valdora* ended her days on the bottom of the sea off Dover, together with the *Aragonite* which struck a mine near Deal. The Royal Netherlands steamship *Simon Boliva* was also lost on the South Goodwins Sands, on 18 November 1939.

The two Southern Railway ferry boats *Hampton* and *Shepperton*, were later joined by the coastal mine-layer *Plover* and the cruiser mine-layer *Adventure* at Dover. The crews were a mixture of either Southern Railway employees or RNVR ratings. Every third day each ship took on board from Dover 300 bags of coal and an equal number of the H11 type mine. By December 1939 they had laid between them twelve thousand mines in the English Channel and the approaches to the Thames Estuary.

This defensive measure soon brought results when the German U-boats U12, U40 and U16 were lost in October. The Germans were quick to sow their own mines using minelaying destroyers which caused havoc among British shipping for months to come.

The mines arrived at Dover by rail and when hundreds of tons of chalk land-slipped onto the track between Dover and Folkestone in November, it completely paralysed the supply route. During the blockage, which lasted for five months, thousands of mines were held in Shakespeare Tunnel, before the mine tunnels at East Cliff were completed. The line was cleared in April 1940, just in time for the Dunkirk sea drama.

While the British were sowing mines, so the Germans were similarly engaged, using E-boats and aircraft during the hours of darkness. The German operation took many weeks to complete, and kept the Dover minesweepers busy for many months.

Dover was now protected by two 9.2-in guns at the Citadel, Western Heights, two 12-pounders at the Langdon Battery, two 6-in on Admiralty Pier, and two 12-pounders on the pier extension. A further two 6-in guns were installed on the breakwater, and two 12-pounders on the eastern arm.

Dover Fire Command Post, controlling these guns became operational on 24 August. When Winston Churchill became Prime Minister, however, a review of

Every third day the mine-laying steamers *Hampton*, *Shepperton*, *Plover* and *Adventure* took on 300 bags of coal and 300 mines. Seamen sleep in hammocks on the train-ferry deck beside rows of deadly mines

the harbour defences caused another 12-pounder to be installed at the Admiralty Pier, with twin 6-pounders and two 4-in going to the breakwater – all installed in the following year.

As early as July the town had taken delivery of the first consignment of the Anderson splinter-proof garden shelters, named after Sir John Anderson, the Home Secretary. The shelter was designed to accommodate at least six people and to protect them against bomb and shell. During Dover's Carnival Week in August, one of them was erected in Pencester Gardens to show the public how to use them.

★ ★ ★

THE MAYOR AND AN EMERGENCY

In the event of an emergency arising, the Town Council have been instructed to 'black out' the town at short notice, and arrangements are accordingly being made for the number of public street lamps to be decreased immediately and for the remainder to be put out at short notice.

Arrangements should also be made by house-holders and shop keepers immediately to ensure that none of their lights of any kind is visible from the outside. In an emergency it will not be permitted to illuminate after dark any room in which adequate screening arrangements have not been made.

All electrical and neon advertisement signs should be turned off each night by the occupier before leaving the premises, and in an emergency these signs must not be used at all. It is strongly recommended that house-holders should obtain now a store of non-perishable foods. There will be no further rehearsals of the Town Siren. If the sirens are sounded in the future, it will be a definite warning that an air raid is expected. An air raid warning will consist of a signal by the sirens of TWO MINUTES' duration of a fluctuating or warbling note of varying pitch.

The ALL CLEAR signal will be a steady blast on the sirens of TWO MIN-UTES' duration. Last, but by no means least, I regret to have to state that over 100 volunteers are still urgently needed for RESCUE, REPAIR and DECONTAMINATION SQUADS alone, and volunteers are still required for almost every other SERVICE. The necessity for those SQUADS to be fully manned and trained in the event of war must be obvious to everybody, and I sincerely trust that this appeal will not go unheeded, as the situation now demands that NATIONAL SERVICE should come first.

In conclusion, I appeal to everyone to remain calm. The Council and their officers have everything well in hand and are prepared for any emergency.

Signed J.R. Cairns *Mayor*
DOVER *28 August* 1939

BLACK-OUTS WILL NOT BE OPTIONAL

Should war come, there will be no option as to a BLACK-OUT. In every part of EAST KENT it will be compulsory. NO SIGN of light from houses will be permitted, and those who offend will be liable to heavy penalties as well as public opprobrium. Dark, well-fitting blinds must be fitted to all windows, and to avoid light showing out the sides it may be necessary to paste strips of opaque paper at the sides of the windows. Even temporary lights will be prohibited. If the streets are darkened and electric torches are used by pedestrians they would have to be directed downwards and used as little as possible. By calling attention to these matters, and pointing out that such regulations will be compulsory it is hoped that future trouble may be averted.

In September that year Dover Police Court began to deal with people who, through carelessness, were now being fined the sum of ten shillings (50p) for

Despite Hitler's postponement of his invasion plans, Dover Borough Police Force was issued with rifles. They were already in possession of .45 calibre revolvers, provided under the special emergency established at the Kent Police HQ in April 1939

failing to observe black-out regulations. Within one year, however, to stem the flow of offenders the fine was increased to £3.

In that same month, six hundred Anderson shelters were distributed in the Tower Hamlets district. Records reveal that Dover was one of the first towns to be issued with the new shelter.

URGENT GAS MASK NOTICE

The following notice has been issued. Persons who have not yet obtained respirators should go as soon as possible to 51 London Road, where they will be fitted and supplied. Respirators for babies and young children under five years of age will not be used yet, but parents should give particulars either by post or personally at 51 London Road, of the numbers and ages of their children under five years of age.

Probably the first black-out fatality was that of William Banks, who was knocked down by a bus near Elms Vale Road, while walking his dog on 27 September. The frequency of black-out accidents increased during the first two years of the war, not least because of the phenomenal military presence.

For ARP purposes the town was divided into sectors, divided again into sub-sectors where wardens' posts were installed. Some posts were specially built, solid small buildings, not much bigger than about 12 feet by 8 feet, within which was a double bunk-bed, a small desk, a couple of chairs, and a telephone directly connected to the ARP Controller in the basement of the police station. It was from these posts that wardens were sent out to investigate incidents in their particular area, either on foot or using bicycles.

ARP posts were a vital link in the Civil Defence chain, and both men and women members were to play a prominent part in the town's war. Rescue squads and First Aid parties worked together in whatever circumstances prevailed. Through the many traumas brought about by enemy action they became dedicated to one cause, eventually to become one workable unit of remarkable efficiency.

Extremely loyal to the traditions of their chosen profession the Dover Fire Brigade remained unyielding towards the new auxiliaries of the AFS. The fire station at Ladywell remained a bastion of orthodoxy.

The AFS, which was formed in 1938, quickly outnumbered the regular firemen after the Munich crisis. Over the whole country there were thousands of men and women who signed up and eventually a plan to nationalize them was made law on 13 May 1941. By August of that year all independent fire authorities were absorbed into the National Fire Service (NFS).

At Dover in 1939, the AFS was spread round the town. It was strategically located at Finnis Hill, in one of the caves, at Southern Autos Garage, Castle Place, the Woodlands ARP Depot, Bridge Street, and at Slip Passage close to the harbour.

First Aid teams largely comprised members of the St John Ambulance Brigade – the Dover Nursing Division which received notice to report to the Royal Victoria Hospital. Gwendoline Curd recalls she was notified at the end of August 1939. This was her first location but since things were quiet she volunteered to work at the Isolation Hospital for one year as they were short-staffed. When things became more active she went back to the Royal Victoria to help in the casualty wards when they were preparing for Dunkirk.

At the tender age of thirteen, Muriel Sidwells helped to assemble civilian gas masks at the St James's Boys' School, off Russell Place. She had just left the Holy Trinity Girls' School when war started. Later, when working nearer home, she found a job with a German of Jewish descent, who had been operating a clean-

Dressed in gas protective clothing and carrying their gas masks, nurses at the Royal Victoria Hospital pose for the photographer on the roof in 1940

ers business. He was eventually interned and the shop closed down, but not before the employees had enjoyed their works outing in a charabanc to Southend-on-Sea. They all arrived home to a black-out practice. Muriel recalls:

> It was eerie to find people trying to find their way around with the help of torches and candles in jam jars. We had fixed our blankets at home so that we could open the door onto the street without showing a light. Tin-helmeted ARP wardens were patrolling the streets, shouting at offenders to, 'Put that light out!' Soon after the Prime Minister's broadcast the air raid sirens sounded. We all went out into the street to watch the ARP chaps dashing about blowing their whistles and telling people to, 'Get under cover!' Of course, it was a false alarm.
>
> At that time there were many Army conscripts in the town. Mum and Dad used to invite some of them to our flat in the evenings to share a cup of cocoa or coffee with us. We even made the ration stretch enough to give them homemade cake and toast. Of course, there was very little for them to do in their spare time but to walk the streets. Many of the shops in the town were already closed, the town of Dover was in darkness and they were so fed up.

Servicemen were later told to carry tin helmets and rifles, as well as their gas masks. Problems soon arose in local cinemas when they found difficulty in squeezing between the rows of seats. Often the ALERT would flash on to the screen and they would have to leave in a hurry.

John Lockyer remembers vividly an unrehearsed mishap:

The Royal Hippodrome next to where we lived above my father's restaurant, The Nook, was then the centrepiece of the street. Its management, no doubt wishing to appeal to the tastes of lusty sailors and soldiers, had almost abandoned the traditional music-hall programmes for which the theatre had been well known, in favour of posing nudes. These ladies, usually claimed to be 'from the *Folies Bergère*', rejoicing in names such as Drina or Peaches Weston. By an oversight no doubt, on the part of my parents, I saw Drina, not on the Hippodrome stage so much as off it. That evening, as the stage curtains were drawn back to the tune 'Lovely Lady', revealing the still nude pose of Drina, something dreadful took place. Not only did Drina move, contrary to the rules of the Lord Chamberlain, but so did the whole of the scenery in which the nude lady was seated. This disaster, not due to enemy action, caused the audience to gasp.

Sailors in the front row of the stalls rose to give assistance as Drina vanished in a welter of broken woodwork and drapery. As the orchestra died, the safety curtain swiftly fell into place and the auditorium became a buzz of voices. Presently the theatre manager, in evening dress, appeared over the footlights to assure everyone that all was well, including Drina. With a wave of a hand he then beckoned to Drina, now decently clad in a pink dressing gown, to howls and whistles from servicemen. The disrupted evening at the Hippodrome was concluded with rousing choruses of 'Roll out the barrell' and 'There'll always be an England'.

CHAPTER TWO

1940

'I Heard the Cry Too'

On Monday 8 January 1940 the first food rationing of World War II began. In spite of all the preliminary warnings, however, the Dover Food Control Office was crowded all day with late-comers who had neglected or been unable to carry out one or other of the necessary formalities.

A report stated: 'Henceforth, the weekly ration, which will be strictly adhered to is 4 oz bacon, 4 oz sugar, and these cannot be obtained without producing the ration book and allowing the retailer to detach the necessary coupons. Margarine, of which there is plenty of very good quality, is un-rationed.'

The rationing of meat was started the same day. The public was advised to choose any butcher they liked, and the procedure was similar to the registration for butter, bacon and sugar. Meat was to be rationed on the basis of value. The weight of the ration would, therefore, vary with the consumer's choice of quality.

After 15 January the Ministry of Food was responsible for the purchase of all livestock offered by farmers for slaughter and it was in complete control of all meat supplies, both home-produced and imported. The principle of 'Share and Share alike,' read one notice, 'is the simple justification for rationing, and the rationing of meat is a logical next stage in the application of this principle to war-time needs.'

In early January, on a particularly foul night with strong gale force winds blowing, two trawlers – *Cayton Wyke* and *Saon*, together with a destroyer – received a message that a crossing of a gap in the Goodwin Sands had been detected on the loop cable, connected electrically to a coastguard station. The three vessels steamed up and down just outside the gap, and near to the treacherous sands, dropping depth-charges. They eventually succeeded in driving a German U-boat onto the western end of the Goodwins.

The skipper of *Saon*, William Mullender wrote: 'We went in and saw the U-boat stuck fast on the sands, but we could not approach it because of the strong gales. A cable ship came out to join us from Dover as we waited for the weather

to ease before trying to save the U-boat. It would have been a great prize if captured intact, the first of the war. But as we watched and waited, the sands slowly
swallowed the U-boat and its crew.'

Thursday 7 March
HIS MAJESTY KING GEORGE VI VISITS DOVER

His Majesty King George VI arrived at Dover by special train. Dressed in naval
uniform he went immediately to the headquarters of the Dover Patrol, where he
inspected the crews and vessels of the anti-submarine and minesweeping flotillas.

He was accompanied by Vice-Admiral B.H. Ramsey and he also inspected
the first contingent of the WRNS who, for the first time, were parading in their
new uniforms, in trim navy blue with caps setting off their white shirts.

The King was piped aboard the converted cross-Channel steamer HMS
Hampton, and saw how the mines were stowed and watched ratings demonstrate

His Majesty King George VI visited Dover on 7 March 1940 to inspect the vessels of the anti-
submarine and minesweeping flotillas. His Majesty shakes hands with CPO J.G. Godwin of HMS
Hampton, who received the MBE from the king

their skills in a simulated exercise of minelaying. He was then taken to see the Boom Defence Party on the eastern arm, after which he went to the castle to visit the underground galleries and tunnels in the chalk cliffs. A heavy snow storm brought the King's visit to an abrupt end but he promised to return.

Civil Defence measures were increasing weekly. There was a large number of vehicles to be maintained by the Dover Corporation in connection with the ARP and AFS services, so the Maxton Tram Depot was adapted into a repair garage. When it was discovered that the sandbags protecting the telephone exchange at the Ladywell Fire Station were inadequate, some steel shutters lined with timber were soon substituted.

A circular from the Ministry of Health suggested that First Aid Posts should come under the charge of a private medical practitioner who would receive £75 per annum for his services. Under the general supervision of the Medical Officer of Health his duties would include the running of the posts, training and arranging duty rosters. At this time arrangements were also made for the whole ground floor of the Royal Victoria Hospital to be used as No. 1 First Aid Post (FAP). In the event of an emergency, however, the upper floors would also be used. By this time all patients had been removed to Waldershare Park.

Another circular, this time from the Ministry of Home Security, requested local authorities to review their ARP and AFS organizations with a view to reducing so far as was possible the paid personnel.

Dover Council's proposals with regard to the minimum paid strength of the various services were as follows:

	Men	Women
First Aid Posts	14	37
First Aid Parties	50	—
Wardens	44	6
Decontamination Squads	7	—
Rescue Parties	33	—
Drivers	24	24
Control Centre	3	14
Messengers (Boys)	2	—

PRIVATE SHELTER ACCOMMODATION

The work of strengthening basements in private houses occupied by persons entitled to free shelter accommodation in whose gardens Anderson Shelters cannot be provided was proceeding.

Communal Shelters will be provided at the following localities: Millais

Road – Mathews Place – Pauls Place – Dickson Road – Leighton Road and Victoria Street.

Public Shelter Accommodation. Since the date of the last report the following additional shelters have been completed and brought into use:

Caves. Adjoining Regent Cinema, London Road.
Basements. Dover & District Co-operative Society Ltd Drapery Dept., Biggin Street, Messrs. F.W. Woolworth & Co. Ltd., 62–3 Biggin Street.
Sandbag Shelters. Chapel Hill, alongside Methodist Church; High Street, alongside Maison Dieu Hall; Tower Hamlets Chalk Pit; at rear of No. 51 London Road.

Other Shelters. Railway Arch, Crabble Road; Charlton Girls' School, Barton Road (outside school hours).

The consent of the Ministry of Home Security for a grant not exceeding £2,500, had been received in respect of Lagoon Garage and Beaufoy's Caves extension and connecting tunnels. The Christ Church Tunnel extension was authorized for a further distance of 60 yards in order to increase accommodation.

Further arrangements were introduced to allow shelters to open when the air-raid warning was given by the police, Special Constables, Air Raid Wardens or some other person living in the vicinity. In addition, at certain shelters a small wooden box with a glass front containing a key, so that in the event of the shelter not being opened on the warning being sounded by the person responsible, the glass could be broken and the door unlocked by anyone wishing to take refuge.

★ ★ ★

When the Regional Commissioner had agreed in principle to the construction of wardens' posts, having internal dimensions of 12 feet by 12 feet, they requested certain changes to reduce costs: (a) The reduction in thickness of the roof from 9 inches of concrete to 6 inches, reinforced with steel rods where no load was likely to be encountered, (b) reduction in the internal height from 7 feet to 6 feet 6 inches, (c) the omission of a cupboard for storage, and (d) a reduction in the cost of a chemical closet from £6 to £3. Dover Emergency Committee elected to refuse the request.

ALIENS IN DOVER

The Home Secretary was asked in the House of Commons, if he could state the number of persons of enemy origin living in the protected areas in which Dover was situated. Sir John Anderson replied:

The time available since this question appeared on the Order Paper has not been sufficient to enable me to obtain information except in respect of the Borough of Dover itself, where there are seven persons of enemy nationality registered with the police all of whom have been placed in Category C by the local tribunal.

House of Commons
10 May 1940

Tuesday 14 May
RADIO APPEAL BY SECRETARY OF STATE FOR WAR

The response to the call made by the Secretary of State for War, Anthony Eden, on the wireless on Tuesday 14 May, for volunteers to join the anti-parachute corps has been extremely satisfactory in Dover.' So read the *Dover Express* article on Friday 17 May. It went on, 'Over twenty names had been given in before 8.00 a.m. on Wednesday, and throughout the day there were long streams at the police station, special arrangements having been made to deal with it. Volunteers came from all classes, and included a general, captains, and several musketry instructors. The C-in-C, Home Forces, requested owners of rifles who are willing to lend them to the Local Defence Volunteers to notify the police station nearest their homes, giving details of type and any ammunition held. At the end of the day (Wednesday) over two hundred people had signed on.

On 18 May Captain W. Moore was appointed to command the Dover Company of the 8th (Cinque Ports) Battalion, and on 22 May a meeting of prospective officers was held and five platoons formed. The following Sunday, 26 May, the first of the volunteers went out on night-duty patrols on the hills and cliffs above the town. Towards the end of July, however, at the direct suggestion of the Prime Minister, who had already made a visit to the town, the nightly duties were transferred to the seafront. For close on four years this nightly vigil continued in all weathers and under varied conditions caused by enemy action of one sort or another.

'If in 1940,' Winston Churchill said, '. . . the enemy had descended suddenly in large numbers from the sky . . . he would have found only little clusters of men mostly armed with shotguns. . . .'

DOVER AND DUNKIRK

It was just ten days after Anthony Eden made his appeal for civilians to take up arms that the German Panzer Divisions stood poised to overwhelm the last sea ports remaining open opposite Dover. Here, the British Expeditionary Force, the French and Belgian armies, were trapped in a small pocket at Dunkirk. The formidable German war machine, like a tidal wave, bored through to the French Channel ports mopping up the pitiful remnants of ill-equipped armies.

Four days before, the British Admiralty had been assembling a vast fleet of vessels, which included the most unlikely water-craft ever amassed. There were motor launches, pleasure boats, lifeboats, yachts, tugs, drifters, trawlers, paddle steamers, and any vessels capable of carrying troops across the Dover Strait. The expectations of this conglomeration of small vessels was unknown.

South-east England was faced with the overwhelming task of evacuating thousands of troops from French soil. Dover, like other sea ports in close proximity to France, was soon to cope with the men brought over by the armada of ships and boats, which in just nine days, rescued some 338,000 British and Allied servicemen from harbour and beach.

On the evening of 26 May the Admiralty signalled the start of Operation Dynamo – the evacuation of troops. The name selected for the operation came

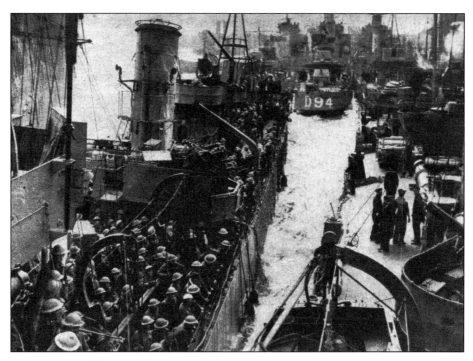

On the last day of the Dunkirk evacuation there were no less than sixty vessels in Dover Harbour. A destroyer, her decks crammed with troops from the beaches, slowly edges towards another berthed alongside the Admiralty Pier

from the dynamo room beneath Dover Castle, above which was the headquarters complex of Vice-Admiral Ramsey who co-ordinated the Dunkirk exodus.

It was a weary and bedraggled force, a large part of which landed at Dover in utter confusion. Although the harbour was considered spacious, having at least fifty mooring buoys in the outer harbour, only the Admiralty Pier was reckoned suitable for the intense disembarkation. Room for manoeuvre within the commercial harbour was limited, but the two Dover Harbour Board tugs, *Lady Duncanon* and *Lady Brassey*, pushed and pulled the ships to and fro from their moorings for either rapid repairs or essential refuelling.

Vice-Admiral Ramsey and his dedicated staff, the rescue ships and their crews, the harbour officials and tugs, the Southern Railway staff, East Kent Road Car Company employees, and townspeople of every vocation, worked ceaselessly. Almost nine hundred vessels, some manned by civilian volunteers, began their epic task of plying to and fro across the Channel, loaded to the gunwales – far exceeding the safety limits, with exhausted troops.

On 31 May for example, 34,484 men were landed at Dover from 25 destroyers, 12 transports, 14 drifters and minesweepers, 6 paddle steamers, 5 trawlers,
16 motor yachts, 12 Dutch Skoots, 4 Hospital ships and over 20 foreign vessels.

The destroyer flotilla leader HMS *Codrington* was ordered on 4 June to evacuate Major-General Bernard Montgomery from the beaches. The fleet oiler *War
Sepoy*, moored in the outer harbour, was almost continuously refuelling every
kind of vessel. Berthed at the eastern arm was the depot ship *Sandhurst*, a mobile
fleet workshop, whose skilled engineers worked many long hours patching up
and making seaworthy damaged ships.

Hitler, realizing that thousands of troops were getting away, ordered air
attacks. A number of the former cross-Channel ferries suffered while laying off
the French coastal ports. The steamer *Canterbury*, for example, took a terrible
pounding at the Mole at Dunkirk. But a few days later, after hurried repairs, she
was once again in the thick of the action.

At the Admiralty Pier the eight berths were soon choked with ships of every
kind. Troops were clambering over the sides from one to the other eventually to

One of several Dunkirk scenes taken at Dover during the evacuation. Troops clambered over the
side of one vessel to reach another, until they eventually reached the quayside, where they were
relieved of their rifles, machine guns and ammunition

reach the jetty. Before their befuddled brains could comprehend they were relieved of their rifles, machine guns and ammunition. Even so, all sorts of weapons were dumped into the sea.

The Marine Station area was, at one time, packed to overflowing. It was here the Dover WVS, YMCA, Salvation Army and civilian volunteers administered tea and sandwiches to soldiers already entrained at the platforms. Whole battalions were assembled and marched along Snargate Street to the lines of East Kent buses. As each ship disembarked its human cargo, a tug would tow it clear of the quayside to refuel, before it returned to the carnage on the French coast.

The carnage and tragedy were not confined to the Dunkirk beaches. The little minesweeper *Nautilus* is just one example. It was almost midnight when an Aldis lamp blinked its message from out of the darkness just beneath the castle. *Nautilus* and *Comfort* edged their way from beside the Prince of Wales Pier, and set course for France. They were just half way across the Strait, carefully negotiating the minefields, when they ran into trouble.

Petty Officer Robert Muir recalled:

It was pitch black and suddenly an E-boat loomed out of the darkness. We had the sauce to engage it with our full armament – one Lewis machine gun. I suppose it thought we weren't worth bothering about, for it went off at high speed. Our skipper was rather pleased with our performance, but shortly afterwards there was a terrific explosion and the next we heard were screaming men in the water. We stopped and picked up nine men as they were being swept past us on the tide. *Comfort* picked up about sixteen. They were all survivors from the destroyer HMS *Wakeful* including the captain.

The E-boat had put a couple of torpedoes into her whilst she was returning to Dover with a load of troops below decks. She had been struck amidships, broke her back and sank almost immediately, taking most of her hundreds of troops down with her.

Comfort was ordered to take her survivors back to Dover but in the chaos and confusion, she was to become the victim of a terrible mistake. Shortly after the *Wakeful* went down, the destroyer HMS *Grafton* was also torpedoed, and both she and the fleet minesweeper *Lydd* opened fire on *Comfort*, believing the drifter to be an E-boat. Tragedy built on tragedy, as *Lydd* rammed *Comfort*, then the drifter's crew were machine-gunned in the water. *Nautilus* escaped that horror but later she was hit by a bomb which exploded in the engine room. She began to sink. Made entirely of wood, she caught alight from stem to stern.

The crew were about to be taken on board the *Gracie Fields* paddle steamer when they spotted another paddle steamer, *Sandown*, about to set sail for Dover.

Both *Gracie Fields* and *Sandown* were among the thirty or so river and seaside paddle steamers which had been painted battleship grey and used for mine-laying duties. *Nautilus* eventually got back to Dover but *Gracie* was bombed and sunk. *Pangbourne*, packed with soldiers, tried to get a tow on *Gracie* with her sweep cable but it was too late. *Sandown*, however, seemed to have a charmed life, and survived in spite of being bombed and machine-gunned.

Meanwhile Lysander and Hector aircraft had been used to drop supplies of food, water and ammunition to the beleagured troops at Calais. A heavy sea mist had suddenly developed at Dover on 27 May when a Hector bi-plane of 613 Army Co-operation squadron was returning to RAF Hawkinge. Plt. Off. Jenkyns managed to avoid Shakespeare Cliff, but was unable to gain sufficient height to clear the hill, above which stood the Citadel Barracks. The bi-plane broke up on impact. Jenkyns was thrown clear of the wreckage but L.A.C. Brown died in the rear cockpit.

On the last day of the evacuation there were no less than sixty vessels in Dover Harbour. The paddle steamer *Whippington* is on record for having carried 2,700 men on one trip. During the nine-day period a total of 327 special trains were used to clear 180,982 troops from Dover.

The epic story of Dunkirk, the bravery, the tremendous loss of life, the carnage and the unforgettable, horrific scenes of drowning soldiers, has been told many times. The courage and determination of both the rescued and the rescuers was evenly matched. This spirit of camaraderie seemed to have rubbed-off on to the citizens of Dover. There is little space here to encompass the depth of unselfish support given for the most part spontaneously to the wounded and the dying.

Can we judge the spirit of the townspeople, given so willingly, by just one person? Dr Gertrude M.B. Toland, F.R.C.S., at Dover throughout the war, is remembered for the long hours spent in the operating theatre, working tirelessly dealing with the many victims of the evacuation period. Somehow, her sterling services rendered to Dunkirk survivors and later to Dover people, was never given official recognition.

Sunday, 1 June
EVACUATION OF DOVER CHILDREN

The evacuation of more than three thousand Dover children to Wales, in respect of the Government Emergency Act, and in conjunction with other towns in the south-east, took place without incident. All the children were housed in the urban and rural areas of Monmouthshire in Wales.

The mayor and councillors were at the station to see the children off to their

IMPORTANT NOTICE

EVACUATION

The public throughout the country generally are being told to "stay put" in the event of invasion. For military reasons, however, it will in the event of attack be necessary to remove from this town all except those persons who have been specially instructed to stay. An order for the compulsory evacuation of this town will be given when in the judgment of the Government it is necessary, and plans have been arranged to give effect to such an order when it is made.

You will wish to know how you can help NOW in these plans.

THOSE WHO ARE ENGAGED IN WORK OF ANY DESCRIPTION IN THE TOWN SHOULD STAY FOR THE PRESENT.

OTHER PERSONS SHOULD, SO FAR AS THEY ARE ABLE TO DO SO, MAKE ARRANGEMENTS TO LEAVE THE TOWN—PARTICULARLY

MOTHERS WITH YOUNG CHILDREN
SCHOOL CHILDREN
AGED AND INFIRM PERSONS
PERSONS WITHOUT OCCUPATION OR IN RETIREMENT.

All such persons who can arrange for their accommodation with relatives or friends in some other part of the country should do so. Assistance for railway fares and accommodation will be given to those who require it.

Advice and, where possible, assistance will be given to persons who desire to leave the town but are unable to make their own arrangements.

Information about these matters can be obtained from the local Council Offices.

(*Signed*) AUCKLAND GEDDES,
Regional Commissioner for Civil Defence.

2nd July, 1940.

(393/4177A) Wt. 19544-30 70м 7/40 H & S Ltd. **Gp. 393**

Issued by the Ministry of Information, leaflets dropped through letter boxes on a regular basis. Few people read them but the more discerning put them away for safe keeping

new war-time homes. The first train steamed out of the Priory Station at about 07.45, with 707 children and 54 teachers and helpers on board. The next train, bearing among others the children of the Boys' and Girls' County Schools, left at 09.20, its total complement being 687 children and 59 helpers and teachers. The third train left at 10.40, with 744 children and 64 adults, and the fourth train, the last, left at 12.40 taking 761 children and 58 adults.

The schools went to the following locations:

Blackwood, Monmouthshire (Bedwelty Urban District): Astor Avenue, St Martin's Boys and Girls, St Batholomew's Boys, Girls and Infants, and River Mixed.
Ebbe Vale Urban District: County School for Boys and St Paul's (R.C.) School.
Caerleon Urban District: County School for Girls.
Cwmbran Urban District: Christ Church Boys and Infants, Holy Trinity Boys and Girls, and Pier Infants.
Blaenavon Urban District: St Mary's Boys, Girls and Infants, and St James's Girls.

Seven Tunnel Junction (Chepstow Rural District): Buckland Girls.
Risca Urban District: Buckland Infants.
Ynysddu and Pontllanfraith (Mynyddislwyn Urban District): Barton Road Boys, Girls and Infants, and Charlton Boys and Girls.

★ ★ ★

ANSWER SENTRIES AND DON'T EVADE THEM

An official warning has been issued that people should approach aerodromes, factories, and any other prohibited places, including field works, gun and searchlight emplacements, only by the recognized entrance, where they will be stopped and called upon to identify themselves. Failure to observe this warning may result in the offenders being fired upon. Already persons have been shot for failing to obey the challenge to stop. People at night should keep to the roads and not cross fields.

★ ★ ★

The Minister of Home Security, Sir John Anderson, strongly urged that persons in Dover and particularly those in responsible positions should remain quietly at their posts and carry on their work. Clear instructions will be given to the civilian population when special action is required of them. At present their duty is to go on with their work and refuse to listen to rumours.

★ ★ ★

SAFETY IN RAIDS

If you hear gunfire do not look out, but get down stairs and away from windows. Splinters from our own shells are a danger that can be easily avoided by this means. If the siren sounds you may be far safer in your own home than if you dash through the streets to some shelter.

★ ★ ★

We shall go on to the end. We shall fight in France, we shall fight on the seas and oceans, we shall fight with growing confidence and growing strength in the air. We shall defend our island whatever the cost may be; we shall fight on the beaches, we shall fight on the landing grounds, we shall fight in the fields and in the streets, we shall fight in the hills. We shall never surrender, and even if, which I do not for a minute believe, this our island, or a large part of it, were subjugated and starving, then our Empire beyond the seas, armed and guarded by the British Fleet, would carry on the struggle, until, in God's good time, the New World, with all its power and might, steps forth to the rescue and the liberation of the Old.

Winston S. Churchill
4 June 1940

After Dunkirk, plans to counter any invasion threat by German forces were implemented. Orders were received to remove all signposts throughout the country, milestones were to be uprooted, and the names of streets, roads and railway stations were either taken down or obliterated.

By July the first line of defence had already begun. Temporary road barricades were being hastily erected at strategic positions on all routes into Dover. These original makeshift barriers, using anything local authorities could lay their hands on were, at a later stage, replaced by the more substantial concrete structures. Beach areas were put out of bounds to the general public and miles of barbed wire cordoned off Shakespeare Cliff and the East Cliff areas. Hundreds of anti-personnel mines were literally planted from the cliff edges and back into the open spaces beyond. The public were discouraged from taking their usual short-cuts across fields. Concrete pillboxes and sandbagged machine-gun emplacements were built all over the place. Some were cleverly disguised as either bathing huts, newspaper kiosks or cafés. Eventually the whole system of first line defence became, more or less, an unbroken barrier.

The purists, however, made their disparaging remarks that nothing would stop the German Panzer Divisions. In hindsight, these meagre defences could have been easily blown up had Hitler's invasion force arrived. But if nothing else was achieved, it gave a sense of confidence to the civilian population who were soon to realize they were in the front line, when they had to negotiate the concrete anti-tank blocks, colloquially called 'dragon's teeth'.

While a strong force of civilian labourers, under the direction of the Royal Engineers, was busy erecting these concrete barriers and other defence works, another contingent was engaged on a more secret project at the packet yard in the docks. No one, outside a select circle, knew precisely what was going on. Men toiled on twelve-hour shifts putting together hundreds of miles of small diameter bore pipes, which were laid eventually along the coast, sometimes hidden in the cliff face while others were submerged beneath the water-line. Had Hitler's troops invaded, as was expected, then they would have been met by a conflagration of ignited oil sent down the pipes.

Winston Churchill, the Prime Minister, was particularly anxious about Dover's defences, and several times visited to personally inspect troops and weapons. He was aware of the imminent build-up of the heavy German artillery batteries on the immediate French coast, right opposite Dover. He had already issued instructions that the high ground on either side of the port be fortified with large-calibre guns to fire across the Strait with some degree of accuracy.

Hitler's invasion plan known as Operation Sea Lion, would have crossed the Channel from the French ports to land just west of Folkestone. The port of Dover, of course, was of vital importance to his plans, and highly trained troops were briefed to sweep round to the east and capture Dover. Had he done so there was little in the way of defence to stop him. Dover's gun batteries, such as they were at that time, like those at Singapore, were facing seaward and not able to fire inland.

The Royal Marine Siege Regiment arrived at St Margaret's Golf Course in mid-July, to prepare the site for the installation of the first of two 14-in guns. The gun, named 'Winnie', was fired on 22 August, with the CO Lt. Col. H.D. Fellowes, RM, and Vice-Admiral Ramsey being present. Three rounds were fired on that occasion, and to the delight of the gunners, they were plotted falling within 300 yards of the target. On a purely historical note it is perhaps worth mentioning that 'Winnie' was the first British land gun to fire a shell onto French soil. Many more were to follow during the course of the war, but the extreme accuracy of the first 'shoot' was, indeed, a fillip to the batch of inexperienced gunners. Of course, there were the sceptics who voiced their opinion that it was 'more luck than judgement'.

The sister 14-in gun named 'Pooh', after A.A. Milne's *Winnie the Pooh* was not in place until November, being installed near Hog's Bush, St Margaret's. Similarly manned by the Royal Marines, 'Pooh' joined in with 'Winnie' to bombard the German long-range guns of infinitely larger calibre, whose batteries were located between Calais and Boulogne. Perhaps the most famous of these German guns was *Batterie Lindeman*, possessing three 16-in guns; *Batterie Todt* with four 15-in guns; *Batterie Grosser Kurfurst* with four 11-in guns, and the four railway-mounted artillery of 11-in guns.

It was the K5 railway-mounted guns which first fired on British convoys passing through the Dover Strait, long before the remainder were encased in their huge concrete casemates on the French cliffs. At that time the British had not installed any guns capable of returning accurate fire. Churchill was incensed with the lack of retaliatory artillery, and in September three new batteries were constructed in the Dover area especially to stop German shipping from moving freely along the French coastal waters with impunity.

The first of these, installed at Fan Bay, were three 6-in guns with a range of 25,000 yards; the next was the more important South Foreland Battery of four

Photographed on 12 August 1940 this
K5 – 280mm railway gun near Calais
was the first German long-range
artillery piece to fire on Dover

9.2-in guns with a range of some 31,000 yards. Last, but by no means least, and
certainly more important still, was the installation of the Wanstone Battery, the
heaviest so far with two 15-in guns with an extreme range of 42,000 yards. Fan
Bay was ready for action in February 1941; South Foreland was next on the list
of 'ready for action' in October that same year, but the Wanstone guns did not
appear on the 'ready for action' list until June 1942.

In order to ease the congestion on the French railway network the Germans
were obliged to send small convoys of cargo ships and tankers through the Dover
Strait, thus providing innumerable targets for the British heavies. Very soon,
however, the Germans were reduced to sending the ships by night.

Later in the war the Dover heavy guns used a new radar system which enabled
enemy shipping to appear on the radar screens with uncanny accuracy. Range,
direction and speed were automatically calculated and the Dover batteries were
able to spot and pick up enemy ships by night or in thick fog.

In addition to the British static guns were three rail-mounted 13.5-in guns
named respectively 'Gladiator', 'Sceneshifter' and 'Piecemaker'; all three had

been relics of World War I. 'Sceneshifter', manned by the Royal Marines, was the first to arrive on 18 September 1940 and was hidden from prying eyes in Guston railway tunnel. Each train was hauled by diesel engines operated by the Royal Engineers and comprised wagons for shells, cordite charges, maintenance and living accommodation.

★ ★ ★

A poem appeared in the *Dover Express* written by an unhappy mother.

Home from morning school they come,
Shouting 'What's for dinner, Mum?
And what's for After's? Rice again!
That blinking stuff gives me a pain.'

Dad, his shoes are through again,
I've mended his trousers – but in vain,
Just look at those mud marks on my floor,
Don't think I'll polish any more.

What's this in his trouser pocket?
Some marbles, a damp squib and a rocket
That's been let off – a piece of string
Oh, and that's not everything.

A piece of plasticine I find,
And – looks like toffee to my mind,
That fondly to the lining clings,
And what? Some of my curtain rings.

'MUM – we're going to be evaporated,
teacher said,
Could I stay up, not go to bed
So early, I've such a lot to pack,
And could you make me a haversack?'

Now they have gone, dear girls and boys,
I sit and sort out all the toys,
That once I grew so cross about,
Threatened so often to throw them out!

'MUM – we're going to be "EVAPORATED", teacher said, could I stay up, not to go to bed so early, I've such a lot to pack, and could you make me a haversack?' Teachers assemble their 'tadpoles' who are about to entrain for Wales in June 1940

The tears fall on a money box,
'Dad, buy me one that really locks,
So's I can save up for a bike
I've seen one that I think I like.'

No 'comics' now upon the floor,
No finger marks upon the door,
The whole house has a hollow ring
Its neatness is an empty thing!

★ ★ ★

SURRENDER OF FIREARMS

It is believed that there may be a number of persons who have firearms or ammunition in their possession without proper authority and that they would be willing to surrender these to the police but for the fear of prosecution.

However, it is already the practice of the police to accept without formality any firearm or ammunition voluntarily surrendered, and there is, therefore, no reason why people should be put off by apprehensions of this kind. The C-in-C Home Forces has already asked all who have 12-bore cartridges in their possession to hand as many as possible into the nearest police station, for re-distribution to the Local Defence Volunteers.

Friday 5 July
17.47 – HES

No ALERT had been sounded – on this, the first day of enemy action to affect Dover. Although a few tentative bombing raids had occurred elsewhere, the nearest at Ramsgate, the bomb which fell in the harbour came from a lone Heinkel 111. Observers noted the aircraft did not show any sense of urgency as it flew away over the Channel.

Three days before, however, Hitler had issued his first directive for the invasion of England which contained details of intense planning at High Command level.

But earlier this day another Heinkel 111 was shot down by Spitfires of 65 squadron, crashing into the sea near Lydden Spout. *Oberfw.* H. Frischmuth and *Uffz.* G. Wagner were taken prisoner by soldiers. *Uffz.* R. Marcklovitz, *Gefr.* F. Burger and *Gefr.* F. Martinek died in the crash, their bodies were later washed up on the beach near Shakespeare Cliff.

Saturday 6 July
05.15 – HES

In the first air raid on the town no siren had sounded, and the first indication that anything was amiss was the machine-gunning of the St Radigund's ack-ack gun site. Bombs were dropped almost simultaneously from the enemy bomber which fell in a straight line from the Abbey ruins to Buckland. Telephone wires collapsed and slates and windows were damaged, but there were no casualties. Sentries saw the raider fly over the town quite unmolested, and when the searchlights eventually flicked on the bomber had disappeared over the sea.

Ack-ack units deployed at the time were few in numbers, by far the greater propor-tion of AA Command units were located on permanent sites using hutted accommo-dation, with a back-up of mobile units which could be moved to any area as required.

The first Heavy ack-ack regiment which moved to the Dover area in early 1940, using the 3-in open-sight guns, consisted of five sites numbered from D1 to D5. Each of these sites was permanent and D1 was located on the Western Heights above Farthingloe Farm, close to the Citadel Battery; D2 was located east of the Langdon Battery site; D3 was opposite the rear entrance to the Duke of York's Military School, at Frith Farm; D4 was on high ground to the north of the St Radigund's Abbey ruins, and D5 was located on the Marine Parade. This latter site was found unsuitable because of enemy air raids and shelling. When the 3-in guns were eventually replaced by the 3.7-in D5 site was moved.

Sunday 7 July
15.55 – HES

The *Luftwaffe* was making reconnaissance sorties along the south and south-east coast. A convoy of ships passing through the Dover Strait came under attack. A Dornier 17 unexpectedly released a single bomb into the harbour and then left. Ack-ack gunners were taken by surprise and just watched the receding aircraft without firing a shot.

Scrambled from nearby Hawkinge airfield, 79 squadron set course for Dover. The CO Sqn. Ldr. D.C. Joslin, was last seen climbing steeply to catch up with the rest of his squadron. But he never made it. He died in the cockpit of his Hurricane when it took the full blast from a prowling Messerschmitt. His aircraft was found in a wood at Chilverton Elms, Elms Vale, on the outskirts of the town.

Monday 8 July
CONVOY ATTACK OFF DOVER

Convoys were steaming through the English Channel in perfect weather conditions. Timed to pass Dover just after midday they were attacked by the *Luftwaffe*. Once again 79 squadron scrambled from Hawkinge. Approaching the convoy's position they were 'bounced' by enemy fighters. Plt. Off. J.E.R. Wood's Hurricane was the first shot down in flames. He was later picked up from the sea by a naval launch but had died. Fg. Off. E.W. Mitchell died in the cockpit of his burning Hurricane when it crashed at Temple Ewell. The remains of the aircraft burned for over one hour and the pilot was only identified by checking the gun numbers.

Wednesday 10 July
FIRST DOVER CASUALTY

Now officially recognized as the start of the Battle of Britain, Fighter Command had been heavily involved in the past few days with many raids. When the convoy *Bread* was approaching Dover, heavy dog-fights ensued, involving more than one hundred aircraft. Bullets and cannon shells, spent cartridges and debris, fell from the sky like confetti.

It was fortunate that only one casualty occurred. An ambulance driver received a bullet wound to his leg. George Knight was standing in a doorway in Matthew Place, near his vehicle, while the dog-fights were taking place overhead.

Saturday 13 July
17.15 TO 18.25 – CONVOY ATTACK OFF DOVER

Another convoy was passing Dover escorted by armed trawlers. Junkers 87 dive-bombers, with a strong escort of Messerschmitt fighters, made their screaming dives upon the slow moving merchantmen.

Hurricanes were patrolling off Dover. Anti-aircraft guns opened fire at everything in sight, and managed to claim a 64 squadron Spitfire flown by Sgt. A.E. Binham. He made a forced landing back at Hawkinge. Then 56 squadron lost three Hurricanes in the mêlée and two Messerschmitts were seen crashing into the sea.

Sunday 14 July
15.00 TO 16.26 – CONVOY ATTACK

There were small convoys steaming through the Strait in both directions. Destroyers, trawlers and other small craft, were making sure the merchantmen kept strictly to the mine-swept lanes. Overhead the Hurricanes and Spitfires patrolled. Again the Stuka dive-bombers attacked and the inevitable dog-fights took place. One was seen to crash into the sea while two others limped back to France severely damaged. Plt. Off. M.R. Mudie's Hurricane was set on fire. He baled out of his stricken fighter within sight of the harbour and was picked up by a trawler. He died, unfortunately, on the following day.

HMS *Vanesa* was hit, just to the west of Dover. Her engine stopped, and she was towed into Dover by the tug *Lady Duncannon*. She was out again shortly afterwards with *Lady Brassey*, to bring in another victim – the SS *Balder* of Bergen, badly damaged at the stern.

The whole action was observed by the BBC commentator Charles Gardner from the cliffs. His broadcast that same evening on the nine o'clock news, was later relegated to the style of a football commentary. Gardner's now famous commentary led to many criticisms of its bad taste. The following letter was received by *The Times*:

Sir,
As a pilot in the last war, will you allow me to record my protest against the eye-witness account of the air fight over the Strait of Dover, given by the BBC in the news on Sunday evening, 14 July. Some of the details were bad

Art Menken, the American news-reel cameraman of *March of Time* fame, shoots sequences during the Battle of Britain, from his high vantage point on Shakespeare Cliff. Soon after this picture was taken Art left for America by Clipper flying boat, via Lisbon

enough; but far more revolting was the spirit in which these details were given to the public. Where men's lives are concerned, must we be treated to a running commentary on a level with an account of the Grand National or a Cup Final? Does the BBC imagine that the spirit of a Nation is to be fortified by gloating over the grimmer details of fighting?

Friday 19 July
12.19 TO 16.54 – HES

The sirens sounded in the town when the destroyer HMS *Beagle* was being attacked outside the harbour by a strong force of Stuka dive-bombers. Although not hit she suffered severe damage. Three hours later the harbour came under attack by another strong force of dive-bombers with a fighter escort. Dornier 17s also appeared to drop over twenty bombs across the harbour installations.

This particular attack clearly indicated to the Admiralty that Dover was no

Stuka dive-bombers attack
Dover Harbour in July 1940,
their silhouette clearly seen
amidst the anti-aircraft shell
bursts. This original print was
stuck firmly to the glass of the
picture frame

place for warships to lay at anchor. Bombs fell across the whole harbour. The
War Sepoy, an oil tanker supplying fuel to naval ships, broke her back when a
bomb exploded close to her. She was later designated unrepairable. The destroyer *Griffin*, the tug *Simla* and the drifter *Golden Gift* were all damaged. There
were no casualties reported.

That morning 141 squadron, flying the Boulton Paul Defiant fighter, had
scrambled from RAF Hawkinge to patrol in mid-Channel. They were attacked
by Messerschmitt Bf 109s of III/JG51. The rest is history. Only four Defiants
returned to Hawkinge, and two of those were so severely damaged they were
immediately struck off strength. One of them, however, with the 'Cock-o'-the
North' motif painted on its engine cowling, ablaze from stem to stern, skimmed
the waves to reach the comparative safety of Dover. Unable to regain height, the
Rhodesian-born pilot Flt. Lt. D.G. Donald guided his severely damaged aircraft
over the town until it crashed at Elms Vale. Both he and his gunner, Plt. Off.
A.G. Hamilton, were killed instantly.

A letter to the *Dover Express* outlined the traumatic events experienced by some adult evacuees persuaded to leave their homes.

Dear Sir,

Leaving Dover, as evacuees on 27 June 1940, for Pembury, we duly arrived about 6.00 p.m. There we were treated well and looked after properly. Then came the transfer. We left Pembury on Saturday 6 July for Weston-super-Mare, at which place we arrived soon after 5.00 p.m., and from there travelled on to Axbridge, arriving about 7.00 p.m.

They received us with the order of women at one table, and men at the other. Our refreshments consisted of a pint pot of tea and bread and margarine. After that we wanted to join our wives for half an hour, but were not allowed to do so. On the following Sunday morning we thought that our wives would join us, but, to our surprise, we were not allowed to even speak to them in the dining-room. One gentleman got up to speak to his wife, but was told to sit down again, and there was to be no talking at the tables.

We found out that we were inmates of the Institution and were under their rules. After speaking to the Master, we were allowed two hours in the afternoon in the church with our wives, but, to their surprise, the Matron wanted to put them in inmates uniforms, which the women refused to do. On the Monday we were given half an hour with our wives, when we discussed whether we should submit to the rules or leave the Institution, and we all came to the conclusion that we would get back home to Dover. One lady, an expectant mother, who came with us, would not stop and left the same night. One husband lost his wife from the Saturday until the Monday. The Master found her some 45 miles away. Another chap lost his sister who was eventually found by the Master at Taunton.

The only freedom we had was to walk around a yard, which was covered with granite chips. Those over sixty-five years of age would be allowed out only once every fortnight. That would have been our position for the duration of the war. All freedom gone!

Could anyone put up with such treatment for we did not ask to be sent away, and I think it is disgraceful to treat us old people in such a manner. My wife could have gone out once a week, in twos, and in the charge of a nurse.

Signed J. Binks
1 Gloster Way, Dover.
12 July 1940

★ ★ ★

Six feet seven inches tall Police Constable 'Tiny' Punter, of the Dover Constabulary, makes
friends with two youngsters in an underground shelter during an air raid

A correspondent wrote in *The Times*:

Here, in this typical coastal defence area a new and more definite meaning attaches to what had become a somewhat loose phrase – the HOME FRONT. The swift and relentless march of events has changed almost beyond recognition the picture that was drawn of this residential seaside resort. Today the HOME FRONT in these parts means guns in action.

The people of this town have grown accustomed to air raids, and there is an element of carelessness in that popular attitude that is causing grave concern to the authorities.

In the past weeks there have been frequent day-light air attacks on shipping and large numbers of people have rushed to the seafront to watch the battles. One day last week a policeman came to one group, reminding them that, 'They all had to lie flat on their stomachs in the road the other day to escape the machine-gun bullets, and if they had not they would all have been killed. It's a crowd like you that they shoot at.' The group was unmoved, 'We've heard that before,' someone was heard to remark.

Alderman F.R. Powell, chairman of Dover Education Committee, said, 'I have done my best to persuade the mothers to send their children away. But if a shell falls on one of the schools while children are at lessons, parents will have no one to blame but themselves'

Saturday 20 July
13.38 TO 18.51 – HEs

Merchantmen of the western-bound convoy CW7 (*Bosom*) had already passed
Dover and were in sight of the Dungeness promontary. The destroyers of the 1st
Flotilla *Boreas*, *Brazen* and *Windsor*, and the armed trawler *Lady Philomena*, were
escorts. They came under attack by Stukas, escorted by an even larger force of
Messerschmitt fighters. Hurricanes and Spitfires were climbing towards them.
The inevitable dog-fights developed which ranged far and wide but the Stukas
were wheeling over the convoy like bees over a honey pot.

The destroyers made smoke immediately to screen the ships. Just about every
anti-aircraft gun in the vicinity opened fire. Then *Brazen* was bracketed by a
stick of bombs, killing one crew member and injuring four others. She came to
a standstill when further bombs exploded at her stern. When the attack ceased
she was taken in tow by a Dover tug. Meanwhile the coaster *Pulborough* had
been sunk but not before her crew were taken off by *Lady Philomena*. The coaster *Westown* was severely damaged and made her way back to Dover for safe
refuge. *Brazen*'s number H80, in white letters and numerals, had almost been

Stuka dive-bombers were soon to demonstrate the vulnerability of British merchant ships in the
Dover Strait. During this determined attack the destroyers HMS *Boreas* and *Brilliant* were forced
to return to Dover harbour with severe damage

stripped from her scarred hull. She was taking in water too fast. Her cable was released, and she sank within sight of Dover.

Thursday 25 July
12.09 TO 20.11 – HES

In a clear blue sky during the evening, a strong formation of JU87s and JU88s, escorted by fighters, were soon to demonstrate not only the vulnerability of merchant ships in the Dover Strait during daylight, but also the destroyer flotillas. The two destroyers *Boreas* and *Brilliant* – both heavily damaged, were forced to return to the doubtful safety of Dover Harbour. The heavily mauled merchantmen of the CW8 convoy scattered in disarray, completely ignoring the minefields.

Journalists rushed to Abbots Cliff to watch the battle. Ship losses included the coasters *Corhaven, Polgrange, Leo, Henry Moon* and *Portslade*. Several other coasters, showing signs of damage, returned to Dover. The small coaster *Summity*, laden with cement, had been hit three times. Two of the crew had been killed and several others wounded. She managed to beach on the rocks at the foot of

Watching an air battle over Dover from the cliffs in August 1940 are American journalists, accompanied by a naval attaché (centre). The girl on the left is Virginia Cowles of the *New York Herald Tribune*, and on the right with the tin hat, is Helen Kirkpatrick of the *Chicago Daily News*

Shakespeare Cliff. Military Police, using a small hut near the sea wall, joined Alf Smith and Jack Funnel in their rowing boat to rescue the crew. The skipper, Captain Milton, with a blood-smeared face, was taken to 24 Old Folkestone Road, where the Pritchard family cleaned him up.

While the dog-fights were wheeling overhead, bombs were dropped across the outer harbour. Occasionally, either a Messerschmitt, Hurricane or Spitfire dived into the sea – lost without trace. The vulnerability of the merchantmen was unquestionable, but the vulnerability of our fighters was quite another matter. Both 54 and 64 squadrons joined in the fray. Two enemy fighters and one Stuka plummeted into the sea, while six Spitfires and two Hurricanes were lost.

Saturday 27 July
12.31 TO 18.37 – HES

In the early hours thunder threatened, and it was not until midday that the first enemy attack on Dover materialized. Messerschmitt fighters, both the twin-engined Bf 110s and the Bf 109s, escorted the Stukas to make a sharp, high-speed attack on the harbour. The anti-aircraft guns opened fire, but in ten

The water in Dover harbour erupted in huge spouts as the Stuka dive-bombers made their characteristic, screaming dives. Minesweepers and smaller craft bobbed about like corks on a pond

minutes the ALL CLEAR signal sounded. The ALERT went off again just after 14.30 when more Stukas suddenly appeared out of the sun. They peeled off, one after the other, diving almost vertically to release their bombs from about 1,000 feet. Huge plumes of water rose up into the air while the sky became pock-marked with exploding ack-ack shells. Ships pitched and rolled in the disturbed water, and the destroyer *Walpole* was put out of action.

A second wave of Stukas arrived two hours later to repeat the earlier performance. Anti-aircraft guns put up a fierce barrage, which caused most of the bombs to fall outside the harbour walls. A third raid was more successful.

Tied up to the eastern arm was the flotilla leader HMS *Codrington*, the destroyer which had conveyed the Dutch Royal family from Ijmuiden to Harwich on 12 May when Holland was overrun by the Germans. She had also carried H.M. King George VI to France and back on 10 December 1939.

She was lying alongside the Royal Navy supply ship *Sandhurst*, when a stick of bombs exploded beside her. The underwater explosions broke her back and she began to settle in the water. *Sandhurst* was heavily damaged by exploding ammunition going off on the crippled destroyer's deck as she sank.

When the news broke that several vessels of the Dover flotilla had been either damaged or sunk over the past few days, the Admiralty decided to move the vulnerable destroyers to safer ports. Their decision was helped by the recent RAF reconnaissance photographs which showed the Germans preparing their heavy coastal gun sites near Calais.

Monday 29 July
07.19 TO 08.25 – HES

Swingate radar revealed a build-up of enemy formations over France. When the sea mists dissipated, over forty Stukas with escorting fighters were heading for Dover. Fighter Command scrambled its nearest squadrons to intercept. The harbour soon erupted with huge water spouts as the dive-bombers made their characteristic, almost perpendicular screaming dives. The little minesweepers bobbed about like corks on a pond.

The anti-aircraft guns put up a formidable barrage. There was little time to identify individual targets. Hurricanes, Spitfires, Messerschmitts and Stukas, wheeled in the cloudless sky like a horde of locusts. Bullets and cannon shells ripped along the harbour walls. Every Royal Navy ship fired its two-pounders, pom-poms and Lewis machine guns. The townspeople ran for shelter.

HMS *Sandhurst* was raked with cannon shells from bow to stern. By 07.45 four Stukas had been shot down, quickly followed by a Hurricane and a Spitfire. The 10,000-ton depot ship was nearly lost when set alight by incendiary bullets.

The 10,000-ton naval supply ship HMS *Sandhurst* was attacked by Stuka dive-bombers on 29 July 1940. Dover firemen tackled the twelve-hour blaze. Disregarding the torpedoes, ammunition and fuel oil in the holds which threatened to explode at any minute, three firemen were later awarded the George Medal

It was also feared the ammunition and torpedoes in her holds would explode. For over twelve hours Dover firemen poured thousands of gallons of sea water into her holds, and sprayed foam over the superstructure. Then they discovered they were surrounded by oil leaking from a nearby ship. The *Sandhurst* survived, and two weeks later, while Dover firemen pumped out her holds, she was towed to the Thames for repairs.

Friday 9 August
17.11 TO 17.32 – DOVER BALLOONS ATTACKED

In late July No. 961 Balloon Squadron, RAF, arrived from 1 Balloon Centre, Kidbrook, to supplement the Dover defences. Perhaps unwittingly, they became more famous than any other in the British Isles. The success of any balloon barrage was to keep hostile aircraft above a certain height restriction, thus denying accurate bomb-aiming.

This tranquil scene of Granville Gardens in 1940 was soon to erupt in frenzied activity when Messerschmitt fighters suddenly appeared.
Incendiary bullets and cannon shells seared into buildings like hot pokers.
Barrage balloons were easy targets

'A' Flight had their HQ at the Dover College, while 'B' Flight used the old Castlemount School. Later on both headquarters were based at the Girls' County School, Frith Road.

Balloons and the ancillary equipment were strategically sited near the long-range guns at Broadlees Meadow, at the Boys' County School playing fields, Astor Avenue, the Crabble Athletic Grounds, Connaught Park, Cherry Tree Avenue, Granville Gardens, Aycliffe and the Admiralty Pier. Others were carried by minesweepers and small craft, used to escort convoys through the Strait.

The reason for 961's notoriety was the frequency with which their balloons were shot down in flames by the indomitable Messerschmitt fighters. It happened almost every day during one particular period, and had become a sort of ritual. This Friday was no exception. *Luftwaffe* pilots seemed to enjoy the challenge, openly defying the ack-ack to shoot them down. In hindsight, however, the whole exercise was both foolhardy and unproductive for some of Germany's élite fighter units.

When the yellow-nosed Messerschmitts appeared, airmen of 961 Balloon Squadron dived for cover in their flower-bed trench in Granville Gardens. Thin corrugated sheet-iron, however, was no match for well-aimed machine-gun fire

As for 961's personnel they simply put up another new balloon as quickly as possible. But all too frequently balloon cables snapped in high winds, and runaway balloons careered across the town and port trailing their wire cables, dislodging chimney-pots, and causing havoc on roads and railways.

Sunday 11 August
07.45 TO 08.42 – MESSERSCHMITT ATTACK

German fighter sweeps were operating along the south coast on most days. Many of them were made at extreme low level and the two fighters which managed to shoot down a couple of barrage balloons had entered British airspace before anyone was aware of them. The sirens went off just before the first balloon caught alight in a shower of sparks at the Crabble Athletic Ground. The next to do down in flames was swaying above Cherry Tree Avenue. Then the gasworks buildings in Union Road came under a fusillade of cannon shells. The fighters disappeared as quickly as they had arrived, leaving behind damaged houses in Randolph Road and burning sheds at the gasworks. There were only two slight casualties reported.

Soon afterwards a couple of twin-engined Messerschmitt Bf 110 fighter-bombers made a lightening attack on the harbour. No significant damage was reported. Then a strong force of single-engined fighters flew in a few hours later. During the inevitable dog-fight Plt. Off. P.C.F. Stevenson was shot down in his Spitfire. He managed to bale out and was picked up from the sea by a passing minesweeper. Captain Arnold, RA, in charge of the guns on the eastern arm, blazed away with a Bren Gun that was 'acquired' from the skipper of HMS *Sabre* when it had arrived from Dunkirk. Although Arnold afterwards declared that he never hit anything, he said, '. . . it was good for morale.'

Monday 12 August
10.11 – SHELLS

Part of Goering's plan of attack, outlined in Hitler's Directive No. 17, was to launch air attacks against our front-line airfields and radar towers on the coasts. These attacks were known as *Adlerangriff* (Attack of the Eagles), and *Adler Tag* (Eagle Day) was due to start on 13 August. The *Luftwaffe* were out in force along the coasts the day before Eagle Day, and there were many skirmishes around Dover.

No ALERT had sounded when an explosion occurred at St Radigund's Road, just after 10.00. A couple of minutes later there was another at Minnis Lane, then others at Prospect Place, Victoria Street and Noah's Ark Terrace.

Military observers were scanning the clear, blue sky for enemy aircraft, while gunners ran to their positions. The huge radar towers behind the castle came under attack from Stukas. Fortunately the towers remained standing although feeder cables were severed in many places and some small wooden huts collapsed in the blast.

As for the mysterious explosions in the town, they came from the first shells fired onto British soil by the German long-range guns. The more permanent concrete gun emplacements were still being built, and these shells had been fired from the 280-mm K5 railway-mounted guns, operating on existing French rail track near Sandgatte.

Four houses were demolished in Noah's Ark Road. Casualties were recorded as five, three seriously injured and two fatal. Thirty-eight-year-old Helen Barker, a member of the St John Ambulance Brigade, lost her life in St Radigund's Road, as did Alfred Reid, who was so seriously injured he died before reaching the casualty hospital in Union Road. Helen's husband was driving the ambulance that was sent to the incident.

Rescuers attending the demolished houses found the first was unoccupied. At No. 2 the occupant and her daughter were found in their shelter suffering from shock. The occupant of No. 3 was also in a shelter, but the man in No. 4 was in his bedroom when the building collapsed around him. He only suffered slightly.

Wednesday 14 August
11.57 TO 14.21 – HES

Enemy aircraft was reported by Dover radar forming up over the Pas de Calais. The sirens sounded. Stukas, Junkers, Heinkels and Messerschmitts comprised this massive aerial armada. It was met, fortuitously, by four of our fighter squadrons. As could be expected, with about 200 aircraft meeting head-on over Dover, a tremendous air battle ensued. Several bombs were jettisoned over the harbour. During this mêlée a small group of enemy fighters detached themselves from the main force to shoot down eight balloons. These deflated 'pigs', as they were sometimes called, fell over the town, their cables dragging through the deserted streets taking with them fences, trees and chimneys. Beaconsfield Road was blocked by one of them for over two hours. Two Hurricanes plummeted into the sea – their pilots lost, but four Stukas were shot down and another four Messerschmitt Bf 109s. Perhaps the saddest loss was the unarmed South Goodwin lightship, dive-bombed and sunk by Stukas. There were no casualties reported in the town.

Sunday 18 August
10.00 – IBS

Canisters of incendiaries were dropped from a German bomber as darkness fell. It was the end of a disastrous day for the *Luftwaffe*, which had lost more aircraft than they were willing to admit. No ALERT had sounded when individual bombers penetrated our defences on widespread nuisance raids. Searchlights flicked on while ack-ack gunners tumbled from their beds. White-hot incendiaries straddled Castle Avenue. Some had fallen within the castle grounds. The AFS and Dover Fire Brigade managed to bring the small fires under control within the hour. There was little damage and no casualties.

Monday 19 August
15.05 TO 15.25 – HES

Dover radar indicated about sixty enemy aircraft, strung out at 20,000 feet between Dungeness and the North Foreland. The anti-aircraft gun barrels swung round and elevated to almost their maximum height. The crews waited intently for the order to fire. The drone of aero-engines, unmistakably German, filtered down through the cloud base. The drone of engines gradually moved away to the east. Everyone relaxed. Gun barrels returned to their horizontal positions.

Then just after 15.00 two Junkers 88s, at no more than 1,000 feet, swept in over the cliffs between St Margaret's and Swingate. High explosives fell on the vacated married quarters in St Margaret's Road, on Edinburgh Hill, Northfall Meadow, behind Victoria Park and at Castlemount. Blast damage was quite severe but there were no casualties reported among the civilians. The reverse was the case when bombs fell exploding within the castle grounds. There were several military casualties. Telephone wires were a complete shambles and were strung over trees like spaghetti.

Thursday 22 August
11.00 TO 23.20 – SHELLS

By August 1940 German High Command had assembled an impressive artillery of the K5 long-range railway guns. Their prime task was to bombard British shipping and selected military targets. In addition, they were involved with Operation Sea Lion, and would have dominated the narrow waters, even before the invasion fleet was to sail for England.

This particular outbreak of shelling was aimed at a convoy called *Totem* slowly passing through the Strait. The ships crews, not unnaturally, thought they were being attacked by unseen aircraft from above cloud. The 80-minute bombardment, however, failed in sinking any ships, although several shells over-reached their target and fell in the outer harbour.

No ALERT had gone off, but at 21.00 two shells struck No. 103 Maison Dieu Road. Two people were being rescued from the damaged building when the siren sounded. About 15 minutes later another shell exploded on Garden Hall in Cherry Tree Avenue, and further shells straddled Valley Road, River, where Nos. 2, 3 and 4 Valley Road were severely damaged. About twenty minutes elapsed before other shells hit the gasworks, severing all supplies to the town and starting fires. While the AFS attended at that scene, St Barnabas Church was severely damaged by another shell.

Military authorities estimated that over thirty shells had hit the town, resulting in seven people being seriously injured with a further two slightly injured.

★ ★ ★

It was on this day, incidentally, that Air Marshal Arthur Harris sat on an Air Ministry meeting to organize the long-overdue Air Sea Rescue Squadrons. Hitherto any rescue attempts of pilots and air crew from the sea had been a hit-and-miss affair, and the loss of pilots through drowning had caused much anxiety.

Eventually No. 27 M.C.U. (Marine Craft Unit) was established at Ferry House, Dover. Using HSLs (High Speed Launches), the RAF now shared their duties of rescuing 'ditched' airmen with the Royal Navy's RMLs (Rescue Motor Launches). In addition to the specially designed and equipped RAF craft, there were other ships to assist airmen in distress. Not least were the armed trawlers and minesweepers on convoy escort duties.

Launches were berthed in the Ferry Dock, sharing facilities with the Coastal Force Motor Torpedo Boats (MTBs) and Motor Gun Boats (MGBs). In 1941, when the RAF was increasing its operational sweeps to attack enemy installations in France, the ASR boats were at sea most of the time. They usually waited at pre-arranged rendezvous positions, either at the North or South Foreland, Goodwin Sands or at Dungeness.

Sometimes the launches were moved to the so-called Submarine Pens at the Camber. Wellington Dock was another venue where boats tied up in close proximity to the stage door of the Royal Hippodrome. Crews would often visit the stage bar where they rubbed shoulders with the current stars.

The danger of attack by enemy fighters was always present. German pilots ignored the yellow-painted decking. Defensive armament on the earlier boats was two Lewis machine guns, one in each turret, later replaced by twin Vickers. The final improvement was to re-locate the Vickers astern and have gas-operated Brownings in the turrets.

In most weather conditions, negotiating minefields often followed by menacing E-boats and being shot up by enemy fighters, the ASR crews performed magnificently in saving life.

Saturday 24 August
10.05 TO 16.02 – HES – SHELLS

Dawn broke fine and warm with a cloudless sky. People out shopping ignored the siren that sounded just after 10.00. Dover radar showed a big raid building up over Cap Griz Nez. The sky became black with enemy aircraft gradually moving towards Dover from between 12,000 feet and almost 20,000 feet. The formation split into two separate groups, one heading further inland while the other made for Dover. The Dover raid was intercepted by our fighters and the formation broke up. In the event only two bombs fell on the town, others

Escorting JU88s attacking RAF Manston on 24 August 1940, *Oberfeldwebel* F. Beeck, of 6/JG51, managed to crash-land his Messerschmitt BF109E-4 after combat with Hurricanes of 32 squadron, beside the A258 Dover to Deal road, at 12.55 p.m. The pilot was captured unhurt

exploded in fields on either side and in the sea. One high explosive fell in Malvern Meadow causing little damage and no casualties, but the other made a direct hit on 31 Avenue Road.

A crowd soon gathered at Avenue Road where the police had erected a barrier. Wardens and policemen were searching the wreckage while ack-ack shells burst over the town. RAF fighters were flying through the barrage despite the danger, the pilots intent upon shooting down their quarry.

There was a shout from a tunnel beneath the debris when a six-month-old baby was found still alive in a pram. Then they found the mother, nineteen-year-old Ruby Tallent – dead. Her six-year-old sister Pearl was found unhurt on the settee.

Plt. Off. J. Lockhart's Hurricane tumbled over onto its back when an ack-ack shell exploded beneath it, but he managed to crash-land at RAF Hawkinge. A launch left the Prince of Wales Pier to pick up Plt. Off. C. Stewart who had baled out of his Spitfire.

At 15.00 another dog-fight happened over the town. Barrage balloons were swinging on their cables and were as much a menace to our fighters as those of the enemy. Plt. Off. K. Pniak, a Polish member of 32 squadron, baled out of his

Hurricane just before it dived into the Camber. Alert gunners on the eastern arm fished him out of the water. Pniak remonstrated with his rescuers who were about to send him to hospital. His persuasive Polish tongue got him a lift in an army staff car which took him back to RAF Hawkinge. Almost an hour later he was shot down again, crashing at Rhodes Minnis near Lyminge. This time he went to hospital.

Most of the day's battles were being fought further inland. At 16.02 a shell exploded near Yew Tree Cottage, River, damaging several properties. There were no casualties.

In the evening RAF bomber squadrons launched attacks on the German invasion barges lying in the French ports. A Blenheim of 53 squadron, based at Detling, was returning from the raid. The barrage balloons were still up and the inevitable happened. The Blenheim struck a balloon cable near Astor Avenue.

PC Bill Maycock had just arrived home at 15 Chevalier Road, Elms Vale, when the plummeting bomber spun into his home. Thirty-one-year-old Bill, police boxer, swimmer and water-polo player, died with his wife Mary when the house collapsed.

The rescue teams took many hours to find them in the debris. It seemed fated that Bill and Mary should die together. For not only had he just arrived home, but Mary had returned that week from Southall, where she had been visiting her two children. She was due to return the following day.

The charred remains of the Blenheim crew, Fg. Off. Rochford, the pilot, Sgt. Briggs and Sgt. Brook, were recovered the next day. Several houses were badly damaged when the Blenheim's fuel tanks exploded. There were two people injured.

★ ★ ★

LAND-MINE TRAGEDY

EARL GUILDFORD'S SON AND DAUGHTER KILLED ran the headline in the *Dover Express*.

We regret to record the deaths of Lord North, son and heir of the Earl of Guildford, of Waldershare Park, and his sister, Lady Cynthia Williams, the Earl's only daughter. They were killed on Sunday, 25 August 1940, when they trod on a land-mine. Lady North was found seriously injured.

The party were taking a walk in the grounds at the time and ventured into a prohibited area surrounded with barbed wire. So violent was the explosion that it could be heard several miles away.

Lord North, who was 38, was descended from the Lord North, Prime Minister of England from 1770 to 1781. Giving evidence at the inquest, PC

Lutman said, 'There were no notices displayed warning the public of the minefield, although it was surrounded by barbed wire.' Pieces of clothing and a handbag were all that remained as evidence of the tragedy.

★ ★ ★

CAVE LAW

Some people who love that sense of absolute security which is to be obtained from being in one of Dover's many deep cave shelters, are taking an unfair advantage of the facilities available. It is absolutely forbidden for them to 'stake a claim' to any particular part, and to leave articles of furniture, rugs, blankets, etc., in the caves.

In the first place, it is most likely that illness and death will quickly result if blankets, etc., are allowed to remain in the damp atmosphere of underground passages. Rheumatism and lung diseases are certain to come to those who do this. The chance of being bombed is, in comparison, about a thousand to one against.

A second reason why this use of caves is prohibited is that if too much room is taken by the few, the shelters will not provide adequate protection for the many who, whilst carrying on their work, may in an emergency have to make use of shelter. Another rule that is likely to be more strictly enforced soon is that those coming early must go right into the interior, and not block up the part near the entrance.

In Winchelsea Tunnel the dangerous practice of making use of oil stoves has been reported. Owing to the strong current of air, there is a danger of fire and a little carelessness might make the place a blazing furnace.

The few people who feel that they can only rest in these caves, and haunt them, would be well advised to leave Dover, if they cannot pull themselves together. Too many parents are keeping young children here. They are an anxiety to themselves and a liability to the authorities responsible for Air Raid Precautions.

Dover Express Editorial

Wednesday 28 August
15.53 TO 17.47 – CHURCHILL'S VISIT

Winston Churchill travelled down to Dover on a snap visit to inspect the deep casemates beneath the castle in which were the plotting rooms for all three services. Standing on the balcony overlooking the harbour, he witnessed a

The Prime Minister, Winston Churchill, visited Dover on numerous occasions. Seen here on 28 August 1940, at the entrance to the deep casemates beneath the Castle, he was accompanied by Dover's Mayor 'Jimmy' Cairns, with Churchill's bodyguard Inspector Walter Thompson walking behind

dog-fight over the Channel. He also saw the firing of a Parachute and Cable (PAC) anti-aircraft device from the Admiralty Pier. PAC was a bizarre invention designed to supplement the small arms to combat low-flying enemy aircraft. Theoretically, the rocket projectile would reach a height of about 600 feet trailing a wire behind it.

A sudden jerk of the wire released a small parachute with a small explosive charge attached, hopefully in the path of an enemy aircraft. While Churchill watched, rockets hurled into the sky in all directions. Most of them crossed the path of another, allowing the wires to become hopelessly entangled. The combined weight of enmeshed wire, spent rocket and parachute, caused the contraption to plummet to the ground. One of them fell in Snargate Street, and went through the roof of the *Dover Express* office. It was quickly followed by another which bounced in the street and shot through the window of Weirs chemist shop.

Churchill watched the fighters in combat with intense interest, following the action through a pair of naval binoculars. He was later informed that an aircraft

Hauptmann Artur Dau, shot down by Sqn. Ldr. Peter Townsend on 28 August 1940 near Hougham, Dover, speaks to P.C. Hills, while Jack Wood of the local Home Gaurd, Cyril Souton, ARP (in tin helmet) and Mr Worrall, look on with interest

had crashed behind the castle. He asked to be taken there. He was accompanied by Inspector Walter Thompson, his personal bodyguard, and several army officers, and visited the site where a Messerschmitt Bf 109 had crashed and disintegrated. Churchill enquired, 'Is he one of their lads?' When told that it was, he replied, 'Good! That's another on the long list.'

Saturday 31 August
07.59 TO 11.30 – CANNON SHELLS

The sirens went off just before 08.00. Of the four enemy formations reported by radar heading for Dover, one of them broke away while the others continued inland.

Twenty-two balloons were swaying in the early morning breeze, waiting to be shot down by the audacious Messerschmitts. Four of them, their engine cowlings painted yellow, suddenly appeared from out of a hazy sun. They began, systematically, to shoot the balloons down – one by one.

Told that an aircraft had crashed at Church Whitfield, the Prime Minister asked to see it. 'Is it one of their lads?' he enquired. When told it was, Churchill replied, 'Good! – That's another on the long list'

The equation of approximately £5,000 per fighter, against more than a dozen balloons for the same price, just did not add up. The value of a fully trained fighter pilot, with such high losses, must have been incalculable.

Reginald Foster, special correspondent for the *Daily Herald* wrote:

> Most of the pilots in the 'balloon potting squad' seemed to be crack men. Their daring wins admiration, even from the balloon men who have to run out and struggle with thousands of feet of twisted wire and burning fabric before a new balloon can be run up. 'You knock 'em down, we put 'em up,' is the motto of the balloon barrage men, chalked on the side of their lorry.

The first balloon to go down was that above Admiralty Pier, the next at the Dover College ground. One fell in flames at the junction of Folkestone Road and Elms Vale Road, and set light to 189 Folkestone Road.

Incendiary bullets and cannon shells seared into buildings like red hot pokers. A middle-aged woman at the Globe Inn, Peter Street, was hit in the thigh but refused hospital treatment. The man who was hit in the chest while standing at his front door in Noah's Ark Road, was carried off on a stretcher. Another house-fire occurred at 162 Lewisham Road. Stray cannon shells ripped into the roof when the Crabble Athletic Ground balloon came down in flames.

The Dover College balloon had fallen behind Boots the Chemist, and

There were twenty-two barrage balloons flying above Dover, just swaying in the early
morning breeze, waiting to be shot down by
the audacious yellow-nosed Messerschmitts.
Reginald Foster was the *Daily Herald* correspondent in Dover, and often called them
the 'balloon potting squads'

F.W. Woolworth's store. Small fires broke out in a number of streets. The matron
at the Isolation Hospital phoned to say a burning balloon had dropped in the
grounds and every building had cables wrapped round it.

The Record of Incidents page states:

10.11 hrs – Cannon Shell – 41 Edred Road. 2 casualties, 1 male and 1 female.
Injuries caused by taking a cannon shell into house, and male casualty hitting
it with an axe. Injuries to legs. Not detained.

Sunday 1 September
10.46 TO 12.14 – MESSERSCHMITT ATTACK

Dover radar showed the inevitable build-up of enemy formations assembling
over the Pas de Calais. The siren went off just as enemy fighters came in to
shoot down the balloons. Ack-ack gunners had already been 'stood to' since

before breakfast. Four ME 109s suddenly appeared over the harbour area. The high-speed whine of aero-engines under full power, coupled with ack-ack gun fire and the ripping sound of machine guns, sent people running for shelter. Bullets struck windows, masonry and streets but young boys peered out from behind walls to watch the action. They became expert in aircraft identification and knew instinctively the difference between one type or another. In the streets, hands on hips, and with the confidence of youth, they would shout at the top of their voice, 'It's Jerry!' or 'They're ours!'

On the following day a Messerschmitt Bf 110 was shot down in combat to crash-land near St Radigund's Abbey. The pilot, Lt. G. Schipper set light to his aircraft before being captured. The other crew member, *Gefr.* T. Schockenhoff, had managed to bale out. He was later captured unhurt at Alkham.

★ ★ ★

At Dover Police Court on Monday 2 September, twenty-three-year-old Julianne Meszaros was summoned for being in the protected area of Dover, on 31 August 1940, without written permission from the Chief Constable of Kent, contrary to the Aliens (Protected Areas) (Part 4) order 1940. She was seen at 15.00 on Saturday, at Dover Priory Station, by a police constable. He asked if she had permission to be there, and she replied, 'No.' She was in possession of her passport and Aliens Registration Certificate, which left no doubt that she was an Hungarian subject. When asked her object in coming to Dover, she said she wanted to get a boat to return to Hungary. She was committed to prison to await internment.

★ ★ ★

CHILDREN STILL IN DOVER

Councillor Walker said, at a council meeting, he understood that there were about eight hundred children in the town. Could not something be done, he said, about letting the children have home lessons? The Chairman replied that they had not got the staff to deal with it. All the staff were in Monmouthshire. Councillor Walker said that he meant they might have books at home so that their parents could help them. The Chairman said that all the books had been sent to Wales. Councillor Law remarked that parents should be made to send their children away.

Saturday 7 September
15.49 TO 19.00 – HES

This Saturday was Goering's blitz on London. Fine and warm, nearly a thousand aircraft had assembled in one huge tactical force to advance towards the Thames Estuary. In essence, it was the biggest aerial armada yet seen, a colossal tidal wave of bombers and fighters.

Dover's dwindled population speculated on the dreaded invasion, and asked each other, was this the pre-invasion onslaught, to be followed by hundreds of landing craft spilling out their stormtroopers onto British soil?

The concentration of invasion vessels in the French ports – ever increasing – caused the Air Ministry to issue its Invasion Alert No. 1 (Attack Imminent) code-named 'Cromwell'. Dover watched and waited but nothing happened until after 16.00. Heading back towards the French coast, a Heinkel 111 was attacked by our fighters. It dropped its bomb load into the harbour, causing neither damage nor casualties.

This RAF reconnaissance photograph shows the concentration of Hitler's invasion barges in Boulogne harbour. Further barges and troop-carrying vessels were also massed at Calais, Dunkirk, Ostend and Zeebrugge

Oblt. Gotz in his damaged ME109, however, made a forced landing near St Radigund's Abbey, where he was captured by troops. His damaged aircraft was later removed by an RAF Recovery Unit and deposited in a field near Barham.

Sunday 8 September
11.15 TO 13.22 – HES – IBS – UXBS

Reichsmarschall Goering's successful attacks on London had born fruit. Much of the East End of the city, especially the docks, had received a considerable pounding. When dawn broke, Londoners crawled out of their shelters to see large parts of their city in chaos.

It is not known if the Heinkel 111s were briefed to attack Dover, or if they had been turned back by our fighters. In any event, bombs fell on open land near Elms Vale, shattering windows in St Martin's School and Markland Road. High Meadows, behind the Boys' County School, erupted when around ten bombs exploded. A shower of incendiaries just fizzled on the ground.

An hour later three more exploded at Aycliffe, one in front of the King Lear public house, the other two behind it. Sixty-two-year-old Cyril Tozer was working on his allotment on the north slope of Shakespeare Cliff. Paddy Hennesey had been reluctant to join him. Later he was asked by Ray Pidgeon why he declined to visit his allotment that morning, he replied, 'Sure – and was it not just instinct bejasus! The foist landed in the grounds of the King Lear, the second killed poor Mr Tozer on his allotment next to mine, and the third – would you believe it? – has blown out one side of me lodge!'

Monday 9 September
00.01 TO 23.43 – HES – SHELLS

During a thunderstorm just after midnight, lightening struck the balloon cables. It was a most spectacular scene: vivid bright blue rods of electricity ran down to the earthing pins, while airmen, roused from their billets, started to winch the balloons down. One of them near Astor Avenue snapped its cable and came down in Church Road, taking half a dozen chimney-pots with it.

Soon afterwards enemy bombers put in an appearance. High explosives fell at Temple Ewell, damaging Woodside View and Redvers Cottages. Although only one female was slightly injured, the complete telephone wire system was brought down.

The sirens sounded again just before 17.00. Long-range shells were falling in the sea off the harbour. The first shell to reach the town exploded at the entrance to Shakespeare Tunnel. It caused a railway signalman to vacate the shattered signal box

The Citadel fortifications, Western Heights, serves as a backdrop to one of 961 squadron's barrage balloons being hoisted from the north slope of Shakespeare Cliff. the King Lear public house is the building on the left

in a hurry. Then four more arrived simultaneously. One hit the Burlington Hotel, taking out part of the structure and starting a fire on the upper floors. Rescue teams took several hours to penetrate the rubble, where they later found fifty-four-year-old William McDonald's body. When another shell exploded on 5 Monins Road, it killed Ernest Wiltshire. Several houses were damaged at Park Avenue but no casualties resulted. Charles Goodbourne happened to be passing Taylor's Garage in Elms Vale Road when a shell exploded which killed him instantly. Later, when the ruins were further investigated, they found seventeen-year-old Basil Wells who was seriously injured. He died later in hospital.

There was a two-hour lull in the shelling before it restarted. The first, in this second batch, exploded at Chitty's Mill, bringing down a huge wall into Granville Street, where several dwellings were severely damaged. Two more fell at the junction of Old Park Road and Brookfield Avenue, shattering the roof of the Scottish Laundry.

The blast of the shell explosion at Chitty's Mill almost ruined the rear of the Admiral Harvey public house in Bridge Street. Frank Rogers the licensee, and his wife, were both injured and taken to hospital. Mrs Rogers had suffered a fractured arm, but Frank died of his injuries the following day. Curiously he is not mentioned in the lists of civilian war dead.

Wednesday 11 September
15.11 TO 22.53 – HES – OIL BOMB – SHELLS

The sirens sounded soon after breakfast-time when a gaggle of ME109s flew in to shoot down balloons. Ack-ack fire was irregular because some of the fighters were at extremely low level.

The sirens went off again about 15.00 in the afternoon. This was the day when Dover was not only bombed but simultaneously shelled. There were

American journalist Guy Murchie of the *Chicago Tribune* recalled: 'I expected to land on the next floor, but, to my surprise, I kept falling for many seconds.' The wrecked Seamans Hostel with the Grand Hotel on the right

about twenty bombers over the town and the attack resulted in considerable damage to business premises and dwellings. A later report suggested that in comparison with the weight of bombs dropped and explosives used the loss of life and number of casualties were comparatively light. The fact that German long-range guns opened fire on the town while their bombers were still overhead remains an extraordinary tactic.

The oil bomb which fell on 46 Leyburne Road not only started a fire but also the whole proceedings. Within a few minutes Nos 14, 15 and 16 Laureston Place were just ruins. Then a stick of 250-kg bombs straddled Liverpool Street and St James's Street, where the school building collapsed, and another stick of bombs struck the west wing of the Grand Hotel.

Newspaper journalists had been staying at the Grand since hostilities began and some were trapped in the wreckage. Nineteen-year-old Robert Harvey was buried so deep in the rubble that his body was not recovered until ten days later. The Seamen's Hostel, a large three-storey building in Wellesley Road, took the full impact of a large calibre bomb and was completely wrecked, trapping people inside. Fifty-nine-year-old William Cook, and his twenty-eight-year-old son Ernest, both lost their lives, and three generations of the Richardson family died in the devastated Sussex Arms public house.

Twenty-year-old mother Lena Amos had thrown herself over her five-month-old baby daughter, at 1 Townwall Passage. Jack Hewitt recalled:

> I was party leader in charge of a four-man first-aid party. Down the road a stoker in the Royal Navy was tunnelling into debris at Camden Crescent. He brought out at least one dead woman. He had taken off his tunic and put his kit-bag down. He later discovered someone had stolen it.
>
> We were about to leave the scene of devastation when Fred Mottershaw, one of our party, said he thought he could hear a baby crying. We all stood still to listen, and I heard the cry too. I suppose we should have called the rescue squad who were further down the road but they were too busy. So I started to tunnel through the debris of two houses in Townwall Passage. I suppose I was tunnelling for about thirty minutes, under tons of rubble, when I found the little girl. Her mother was dead but her arms were around the child to protect her. I scraped away the rubble from around the baby and gradually made enough room to carry her out. I passed her to the ambulance crew and little Jean Amos was taken to hospital.

The work of the rescue teams and others was admirable but in view of the mass of debris in some places it was quite impossible to reach people who were believed trapped.

Jack Hewitt, Leader of the First Aid Party, and member of the St John Ambulance Brigade (Dover), tunnelled through debris at Townwall Passage on 11 September 1940 to rescue five-month-old Jean Amos

Conspicuous courage and resource was shown by stoker George Lowe, who had tunnelled under a huge pile of wreckage 15-feet high to extricate the licensee, the sole survivor at the Sussex Arms. The whole time he worked in an incredibly small cavity. He was in constant danger of being crushed by the collapse of a huge chimney breast which leaned precariously on the pile of rubble.

After that ordeal it became known that a woman was similarly imprisoned. Lowe immediately volunteered to crawl under the rubble to locate her. Mrs Terry, mother of Lena Amos, and grandmother of little Jean, was finally rescued after three-and-a-half hours in total darkness. She had displayed considerable fortitude throughout the long rescue attempt, unaware that she had lost her other daughter, fifteen-year-old Doris, found dead on arrival at hospital.

It was in February the following year that the *London Gazette* announced the award of the George Medal to Stoker 1st Class, George W. Lowe, for his gallantry in saving lives.

Many years later Jack Hewitt learned that he had been recommended for an award for his part in the rescue at Townwall Passage. Enquiries revealed it had been turned down because he was not a member of the rescue squad. He had been a First Aid man!

When a woman was finally dug out of her wrecked home after many hours in complete darkness she was heard to say, 'Here's a nice mess for me to clean up!'

A large number of military personnel was brought into the town to help, but even before they arrived some splendid work was done by many volunteers regardless of droning enemy aircraft overhead.

A bomb failed to explode when it made a large crater in Folkestone Road, near the entrance to Priory Station goods yard. Residents were immediately evacuated and the Bomb Disposal Squad sent for. Gas, water and electricity services were broken, and the crater filled with water until the stop valve was shut off. But control of escaping gas was not so simple. Fred Haywood, a gas company employee and a member of the Home Guard, was still working in the crater at 23.15 that night when the bomb exploded.

Another stick of bombs had fallen across the seafront. Councillor John Walker and his dog took shelter beneath his boat, which was always drawn up onto the beach. He died with his pet when the boat blew to smithereens.

After many hours in total darkness one woman, when she was finally dug out of her wrecked home, stood up to survey the chaos. She was heard to remark, 'Here's a nice mess for me to clean up!'

Running parallel to the seafront, Liverpool Street, seen here after the bombing raid on 11 September 1940, was to almost disappear when shells rained down on the town later in the war. Post-war development erased the street completely

Foreign service correspondent for the *Chicago Tribune*, Guy Murchie, and Stanley Johnstone from the London office of the same newspaper, were talking with two naval officers on the top floor of the Grand Hotel when a bomb brought down the complete west wing. They were shunted with falling masonry some 50 feet as each floor collapsed. Murchie later telephoned his story to London. It appeared in the *Chicago Tribune* the following day.

I held my arms over my head instinctively. Everything went black. I was fully conscious as the floor fell away under my feet. . . . I expected to land on the next floor, but, to my surprise, I kept falling for many seconds. . . . Then I landed. . . . Gradually, the air grew lighter as the smoke and soot settled. And I could see that I was tangled in a mass of timbers. The remaining jagged walls towered upwards some 50 feet, and I was acutely aware of the possibility of one of them falling on me. I climbed out of the debris, elated to be alive. Then I saw Johnstone climb out near me. His face was black with soot. We shook hands. I heard a girl calling, 'Please help me. Please get this beam off me.' She was about 20 feet away. Her face was black, but I recognized her as the pretty hotel receptionist Patricia Treadwell.

Guy Murchie rescued the hotel receptionist by sawing away the timber. He concluded his report:

> The injured girl is now in the next bed to my own after being given a pain-killing drug and being prepared for an operation. I have just heard that one of the naval officers with me in the hotel survived with a few cuts on the head. The other is feared dead. Bombs and guns are still booming as I write.

The first shell to hit the town demolished the passenger footbridge at Priory Station, while another fell in Hawkesfield's Yard. Two houses were demolished in Snargate Street, then two more exploded near the Lord Warden Hotel and the Marine Station. Other shells reached the Elms Vale area and the Citadel Barracks, where an Irish guardsman was killed by a piece of shrapnel. Selbourne Terrace and the Westmount Junior School were also hit.

Friday 13 September
14.50 – HES

Rain and low cloud spread like a blanket over the Dover Strait. There was no ALERT warning given when, at 15.00, a bomber appeared over the town. Military observers quickly identified the machine as a Blenheim. The ack-ack gunners held their fire.

Well above the height of the balloons it dropped SC250-kg bombs across Whinless Downs. The fall of bombs spread into Markland Road, where Nos 113 and 115 erupted, sending bricks and tiles flying about. Then Nos 230 and 232 Elms Vale Road were wrecked in the same way. Several houses were damaged by blast. Five people were treated for slight injuries but there were no fatalities.

It was known to the authorities that some British aircraft, left behind on French soil after the evacuation, were being used by the *Luftwaffe*.

Sunday 15 September
11.35 TO 13.07 – HES

Annually celebrated as Battle of Britain Day – on a par with Trafalgar Day in the British calendar – it was the climax of the intense air battles fought over the British Isles. Although Hitler's invasion plans were put back, yet again, the invasion was still regarded as imminent. The RAF kept up their bombing of barges and landing craft lying in the French ports.

Dover was still regarded as Britain's foremost salient in the coastal front line. People further inland, especially Londoners, conceded that Dover, separated by only twenty odd miles of water, was a special danger zone. Here there was greater variety and continuity of action. There was little relief from the tension of war when bullets and cannon shells ripped into buildings without warning.

One visiting journalist wrote:

> Sometimes I feel that Dover is too crowded with its civil population, including children. I feel uneasy at the sight of cinemas and theatres opening as usual in the teeth of guns and bombing aeroplanes. Yet it produced a glow of pride. Here was the very illustration of the grim and gay mood the Prime Minister had asked for. The anti-aircraft gunners and balloon barrage personnel, the minesweeper crews and naval men all unflinching and lighthearted at their posts – like the hairdresser who trimmed my hair, the waitresses and telephonists at the hotel.

As the early autumn mists rose from the fields it became a fine day. Before long the ack-ack gunners could only stand and stare at the mass of enemy bombers so high in the bright, blue sky. Just after 11.00 nearly one hundred Heinkels and Dorniers swept over the coast to the west of Dover.

Just before midday a single Dornier, probably turned back by the tremendous Fighter Command presence near London, decided to unleash its bombs over the town. Fortunately they fell in an area previously evacuated. There were no casualties and very little damage.

The greatest tragedy of the day's events was when another Dornier dropped bombs over the harbour. A number of trawlers were tied up against the Admiralty Pier. HMT *Botanic* was hit, which killed the skipper and five ratings, seriously injuring several others.

Monday 16 September
07.34 TO 11.06 – UXBS – SHELLS

It was the kind of day that sailors call 'dirty weather' – a strong sou'wester blowing with heavy sea mists restricting visibility. Despite these conditions a number of bombs were dropped at about 08.30. Strange to relate, not one exploded. Two buried themselves in soft ground near the balloon site at Elms Vale. When the airmen realized what had happened they scrambled for safety. Two others fell in Elms Vale and near Chevalier Road, and another two sank into the allotments at Astor Avenue. The whole area was evacuated and the police put up barriers. It was about 11.00 when just two shells exploded. One hit the bank opposite 24 Victoria Park, while the other demolished the Sea Baths on the seafront, where there were six military casualties.

Sporadic attacks continued. The sirens sounded two and sometimes three times each day. Incendiaries were dropped near Green Lane on the following day. Searchlights probed the night sky while the heavy ack-ack guns opened fire.

Monday 23 September
04.10 TO 10.57 – HES

Servicemen were watching the latest films in the local cinemas when they were suddenly recalled to their units. Soldiers, sailors and airmen tumbled out into the streets. Civilians left behind in their seats wondered if the Germans had invaded.

The Royal Hippodrome had been closed since 9 September. It had opened for just one day then closed again because of electricity failure. It had managed to re-open this Monday, with a reduced audience and a poor billing. The Farthingloe ack-ack gun site had been bombed. Damage or casualties were not revealed. When an ack-ack shell exploded in St James's Street, Thomas Kemp was injured by a shell splinter. Protesting vehemently he was rushed to the casualty hospital for treatment.

Thursday 26 September
14.35 TO 16.50 – SHELLS

Sixty-two-year-old Edith Cameron never even heard the sirens wail. It only sounded after the first shell demolished her home at 10 Church Street. Part of the house collapsed inwards burying her completely in the debris. Living next door at No. 12 was twenty-year-old James Holman. He was found about an hour later seriously injured in the ruins. He died the following day. The only other shell to reach the town had exploded opposite the Yacht Club on the beach.

★ ★ ★

Hardly any German agents in Great Britain were in 'position' before the war started. Nearly all of them, and there were a few, came during the war. Hitler had regarded England as racially related to Germany and as early as 1935 had prevented any spying in Britain. He was conscious of the fact that spying in Britain would, if discovered, put in jeopardy his policy to dominate the world.

Perhaps the only natural source of spies in Britain at the time was Oswald Mosley's British Union of Fascists. As early as May 1940, the journalist George Darling had named several well-known members of the Anglo-German Association and the organization called The Link, reputed to be the most out-spoken pro-Nazi clique in Great Britain.

On Friday 19 July Captain Robert Cecil Gordon Canning, MC, who had lived in Sandwich, was arrested in London under the Apprehension of Aliens Act Section 18b. Also arrested with him was a local wealthy landowner called Rice. Soon afterwards a man and a woman were observed questioning service-men in the bars of the Cliff Hotel and the Hope Inn at St Margaret's. When arrested by the local police it was discovered they had visited Germany only eighteen months before the war began. Police found a rifle and ammunition under a mattress at Brown Cottage where the couple were staying. Although both denied being spies they were regarded as pro-German sympathizers and were jailed to await internment.

Prior to Hitler's proposed invasion in September 1940, four enemy agents were picked up near Dymchurch, to the west of Dover. The incompetant four-some, ill-trained and lacking the rudimentary knowledge of survival in a foreign land, were all in custody within thirty-six hours of their having set foot on English soil. Three were hanged at Pentonville Prison, London, while the other was detained under Section 18b.

One of the more successful agents was the Dane, Hans Hanson, who para-chuted into England in 1940. His connection with Dover centres around his radio reports transmitted to the *Abwehr* in Hamburg confirming troop move-ments in the Dover area just before D-day. There were several agents operating in the south-east ports but not one of them could be regarded as legitimate. Each of them had come under the control of the British, and information passed to the *Abwehr* was first vetted by British counter-espionage.

Friday 27 September
08.37 TO 16.43 – HES – SHELLS

Blips on Dover radar screens gave the sign of bomb-carrying Messerschmitts on course for targets further inland. Our own fighters were waiting and broke up the formations. Enemy aircraft scattered in all directions dropping their bombs indis-criminately over the countryside. Dover received only one bomb. It fell in Harold Street, demolishing the AFS emergency water tank and seriously injuring one man.

Long-range shells began to arrive at about 15.30. The first exploded at Victoria Park, bringing down vital military telephone wires. Two more straddled the harbour and East Cliff, where one house was partly demolished. The second salvo plopped into the harbour near the eastern arm where a huge spout of water cascaded over terrified gunners. Stables were demolished at the old Castlemount School, and when the last shell exploded at Connaught Park, an Army Captain was reported killed. Civilian casualties suffered only minor cuts and bruises.

Sunday 29 September
11.32 – HEs

Several high-flying enemy formations were observed flying above cloud. Ack-ack guns opened fire immediately, even before the sirens had sounded. Only one bomb fell, and that demolished a building in Northfall Meadow, where it was stated the ATS was billeted. Casualties were not mentioned.

London newspaper men seemed to be enjoying themselves at the Royal Oak public house, Capel, on the outskirts of the town. The Marquess of Donegall, writing in the *Sunday Dispatch* said, 'So you and I are in the middle of some nice pork with real crackle when there's a big "plonk". "A shell, boys!" says the *Daily Mail*. "Nonsense, Ack-Ack," says the *Evening News*. "Sit down, you fools, bomb in Folkestone!" says the *Daily Mirror*. With the net result that everybody leaves the pork, grabs tin hat, gas mask and binoculars, scrambles into cars and is off.'

THE EREBUS BOMBARDMENT

The Prime Minister had looked aghast at the RAF reconnaissance photographs showing the growth of the German heavy artillery along the Channel coast. Intelligence reports in August and September even gave him the number of guns, their sizes, name of battery and the exact locations.

On 25 August he wrote to the First Lord and the First Sea Lord:

I shall be obliged if you will make proposals for a shoot by *Erebus* against the German batteries at Gris-Nez. I was very glad to hear you thought this practicable. It is most desirable. There is no reason why it should wait for the railway guns, though, of course, if they were ready they could follow on with the 14-in at daybreak. We ought to smash these batteries. I hope we have not got to wait for the next moon for *Erebus*, and I shall be glad to know what are the moon conditions which you deem favourable.

HMS *Erebus* was a First World War monitor mounting two 15-in guns. Her first attempt to bombard at night was on 28–29 September, but her captain was forced to abandon the exercise through bad weather. A second attempt was made on the following night, and the Dover tug *Lady Brassey* assisted the monitor to her special buoy in mid-Channel. Once in position, close on 02.00, she opened fire at the Calais area. She managed to send off seventeen shells before being dogged by a technical fault. Further trouble compounded the night's work when spotting aircraft failed to observe the 'fall of shot'. The 14-in gun 'Winnie' at St Margaret's only managed to fire one shell!

This unsatisfactory attempt to smash the German long-range guns brought an accurate response within just a few hours. The second bombardment by *Erebus* was made on 16 October, during which she fired off about fifty rounds. Although it was considered a commendable performance it was never repeated.

Monday 30 September
11.23 TO 11.48 – SHELLS

The usual ranging shell fell outside the breakwater just before 11.00. The siren went off, its warbling note now restricted to one-minute duration instead of the previous two minutes. A shell then exploded at Ladywell, severely damaging the

After Dover's fire station was damaged, it moved to a house called Redstone at Kearsney. Female staff used a bungalow. Left to right: Kathleen Hunt, Evelyn Relf, Sadie Stuart, Tilley Beney, Gladys Gillman and Elizabeth Woods

Westminster Bank, on the corner of King Street and the Market Square, was shell damaged on 30 September 1940, 7 May 1941 and 20 April 1944. The general manager of Tilmanstone Colliery and a naval officer were treated for minor injuries on 7 May 1941, when their car was overturned

fire station where there was one casualty. Burton's the tailors, at 10 Cannon Street, received severe damage, William Dutnell was killed in Barwick's Yard, and Tapley's Garage in Cambridge Road was also badly damaged. When another shell exploded behind 11 Dickson Road, a whole row of terraced houses was only fit for demolition. There were three casualties. Westminster Bank, Market Square, had its front windows blown out by the last salvo, which injured two people. To cap it all, some hours later the navy discovered an unexploded bomb near the dockyard gate.

★ ★ ★

GEORGE MEDAL FOR DOVER FIRE FIGHTERS

The award of the George Medal to three Dover men was confirmed in the first list of awards of the new medal, published in the *London Gazette* on Monday 30

Torpedoes, ammunition and spilled fuel oil threatened to explode at any moment on board HMS *Sandhurst* on 29 July 1940. Three Dover firemen were later awarded the George Medal. Left to right: Deputy Fire Chief C.W.A. Brown, Executive Officer E. Harmer and Section Officer A. Campbell

September. They were awarded to: Executive Chief Officer Ernest Herbert Harmer and Second Officer Cyril William Arthur Brown, both of the Dover Fire Brigade, and Section Officer Alexander Edmund Campbell of the Dover AFS. The official account states that it was 'in recognition of their gallantry on the occasion of a fire caused by enemy action in Dover Harbour and in vessels lying therein, on 29 July 1940.' His Majesty the King was also graciously pleased to give orders for the publication, as having received an expression of Commendation for their services on the same occasion, of the names of:

The Dover Fire Brigade
The Dover Auxiliary Fire Service
Fireman Ernest Alfred Foord (Dover Fire Brigade)
Fireman Edward Jesse Gore (Dover Fire Brigade)
Station Officer Harold Thomas Hookings (Dover Fire Brigade)
Auxiliary Fireman Arthur Thomas Cunnington (AFS)

Auxiliary Fireman Lionel Rupert Hudsmith (AFS)
Auxiliary Fireman John McDermott (AFS)

In the recent large-scale attack by enemy bombers on Dover Harbour, fires were started on ships and oil stores. Air raids continued throughout the day. During the attacks all members of the Dover Fire Brigade and the AFS engaged at the fires did excellent work in difficult and dangerous circumstances and the fires were eventually extinguished.

The individuals named above volunteered to return to a blazing ship containing explosives, in which they fought fires while enemy aircraft were still overhead. At the Technical Institute on Monday 30 September 1940, the Mayor handed to those honoured the official record of the deed, and congratulated them in the name of Dover.

Wednesday 2 October
08.39 TO 12.54 – HES – UXBS

Just after 08.30 enemy formations flew inland at between 20,000 and 30,000 feet, in brilliant blue skies. The heavy ack-ack batteries engaged them. At 11.30 six Messerschmitts, fitted with bomb racks beneath their fuselage, flew in low over the Channel to make a lightening attack on Dover. Undetected by our radar, the Observer Corps post on the cliffs gave the alarm. While telephone wires hummed with messages the first bombs were released on Clarendon Street.

Four houses were immediately demolished in as many seconds, seriously injuring four people. Two more fell almost at the same spot. A huge crater appeared in the road and escaping gas from a broken main caught alight. When the next wave of fighter-bombers struck, their bombs failed to explode. One landed in a garden of the general stores in Longfield Road, another ploughed through a building in Westbury Road, and the last one hit the roadway, then bounced into Belgrave Road School. Residents were evacuated immediately to await the Bomb Disposal Squad.

Visibility in the Strait on the following day was down to about 500 yards. A couple of balloons came down in the high winds to block Lowther Road. It was not the sort of day for moving house, although some bombed-out people were observed trundling handcarts piled high with essential items to safer areas in the town.

Saturday 5 October
15.35 TO 16.47 – HES

The sirens went off when nearby Folkestone was being attacked. Nothing happened in Dover until almost 15.30. Machine gunners, defending the heavy artillery gun sites near St Margaret's, opened fire upon six, bomb-carrying Messerschmitts when they suddenly flew in over the cliffs at low level. The officers' mess and several other buildings at Connaught Barracks erupted as the 250-kg bombs exploded on target. Military casualties were not revealed.

Monday 7 October
09.31 TO 11.33 – HEs

Reasonable weather in October was still good enough to help Hitler's invasion prospects, had he wished to invade. Marshal Goering, however, was finding it more convenient to use new tactics to help demoralize the British people. His bomb-carrying Messerschmitts were being used to great advantage. Once the bomb was released the fighter-bomber immediately reverted to its original fighter role, and was more manoeuvrable to defend itself against RAF fighters.

After the forward-placed balloons had been conveniently disposed of, giving the fighter-bombers free reign to fly at a lower level, they would release their bombs. St James's Street received a pounding. The Parish Hall, St James's School, a shop, the Golden Cross public house and several private dwellings were wrecked in seconds. Mr and Mrs Moore, who ran a small shop, were seriously injured and their little pony, which used to stand outside harnessed to a small delivery cart, was killed.

William Ashdown and Benjamin Botten were both found injured in St James's Street, where they had been repairing the road. They died in hospital later that day. Mrs Clavery of Clarence Street was another casualty, as was the landlady of the White Horse public house. Other bombs fell in Belgrave Road and across the harbour.

Tuesday 8 October
07.19 TO 18.25 – HEs

It was 07.15 when the sirens sounded. Enemy fighters came in low to 'pot' the balloons in advance of a raid. Three hours went by before Messerschmitts appeared. Additional Bofors 40-mm anti-aircraft guns had been moved up on the cliffs to combat these 'tip-and-run' raiders but their effectiveness was limited by their height above sea level. Usually the fighter-bombers were below the height of the cliffs.

The first 500-kg bomb exploded between the Gun Wharf and the Esplanade Hotel. Fourteen houses were seriously damaged. The next was a direct hit on HMT *Burke*, lying beside the Granville Dock. The trawler sank almost immediately. There were several deaths, both naval and civilian – George Dewell,

George Lamkin, John Austin, Cyril Playford, Frederick Stanford and Arthur Young. The latter died in hospital the following day. Six naval personnel were seriously injured.

Just after 18.00 a JU88 bomber dropped seven bombs across the town from Stanhope Road to Maxton, missing the centre of the town completely. Airmen on the balloon site at Astor Avenue had the fright of their lives when a bomb threw up a ton of earth. But there is no recorded reaction of the troops at the Citadel Barracks when their cookhouse was demolished. Only one female casualty was reported at Manor Road. Goering's new tactics placed an even greater strain upon civilians. They accepted air raids as part of everyday life, and were, more than ever, feeling a touch of pride in finding themselves well and truly in the 'front line'.

Thursday 10 October
08.25 TO 19.20 – HES – SHELLS

A smart, low-level raid occurred just after 10.00. Some six fighter-bombers swept in out of the haze. Dubbed 'nuisance raids' by the military the citizens of Dover were not a little complacent about them. It was noticeable that people just used to step quickly into a doorway rather than enter a shelter, to wait for the raiders to pass. Bombs fell above the Priory Tunnel, at the junction of Castle Hill and Connaught Road, while others fell harmlessly in the harbour. There were no casualties reported and very little damage.

Another raid occurred at 15.30. An empty ward at the Isolation Hospital, Noah's Ark Road, erupted into a shower of bricks, tiles and masonry. There were no casualties. The next bomb almost took out six houses and the Prince of Wales public house at the junction of George Street and Chapel Hill. When a bomb struck, to explode on the cliff face behind Athol Terrace, just below the castle, it ripped out the rear walls of Nos. 2, 3, 4 and 5, and brought down tons of chalk. A large proportion of the residents were re-housed. There were no casualties.

Shops were closing and most of Dover's working population was hurrying home when the ALL CLEAR sounded. When sixteen shells fell into the sea and the harbour, many Dovorians felt the German gun commanders knew they were hurrying home. One reached the waterworks, throwing up tons of earth, but the next exploded in St James's Church cemetery. Shattered gravestones and tombs greeted the rescue squad. The Borough Surveyor ordered an immediate clean-up operation. The church looked in a sorry state. A large hole had been blown through the flint walls of the chancel.

★ ★ ★

SIREN FOR SHELLING

'It has been decided that, as from Sunday 13 October, a special siren will be sounded to indicate danger from shelling. The warning will be a warbling signal for one minute, a short pause, and then another warbling signal for a minute.'

Saturday 12 October
12.10 TO 14.52 – HES – SHELLS

Two bombs fell on Park Avenue, at the rear of The Lodge, and some others fell harmlessly in the harbour just after midday. There was little damage and no casualties reported. There is, however, one report which states a shell exploded at Aycliffe, while another report suggests an unexploded bomb had suddenly gone off without warning.

Another entry reads: '12 October 1940. 38 Germans landed during the night. MTBs sunk 2 German trawlers and took off survivors.'

There were several flotillas operating from the Coastal Force Base in Dover in an offensive against German convoys and their escort ships. The force consisted of MTBs, MGBs, and Motor Launches (MLs).

The incident mentioned above, when prisoners of war were taken, was the culmination of an operation by three MTBs. The MTBs were led by Lt. Cdr. A.B. Cole, RN, with Lt. D. Jermain, RN, and Lt. N. Poland, RN, commanding the other two boats. They were on their outward journey when they sighted two trawlers just north of Calais. Cole sent a signal back to Dover asking if any British trawlers were in the vicinity. He received the reply, 'No'. Cole immediately attacked with torpedoes, and both trawlers were sunk. During this action Lt. Jermain managed to sink one of them by dropping a depth charge under it. Almost all of the survivors were picked up and brought back to Dover.

Coastal Force craft, with their limited speed available, began their operations to control the Dover Strait in the summer of 1940, when the French, Belgian and Dutch ports had fallen to the enemy. They usually operated at night, not only against enemy convoys, but more especially against the German E-boats and R-boats, who often ventured into our coastal waters to lay mines or attack shipping.

The three principal types of craft at Dover used either the Ferry Dock or the Camber area of the harbour, the latter often referred to as the Submarine Pens. The base, or headquarters, was located in the former Lord Warden Hotel, re-named HMS *Wasp*, near the Western Docks. It was here that the crews were billeted, where the signals section, plotting rooms and offices were housed. Equally necessary were the maintenance staff who carried out repairs of the internal-combustion engines, maintaining the torpedoes, various types of automatic quick-firing guns, wireless and electrical equipment and many other tasks on a regular routine schedule. Some of these tasks were efficiently done by WRNS, who were billeted at Dover College (HMS Lynx), near the centre of the town.

The MTBs, the heaviest of the boats, their task self-explanatory, were mainly concerned with attacks on enemy shipping. The MGBs, however, were concerned with close fighting with enemy light craft, and especially in close support of MTBs when in action. Slower in speed than the other two, the MLs were used for many different purposes, such as laying mines in enemy waters and taking landing parties of the Combined Operations Commandos to raid enemy positions on the French coast. One of the first of these commando raids took place from Dover on the night of 23–4 June 1940. While no claim was ever made of its success, it was, after all, the first such commando raid made on enemy-held territory; the news spread like wild-fire throughout the country. But the routine patrols, laying smoke screens around convoys, and the invaluable duty of rescuing 'ditched' pilots from a watery grave, hardly made up for the glorious adventures experienced by crews of the MTBs and MGBs.

Friday 18 October
12.12 TO 14.45 – SHELLS

The British heavy artillery opened fire soon after daybreak. The German long-range guns replied just before noon. These actions were often thought by the layman to be duels but in reality the British guns were firing at German shipping. Eight shells of German origin fell in the harbour area, hitting the Admiralty Pier and killing thirty-six-year-old Herbert Trinder, and damaging another trawler. Thirty-two-year-old Sidney Trow was killed while working on the trawler. There were several military casualties when shells fell on Connaught Park and injured three civilians.

Sunday 20 October
11.08 TO 16.37 – SHELLS

Shortly after 11.00 four shells sent up a huge series of water spouts just outside the harbour. The German guns then began to fire at intervals and continued for more than two hours. Later, a naval estimate suggested fifty shells had been fired on Dover. Just before midday a shell took out Nos. 4, 6, and 8 Stanhope Road, seriously injuring Percy Carswell, who later died in hospital. A further twenty houses were seriously damaged. Then Eastbrook Place was hit, damaging the convent, while another shell struck Southern Autos Garage, where the AFS Depot lost much of its equipment.

Albert Ashbee, licensee of the Ancient Druids public house, happened to be walking along St James's Street when a shell exploded on the already-wrecked St James's Parish Hall. He was killed instantly. St James's Church received another battering. A shell bored straight through one wall coming out the opposite side to explode. Another partially demolished Nos 23 and 24 Castlemount Road where there were no casualties.

When Percy Carswell was seriously injured, he and his brother were trying to reinforce their garden shelter. Percy's brother survived but was badly injured. Part of the Burlington Hotel collapsed into Liverpool Street and left a huge pall of dust hovering above the building for over half an hour. Other shells hit Maison Dieu Road, Clarence Lawn, Harold Street, Salisbury House and Castle Hill.

★ ★ ★

COME BACK SAYS MAYOR OF DOVER

The London *Evening Standard* printed the following article:

> The feeling down here is that the threat of invasion is over – at least for the moment. But unless a few of the residents come back from the districts to which they have moved and open up their houses again, it is not going to make much difference to the life of the town. A few people who are in business in a small way have been coming back during the last week or ten days and opening up their premises again. At the moment the life of Dover depends on those who refused to leave and have been carrying on in spite of regular shelling and danger from invasion.

The above report was strenuously denied by the Mayor, J.R. Cairns, in the Council Chamber, when he was questioned by Councillor Gates, who also asked the Mayor, after a heated debate, not to lose his temper! The Mayor replied, 'I have not lost my temper, my dear infallible friend!'

★ ★ ★

Soldiers, sailors and airmen, were fast losing their drinking facilities in Dover. The Burlington Bar had been closed for the duration of the war, and public houses closed by enemy action included the Golden Cross, the Sir John Falstaff,

The YMCA canteen van, known to the troops as 'char and Wad', makes its daily visit to an anti-aircraft gun site near Guston

The Avenue, King Lear, Star Inn, Mail Packet, the Sussex Arms, Ancient Druids, The Angel, King William and the Granville Arms.

★　★　★

'Owing to recent enemy action, the Barnet Hut, YMCA Dover, was severely damaged, and, in consequence, the premises have had to be vacated. In the meantime, and until fresh suitable premises are obtained, the YMCA tea car service is being augmented in order to continue and extend the work amongst H.M. Forces.'

Monday 21 October
12.50 TO 18.52 – HES – UXBS – SHELLS

Low cloud and sea mists covered most of the Dover area. The record of the day's events begins with four bombs being dropped when no warning was sounded. The most serious incident occurred in the Market Square at 12.50. The Market Hall and Museum were seriously damaged when a bomb hit the rear of the building, burying tons of foodstuffs. Another exploded behind the Hippodrome in the dock area, damaging the structure of the old theatre and causing chaos in Northampton Street.

Airmen at the Astor Avenue balloon site watched spellbound as one bomb buried itself in soft ground without exploding. They beat a hasty retreat, leaving their balloon swaying in the breeze. The last bomb struck 9 Last Lane, where Allison's fruiterers in Adrian Street was seriously damaged. Casualties were confined to slight injuries.

At 14.00 the German guns opened fire. They fired at varying intervals, commencing just before the hour, and continued for nearly four hours. The new shell warning sounded only after the first shell exploded in Tower Street, taking out Nos 57 and 63. The whole street was blocked with rubble. Salvos fell to explode as far away as the gasworks at Union Road, while others fell in the Granville Dock, where a sailor was killed and several more injured.

The ALL CLEAR signal had sounded when soon afterwards another shell exploded at Stokes Farm, High Meadows, while another had reached Coldred. People went back to their shelters when Adrian Street received another shell. Pardoners Way was hit by yet another and two casualties were reported at the Clock Tower, Esplanade. Although there were no fatalities PC Saville had been hit by a piece of shrapnel and later had his left arm amputated.

On the following day shells demolished four houses in Norman Street; casualties were listed as minor.

★ ★ ★

MORE POWERS FOR AIR RAID WARDENS

By an Emergency Powers Order, air-raid wardens and members of a recognized voluntary fire-fighting party are given powers of entry and of taking steps for extinguishing fires or for protecting property or rescuing persons or property from fire; such as have already been conferred on auxiliary firemen.

Friday 25 October
21.10 TO 23.30 – SHELLS

By first light the radar screens showed the inevitable 'blips' indicating enemy aircraft over the Pas de Calais. Enemy aircraft came over in waves and met a formidable ack-ack barrage. Dover's balloons were attacked about half an hour before the main bomber formations appeared over the coast. People ran for shelter when bullets and cannon shells splattered along the streets and roads. Three of the Messerschmitts were observed damaged and, trailing black smoke, they aborted their attack. At least one was seen to hit the sea, while two others crash-landed on French soil.

German seaplanes were observed laying a smoke-screen round a small convoy hugging the French coast in the afternoon. Our big guns opened fire on them. It was almost 18.00 when a British convoy was making slow progress through the Strait. The German long-range runs fired on the merchantmen but no hits were observed.

Further shelling took placed at 21.00 – this time the town was hit. The first exploded in the garden of 3 Elms Vale Road and the house was badly damaged. The next one hit Oil Mill Bridge, Limekiln Street, where the unfortunate Victor Abbot, sitting in his ambulance outside the First Aid Post, was killed instantly. Twenty minutes later the King William public house, Tower Hill, was demolished along with several houses. George Decent and Ernest Silk lost their lives there and three others were seriously injured. Five minutes respite then the next shell exploded on the signal office at Priory Station. The blast injured twenty-nine-year-old Arthur Lyus, who died in hospital later the same day. There were five more casualties at the station and the line was blocked for many hours.

Tuesday 29 October
16.08 TO 17.56 – HES – UXBS

Bomb-carrying Messerschmitts were out in force on this day dropping bombs all over Kent. When bombs fell on Dover just after 16.30, there was no clear identification of the aircraft involved. What did become clear, however, was the unusually light calibre of the bombs used. It was known that the fighter-bombers sometimes used 100-kg bombs fitted to special racks on the wings. In any event, the railway line was blocked at the top of Templar Street by one of them, and another exploded between 17 and 19 Folkestone Road. The third bomb failed to explode when it bored down through Lawrence's fish shop in Snargate Street. There were no casualties reported from any incident.

★ ★ ★

Townspeople were informed that all shelters and caves would be provided with sanitation. Elsan Closets were introduced at the Winchelsea Tunnel, Athol Terrace, Oil Mill and Trevanion Caves, and were already issued to the Lagoon Cave. Electric heating was also suggested for other shelters and caves where people stayed overnight. Although by December all caves were to have water stand-pipes installed, it was proposed to install taps and sinks at Winchelsea, Athol Terrace and the Oil Mill Caves.

★ ★ ★

SLEEPING ACCOMMODATION IN PUBLIC SHELTERS

Arrangements have been made to provide SLEEPING ACCOMMODA-TION in the LAGOON GARAGE SHELTER. Application for allocation of sleeping places should be made on FORMS to be obtained at the Public Health Department, Brook House, Dover. Accommodation cannot be guaranteed to everyone who makes application, and the priority will be given to the following classes of people:

Mothers and children who have no adequate shelter at home.
Elderly persons and invalids who have no adequate shelter at home.
Men engaged on work of national importance who have no adequate shelter at home.
Sleeping accommodation will be allocated on condition that applicants will strictly comply with the regulations relating to the conduct of shelters.
Similar arrangements will be made in the near future for providing sleeping accommodation in certain other public shelters.

Signed S.R.H. Loxton, Town Clerk
Brook House, Dover *31 October 1940*

Friday 1 November
17.19 TO 19.02 – SHELLS

Escorting destroyers were laying a smoke-screen around a British convoy. Motor launches were fussing about like mother hens while the rigid-type naval balloons were swaying above like inflated torpedoes. German guns opened fire but gradually the convoy moved westward towards Dungeness and the German gunners lost their target. The HMD *Torbay II* was lost off Dover.

They continued to fire, however, and the next salvo hit the town. Military Hill received the first then the next burst above the Grand Hotel. Within a few minutes a new menace had arrived – the air-burst shell, designed to explode above ground sending out a lethal shower of hot shrapnel in all directions. Further shells exploded over Priory Station, then over Peverell's Tower at the castle, over the harbour and the old swimming baths. Fortunately there were no casualties.

The usual, and more conventional shell still came over between the air-burst type. Houses in Magdala Road and Prospect Place were slightly damaged when a shell exploded on High Meadow. Then the kitchen at Barton Road School collapsed in a heap, leaving another eight dwellings a little worse for wear. Instead of going into the cave at Trevanion a number of people just stood at the entrance, wondering where the next one would strike. They watched explosions occur at Salisbury Road, Balfour Road, Barton Path, Harold Terrace, then one hit the castle moat area, quickly followed by another which exploded on the bank immediately above the entrance to Trevanion Cave. Tons of chalk were dislodged. Albert Cleak was not fast enough on his feet and was killed instantly.

Tuesday 5 November
15.56 TO 17.07 – HES

Dover's new police station in Ladywell was hit by a 250-kg bomb, released by one of two Messerschmitt fighter-bombers which had suddenly appeared over the town without warning. Beneath the police station was the ARP Control Centre, comprising the vital switchboard linking every part of the town and the rural areas; and with large plans showing every street and road, upon which was also marked every ARP Post and AFS Depot. Four War Reserve Constables were later treated for shock. The Mayor was chairing a meeting at the time in the Town Hall. Councillors who were serving in one or other of the Civil Defence parties left in a hurry. The Mayor continued with his meeting quite unperturbed. The other bomb exploded harmlessly on Whinless Down. Unverified reports suggested that German Intelligence knew where the ARP Control Centre was situated. This view was supported by the knowledge that a slick intruder raid, made at low level, by a well-briefed pilot, could place a bomb more accurately on a target than could be expected by a shell fired from the French coast.

Three houses were wrecked on the following day by shells in Malmains Road, and craters appeared in Taswell Street and Harold Road. Only one person was seriously injured.

Monday 11 November
10.00 – HES

There had followed four reasonably quiet days, after a Dornier had bombed the Citadel Barracks early one morning. Neville Chamberlain, the former Prime Minister, had died on 9 November, aged seventy-one.

The shell warning had sounded on numerous occasions when a convoy passed through the Strait. Of course, everyone waited for the inevitable explosions. The time taken for a shell to reach Dover varied from between 60 and 90 seconds. The reason for the variation depended on the charge used to fire a shell of a certain calibre.

When the sirens went just after 09.00, it was an air-raid signal. Ack-ack guns fired at numerous aircraft flying about but nothing happened in the town until just after midday when three fighter-bombers appeared. People watched the first bomb fall on Clout's seed store in Priory Street, almost demolishing the shop, and seriously damaging the Golden Lion public house. It was fortunate that the shops were closed for the lunch-break, because about forty received damage through blast. There were no casualties. The other bombs fell in Connaught Road and at Clark's Nursery in Godwyn Road.

Wednesday 13 November
13.49 TO 14.33 – HEs –UXB

Fighter-bombers were up to their dirty tricks again. They had come in low over the coast at Dymchurch. They continued inland then altered course towards Dover. The sirens went off as they arrived over the town – already facing the Channel to make good their escape before guns could aim at them.

It was unfortunate that a large number of people were in the High Street near the Lagoon Shelter and Beaufoy's Garage. The Salvation Army Citadel erupted with the explosion which sent up heavy masonry, bricks and tiles in all directions. Ten shops and one hundred houses were damaged. Major Pratt, who had been in charge of the Citadel for the past three years, was killed when the roof collapsed. In the shattered High Street lay the bodies of two sixteen-year-olds, Lily Ball and Alfred Cooper. Alfred died in hospital later that day but Lily had already succumbed to her terrible injuries by the time rescuers arrived. William Austin had been talking with Leonard Deverson, the local hairdresser. They were pinned together by crushing masonry and both died of their injuries at hospital. Ex-Sgt. Major George Leggatt, who just three days before had placed a wreath on Dover's War Memorial, was found dead in the rubble.

The High Street was in chaos with gas escaping from fractured mains and thousands of gallons of water ran down the gutters to find its own level. Many items from shop display cabinets were strewn about in disarray. Another bomb fell in the rear garden of 38 Tower Hamlets Road, bringing down chalk onto the railway line. The last bomb made a crater in Bridge Street but failed to explode. The area was immediately evacuated and the Bomb Disposal Squad sent for.

Thursday 14 November
09.34 TO 15.17 – HEs – UXBs

Just after 09.30 the balloons were 'potted', followed soon afterwards by a group of fighter-bombers. Bombs fell at the Old Charlton Road, almost opposite St James's Cemetery gate, while another exploded at Clark's Nursery in Barton Road. Damage was minimal and casualties none.

A more serious raid occurred just after 14.00. Stukas were peeling off to attack the radar masts at Swingate. Pre-warned, the ack-ack gunners were ready and waiting. They fired at everything in their sights with fuses set for 10,000 feet. Bombs were released too early in the dive and the Stukas hastily veered away from the intense barrage. This resulted in many bombs falling wide of their target, some falling near the castle and across the Camber area of the harbour. At least two exploded in the castle grounds while one other failed to explode. East Cliff was showered with stones when the beach erupted, and a direct hit on the drifter *Shipmates* killed two and injured nine others. Henry Marklew who lived in Folkestone Road was seriously injured and was certified dead on arrival at HMS Lynx. The trawlers *Lord Howe*, *Yorkshire Lass* and *Cirrus* suffered damage.

Sunday 17 November
19.35 TO 23.00 – SHELLS

Military authorities counted over forty-five shells falling in the sea. Only one reached the town, which hit Webbers & Robbs in Castle Street, the watchmaker's and gunsmith's, damaging the other shops and dwellings in the area. There were no casualties.

The national newspapers, with almost monotonous regularity, reported the experiences of the long-suffering Dover citizens in their articles. The Editor of the *Dover Express* also suffered a unique embarrassment every week. He was held in the clutches of the Ministry Regulations which prohibited him from reporting on enemy action, but none the less he saw in the national newspapers each day, not only references to every conceivable aspect of Dover's defences, but also the latest incidents. His frustration led him to write many leading articles on the subject. One of them suggested the London newspapermen should be 'kicked out of Dover!'

The Record of Incidents sheet for 25 November records that over one hundred shells were fired on the Dover and St Margaret's areas. Although some fell in the sea and in the harbour, most of them were aimed at the coastal gun batteries at St Margaret's.

The RAF continued to bomb German gun sites and the remaining invasion barges. At night Dover citizens watched the German searchlights probing the sky in clusters over Calais and saw clearly the ack-ack gun flashes. They heard, and felt beneath their feet, the thumps of British bombs exploding. 'We're giving Jerry a taste of his own medicine,' said one Home Guard sentry, who was intensely interested in the spectacle.

Tuesday 26 November
03.12 TO 05.07 – SHELLS

The warning sounded. It was more frightening at night. People got wearily out of warm beds, grabbed a blanket and a thermos flask, then crept out into the cold night air to take shelter in the garden Anderson. They sat in huddled groups, the entrance sealed with a piece of sacking, the oil stove alight and with only a flickering candle to accompany their thoughts.

When the shell exploded behind 17 and 19 Clarendon Place, ripping off roof tiles and smashing windows, people in their garden shelters were plunged into darkness. The candle had snuffed out as if pinched by an unseen hand. It was relit. They waited in silence for the next explosion, wondering if the next shell had their name on it. The ALL CLEAR sounded just after 05.00. As dawn broke they left the shelter and prepared for work. But the risks were the same. During the afternoon of 27 November eight shells fell in the harbour.

Thursday 28 November
12.03 TO 14.15 – SHELLS

A newspaper reported: 'No schools are open in Dover. All the children can do is play in the streets or in the caves and basements which serve as air raid and shelling shelters. These children are receiving no education whatever and Dover's medical officer has given the opinion that their health is imperilled by having to spend so much time in shelters.'

While the shell warning was in force Dover Council agreed to ask the Regional Commissioner to have children of school age compulsorily evacuated. It was estimated that between eight hundred and one thousand children remained in the town.

The first shell arrived just after midday. It exploded close to the Langdon Battery site where there were some military casualties. An hour later another exploded in the Granville Dock, injuring naval personnel. The most serious incident of the day occurred at the Castle Flats, where No. 10 took a direct hit, bringing down most of the front into the road. Over fifty houses and shops were badly damaged.

Rescuers were told a housewife had been in the flat. They tunnelled beneath the rubble until they reached a warm body. They could detect no signs of life. They eventually pulled the body out. Forty-two-year-old Elma Richards, born in France, was given large amounts of blood but she died before reaching hospital.

★ ★ ★

His Royal Highness the Duke of Kent visited Dover on 29 November. Accompanied by an entourage of Army Officers, Civil Defence Services, members of the town's Emergency Committee, and the Mayor, he inspected the long-range guns, the ARP Control Centre and the fire station. Afterwards he visited one or two cave shelters and spoke to people who had taken refuge there during the ALERT. The Duke was then taken to see the all-important Civil Defence secondary Control Centre, located in the Oil Mill Cave. Here, duplicated, were the telephones, large town maps and the incident board. A special room was equipped with bunk-beds and cooking facilities. Occasionally, the control room staff at Ladywell used the secondary control room on a 24-hour exercise.

Wednesday 4 December
13.39 TO 13.48 – HEs – UXBs

Widespread fog had effectively restricted visibility so that enemy air operations were reduced. Although the sirens went off just after 10.00, nothing happened until after the ALL CLEAR sounded, when the first wave of four Messerschmitt fighter-bombers made their lightening attack.

Bombs dropped on the Esplanade, Grand Shaft Barracks, Military Hill South and Snargate Street. Scott & Sons, the dry cleaner's, behind which was the entrance to Scott's Cave, was almost demolished.

The next wave of four released their bombs at Clarendon Place and behind 74 and 137 Folkestone Road. One of them failed to explode and the whole area was evacuated. Four more unexploded bombs were discovered at the Grand Shaft Barracks. The third and final wave flew into a fusillade of small arms fire from the naval ships in the harbour. Bowhill Garage, Snargate Street, lost its front, which fell into the road, and Clarendon Place erupted for the second time. Fifty-four-year-old Emily Foster was unaccounted for – last seen in Snargate Street. Her body was recovered several days later when the entrance to Scott's Cave was being cleared.

Sunday 15 December
19.05 TO 22.13 – *LUFTMINES*

One of the most formidable weapons used by Germany was the parachute mine, which floated to the ground attached to a parachute and exploded just before reaching its target. The explosion, and the resulting damage, was always cata-strophic due to the extreme blast effect. The *Luftmines*, LM1000s, were dropped on this occasion by Heinkel 111s, and while the target is uncertain, they both floated towards military positions. One exploded over Connaught Barracks and the other exploded close to Fort Burgoyne. Both areas were under the military and therefore damage and casualties were not revealed. Nevertheless, 350 shops and houses were damaged in the town.

Bombs and missiles dropped on Dover were principally of the high-explosive type used by Germany throughout their assault on the UK mainland.

The SC (*Sprengbombe-Cylindrisch*) was a thin-cased general-purpose bomb sometimes called the *Minenbombe*. It possessed a high charge of maximum blast effect and usually contained over 50 per cent explosive, used for demolition pur-poses. Published sources reveal that eight out of ten HEs dropped on the UK were of the SC type, between 50- and 2,000-kg.

In 1940 especially, a device called the 'Trumpets of Jericho' was often fitted to the SC type, and was usually made from thick cardboard of First World War bayonet scabbards. They were shaped like organ pipes approximately 14-in in length and gave a fearsome shriek as the bomb fell. This device caused the greatest stress and put fear in the hearts of the civilian population.

The SD range (*Sprengbombe-Dickwandig*), also called *Splitterbombe*, was designed as either an anti-personnel or semi-amour-piercing bomb with a load of about 35 per cent explosive. The fragmentation was more efficient than the SC although it possessed greater penetration ability, largely due to its streamlined casing.

The armour-piercing PC (*Panzerbombe-Cylindrisch*) was usually, because of its heavy hardened cast-steel casing, used against shipping targets or fortified build-ings such as concrete gun emplacements. The explosive charge was no more than about 20 per cent. Originally designed for coastal waters and shipping lanes, the aerial mine (*Luftmine*) was without doubt one of the most devastating weapons used, especially against land targets. The land mine, as it became known to the British public, was attached to a parachute with a high charge ratio of between 60 and 70 per cent explosive, which caused considerable blast damage over a very wide area.

The Incendiary Bomb (*Brandbombe*) was by far the most damaging weapon used by any airforce. Usually of the 1- and 2-kg type, each had a filling of thermite which burned sufficiently to melt steel. An investigation revealed that one ton of incendiaries could devastate over three acres, against only half that area if HEs had been used. Incendiaries were dropped in large metal containers, blown open at a predetermined height by an air-burst fuse, which released hundreds of missiles over a wide area.

Other types of incendiary, similar in appearance to the SC type of bomb were not widely used. The British called them 'Fire-pots' and they ranged in size from the 50-kg phosphorus-filled *Sprengbrand* to the 250- and 500-kg oil-filled *Flammenbombe*.

Saturday 21 December
21.08 TO 23.46 – SHELLS

As Christmas approached there had been little activity, although military observers had recorded 112 shells falling in the sea and in the harbour during the first week of the month. Even this had its lighter side. Bass, whiting, plaice and codling, killed or stunned by the detonations, came to the surface in shoals. Over one ton was retrieved by jubilant gunners off the breakwater.

One shell had badly damaged 24 and 26 Douglas Road, both were later demolished as unsafe. Only three shells landed in the town on this day, causing craters in Taswell Hill and the Crabble Athletic Ground.

Dover was to enjoy five complete days without a bomb or shell falling on the town. Christmas fayre was sparse in the shops and it was no good pretending that trade was booming. Sufficient shops remained, however, to supply everybody and provide their owners with a livelihood. Dover still had three cinemas and one theatre, where at the latter artistes and audience met over a friendly drink in the bars.

CHAPTER THREE

1941

'There's Another Baby There'

The threat of invasion had, more or less, passed away and the task of our coastal gun batteries was effectively to close the Dover Strait to enemy shipping. In order to supply their ports on the Channel and Atlantic coasts of France, the Germans began to send small convoys of merchantmen and tankers through.

The Coast Artillery under Dover Fire Command came under 12 Corps. Its first Corps Commander with the rank of Brigadier was General Bernard Montgomery, a former Dover College boy. He was later replaced by Lt. Col. C.W. Raw, who was to remain in that post for the duration of the war.

Once the Dover defences expanded, and more importantly, the offensive was undertaken to close the Dover Strait to enemy shipping, the new administrative and control staff were provided with a headquarters in the deep tunnels located beneath Dover Castle. These tunnels, sometimes referred to as casemates, were cut into the chalk. They were air conditioned and led off into spacious rooms where all three services had their own operational command posts. The whole system was completely safe from aerial attack and shell bombardment.

The first radar sets supplied for the use of Coastal Artillery appeared in February 1941, and were designed to give early warning of the approach of enemy ships. Depending on weather conditions, these sets were capable of picking up targets at 40,000 yards' range, and sometimes even greater ranges were achieved.

The western entrance to Dover Harbour was now blocked by the wreck of the *War Sepoy*, towed there and sunk the previous September. However, through the continued battering of heavy seas and difficult tides it eventually broke up into three parts.

Vice-Admiral Ramsey quickly acquired another block ship, the *Minnie Larrinaga*, which had been severely damaged in the London docks during the early blitz. This cargo vessel was of no further use and was towed from her berth on the Thames and brought to Dover, arriving in January 1941. She was filled with ballast and sunk directly over the wreck of the *War Sepoy*. The eastern entrance remained open but protected by a floating movable boom, attached to which was an iron mesh below water level to prevent the passage of enemy torpedoes. It was controlled by a naval officer and was opened and closed by a Dover Harbour tug.

At the Prime Minister's insistence, two 6-in guns were installed on the Western Heights, above the town, to increase fire power. They were ready for action in the latter part of 1940. Two 4-in guns were installed on the Knuckle of the eastern arm. Lydden Spout was equipped with three 6-in guns, three 8-in land guns were being erected at Capel le Ferne, and a further three 8-in land guns had been given a site half way between Capel and the Citadel.

All Dover's coastal defence guns, from the 6-in downwards, were designated No. 519 Coast Regiment, RA, and the larger artillery pieces were under No. 520 Coast Regiment, RA. The larger guns, installed to the east of Dover in the St Margaret's area, came under No. 540 Coast Regiment, RA, and consisted of the two 15-in guns, the four 9.2-in guns and three additional 6-in located at Fan Bay. The Prime Minister, in a memo to General Ismay in January 1941, outlined his concern at the delay in installing the new batteries. Despite Churchill's protestations, however, the larger guns were late in reaching 'action stations'.

Monday 6 January
08.24 TO 09.25 – HES

Lightening fighter-bomber raids were more frequent and became a breakfast-time feature along the whole of the south-east coast. The siren went off just four minutes before the first bomb fell at the rear of 38 Mayfield Avenue, close to the Dover – Deal railway line. It is perhaps interesting to note that one of the 13.5-in super heavy railway guns was making a practice run on the railway track at that time. A second bomb, also aimed at the railway line, exploded at the top of Astley Avenue. Damage was confined to roofs and windows which spread into Minerva Avenue and Heathfield Avenue. There were no casualties reported.

Thursday 16 January
01.53 TO 06.03 – HES – IBS

While London was attacked in the early hours, along with many other towns and cities in the Midlands, a lone Stuka dive-bomber, carrying an SC1000 armour-piercing bomb, dived on the castle. Clearly visible in the bright moonlight, the ack-ack guns opened fire. Shell bursts were seen all around the aircraft. It might have been thrown off its course slightly because the bomb fell on Victoria Mews. Castle Hill Road was blocked by debris and every telephone wire had come down with the blast. There were no casualties reported.

Just after 03.00 a Heinkel 111 appeared over the town and released a shower of incendiaries. Fires were started at the Citadel Barracks, Limekiln Street, and in many other parts of the town, such as Strond Street, Belgrave Road, the Ferry Dock, and the most serious fire occurred at the Lukey's Bonded Store Vaults in the Commercial Dock.

★ ★ ★

Lance-Bombardier G.A. Freeman, on the Breakwater Battery, was watching the slow progress of the motor boat *Silver Wings*. It was carrying twenty-nine civilians to the Admiralty Pier where they were employed. It was a particularly foul day and the sea was running high. Suddenly the engine stopped. The high winds blew the boat towards a cable that was attached to the blockship. Freeman knew that if the boat collided with the cable it would most probably overturn in the strong tide. Drifting diagonally out into the choppy sea it was rocking violently and the plight of the civilians onboard was getting steadily worse. A rope was tied around Freeman's waist. He was then helped to slide down the slippery side of the breakwater. Several times he looked like slipping into the icy water far below, but after about twenty minutes he managed to climb over the gunwale of the motor boat. For his gallant action in saving life he was commended in 12 Corps Orders.

★ ★ ★

The Governor of Massachusetts in the United States of America broadcast from the Council Chamber of Dover, Mass., a message of good cheer and hope to Dover, England. The gift of a motor kitchen to the town was also announced – a magnificent piece of generosity from their American friends. He said: 'You in Dover, England, who, looking out towards the shores of France, are in the front line as guardians of Liberty, and we in Dover, Mass., are proud to share with you the same language, the same laws, and the same ideals. As a token of good feeling, we are sending to you a motor kitchen, and hope that it will shortly be seen in your streets.'

★ ★ ★

The King had approved the award of the DSM, in recognition of gallant conduct in action with the enemy, to Warrant Officer Class II (C.S.M.) James McDonald, The Green Howards. When dive-bombers attacked Dover Harbour on 29 July 1940, a sandbag emplacement received a direct hit, with two men being buried. Through blinding and acrid fumes and with bombs still falling in other parts of the harbour, C.S.M. McDonald led a rescue team, and was himself instrumental in digging out the men, one of whom was already dead. On 27 September 1940, while the harbour was being shelled by long-range guns, one shell burst a few yards from C.S.M. McDonald, and his Company Commander, Captain F. Lawson, was fatally wounded. C.S.M. McDonald assisted to place the officer on a stretcher and supervised his removal to hospital while other shells were falling close by.

★ ★ ★

The Prime Minister and Mrs Churchill visited Dover on Friday 24 January, accompanying Mr Harry Hopkins, the American President's personal representative, who was making a fortnight's tour of Britain. The Rt. Hon. A.V. Alexander, First Lord of the Admiralty, was also in the party. They came to see the Coastal Defences, but Churchill, more especially, wanted to see the long-range guns being erected at the Wanstone Farm site.

★ ★ ★

The award of the George Medal to Frederick John Hopgood, Master of one of the Dover Harbour tugs, was announced on Friday 24 January. The official account stated: 'During an air raid on Dover three vessels which lay abreast alongside a jetty, the tug being in the middle, were in danger from burning oil. Hopgood, aided by his engineer and the tug's boy, managed after considerable difficulty to tow all three vessels clear of the danger area.'

Sunday 2 February
13.27 TO 16.20 – HEs

The Chief Constable of Dover, Marshall H. Bolt, received his OBE from the King at Buckingham Palace, and missed the action when three fighter-bombers swept in just after 15.00. Several balloons had been shot down to clear the way for the attack. One of them had fallen on the eastern arm where the gunners tied it to railings. Major Arnold recalled that he acquired a nice, new silver tablecloth for his table. The Shakespeare Inn, Elizabeth Street, was among thirty buildings badly damaged in the explosions. Several army married quarters in South Military Road were also damaged. There were no casualties reported.

Sunday 16 February
14.04 – HES

The Record of Incidents states: '14.04 – Bomb – Farthingloe. Bomb fell on gun site. FAP and Ambulance sent. 3 casualties dealt with by Military.'

A concert party had appeared at Dover's Royal Hippodrome Theatre on 10 February, and was about to give a free concert to gunners of D1 gun site when a bomb exploded. It smashed the stage, buried the piano and damaged the party's car. Mrs Warner, a trained nurse, and wife of the compère, set to work and gave

In silhouette against silver clouds, four JU88s were identified. Ack-ack guns opened fire. The cacophony of sound burst upon the ear-drums as exploding bombs straddled the town. (Above) 390 HAA Battery's 3.7-in ack-ack guns above Farthingloe Farm

first aid to those injured in the blast. When an ambulance had removed the more severely injured, the piano was dug out of the wreckage, dusted off and the show moved to a Nissen hut. There were four women in the party: Tania, the striptease artiste, who also played the piano; Barbara Bentham, singer and dancer; Mabel Walters and Olive Ashley. They had planned to have a meal before the bomb exploded, but all the cook could salvage of their meal was some roast potatoes. The show went on nevertheless.

Friday 28 February
14.11 TO 14.39 – HES

The Langdon Battery had been bombed the day before by a Dornier which suddenly appeared out of low cloud. There were several military casualties. On this last day of February the same thing happened again, when, just after 14.00, another Dornier released four bombs on the town. One exploded on the already-wrecked Sussex Arms, Townwall Street, while the others further damaged properties in Guildford Lawn and Clarence Street. Sections of the seafront railway track were also uprooted.

Friday 10 March
14.11 TO 17.40 – HES – UXBS

There were as many as six ALERTS a day while enemy aircraft attacked targets further inland. During the hours of darkness searchlights and ack-ack guns were busy as townspeople tried to sleep.

Messerschmitts appeared in the afternoon. Granville Gardens erupted and the blast knocked over several airmen on the balloon site. Explosions in Granville Dock decanted hundreds of gallons of muddy water and toppled a telephone kiosk over onto its back. There were no casualties reported.

OPENING THE WOOLTON RESTAURANT

Lord Woolton, the Minister of Food, stated that a Feeding Centre was as essential to a town as a fire station. He said:

> The establishment of community feeding centres, at which good, well-cooked food can be obtained at prices within the range of nearly everybody, is a definite contribution towards our war effort. Its prime purpose is to protect the poorest against food shortages and rising prices. Good, well-cooked meals will be sold at the following prices: Adult dinner, 6d. [5p], sweet extra,

2d. [1p], Child's dinner, 3d. [2½p], sweet extra, 1d. Hot dinners will be served between midday and 2.00 p.m. each day, from Monday to Saturday. Tea, 1d. per cup.

The new community centre was called the Borough of Dover Woolton Restaurant, and was located in St Mary's Parish Hall. Officially opened at 12.30 on Wednesday 12 March, Councillors Gates and Williams entertained the Corporation to lunch. The film and stage actress, Miss Evelyn Laye, performed the opening ceremony and sang a few old favourites.

In the first week over 150 people took advantage of the new restaurant, most townspeople taking their meals home to eat. Its popularity grew so that in just one month nearly 300 meals were being provided.

Monday 31 March
11.10 TO 12.40 – SHELLS

During this reasonably quiet period, work was in progress to clear many wrecked sites of debris and make safe some of the badly damaged buildings.

The siren went off after the first shell exploded at the junction of London Road and St Radigund's Road. Several houses were damaged and one woman was found later in a daze. Obviously suffering from extreme shock, with loss of hearing, she was taken to hospital to recover.

Flashman's Furniture Depository, in Dieu Stone Lane, was hit. Inside was stored furniture, rescued from damaged properties. Most of it became matchwood. When a shell exploded in the Borough Engineer's Yard, Ladywell, a lorry caught alight.

The first of the second salvo demolished 22 Bartholomew Street. Seventy-seven-year-old Rosa Nicholls was found later beneath her wrecked home, and there were three seriously injured casualties. A direct hit on 36 Dour Street sent the whole terrace rocking on its foundations, making it look ready to topple into the street. Water gushed out of fractured mains like fountains and broken gas mains caught alight. Brook House was only slightly damaged when the last shell exploded on the bowling green. Mrs Ashman had a frightening experience: her Anderson shelter suddenly telescoped into just 4 feet, caused by blast. Unable to move even a finger, she was only discovered when her absence was noticed by a neighbour.

Thursday 3 April
15.08 TO 15.25 – LAND MINE

A loud bang was heard. The shell warning went off immediately. Within 15 minutes the ALL CLEAR sounded. A terrible accident had occurred at

Shakespeare Beach. A young Canadian soldier had trod on a mine and had died instantly. In the evening the tragedy was being discussed in the public houses, along with many animated conversations regarding the loss of HMT *Gullfoss*, sunk by a mine on 9 March. Only eleven survivors were returned to Dover Harbour. Twenty-four had been lost, including survivors of the *Keryado* also sunk in similar circumstances.

The conversations led on to discuss HMD *Youngman* and the HMY *Chico*, both boats sharing the honour of shooting down a Junkers 88 (JU88) bomber on 20 March. When HMD *Youngman* returned to harbour it brought with it one wing of the bomber and pieces of the crew which had fallen on the deck.

Dover's 1000th ALERT was sounded on the afternoon of 8 April. Over 400 had been logged since the beginning of the year, giving an approximate average of thirty per week. There were ten ALERTS on the following day and on Good Friday, 11 April, another seven were logged.

★ ★ ★

KENT COUNTY SPITFIRE FUND
THE INVICTA FLIGHT

'The Invicta Flight of aircraft shall be the symbol of their defiance,' said Lord Beaverbrook, Minister of Aircraft Production, in a letter to Lord Cornwallis, President of the Association of Men of Kent and Kentish Men. He was acknowledging a cheque for a further £5,000 from the Kent County Spitfire Fund, totalling £30,000 so far contributed by the fund. Dover's Spitfire Fund had reached £1,370 by 18 April.

On Easter Sunday 13 April dozens of balloons were shot down in flames. Grass was set alight and cables fell across streets. Then the Wanstone Battery site was plastered with shells.

It gradually dawned on the befuddled mind that most, if not all of the publicity given to the plight of the citizens of Dover in the thousands of words which appeared in newspapers and magazines throughout the English-speaking world, not to mention umpteen broadcasts, was pure propaganda. Dover was being harassed by enemy action, and yet had not experienced the intense bombing where whole areas were laid waste. Equally, they had not experienced the awful conflagration that seared the hearts and minds of those who had lived through the blitz in London and the industrial cities.

At the best of times, the emphatic symbolism of Dover's white cliffs was just as dramatic whether you were at war or not. Dover's proximity to the enemy helped to bolster its image in the world's news. But in 1941 journalists in the comparatively safe areas of the West Country were becoming a little curious about that visible and tangible front of the white cliffs.

One curious journalist took a bus ride to Dover from Canterbury, deciding *en route* to look out for signs of normality in the town. He wanted to see for himself the homely signs of curtained windows, children, dogs and flowers in shops. As the bus entered Dover, and until it reached its terminus in the Market Square, he counted eighteen prams, all occupied. There were, of course, flowers, curtained windows and busy shops still in evidence. But he could not help noticing the many scars: roofs devoid of their tiles, hundreds of windows boarded up, and here and there gaps in the rows of terraced houses.

After nightfall, he visited the Hippodrome, where he had drinks with the cast and members of the audience during the interval. During the performance the sirens went off. But no one moved to take shelter. The artistes on stage continued their acts. He was impressed that twice-nightly shows at the theatre must have performed infinite war-service not only to the packed houses but to world-wide audiences who saw through the eyes of visiting journalists.

On his way back to Canterbury he thought maybe the children and flowers and the cosy gilt of the music hall was just historic folly. But he had found the semblance of normality he had been looking for. As the bus climbed slowly out of Dover he heard the 'crump, crump' of shells exploding. The bus conductor remarked, casually, 'We left just in time!'

Thursday 24 April
08.21 TO 12.15 – HES

The shell warning had gone off four days before when the Germans noticed a large merchantman slowly passing Dover at about midday. Six shells reached the town boundary, two exploding on the Citadel Barracks, two more at the Farthingloe gun site, and the last two falling on the Shakespeare Beach. There were no casualties reported.

Enemy fighter-bombers were still making their individual raids, and the one that occurred at Dover at 08.30 on Thursday morning caused some speculation by military authorities.

Did the pilot know the real location of 961's Repair Depot, situated behind the Dover Engineering Foundary? The balloon barrage was obviously a thorn in the side of low-flying enemy aircraft. Perhaps we will never know. But the fact remains tantalizingly controversial. Just one bomb fell to explode on the RAF Repair Depot. The fighter was observed to jink this way and that, avoiding the other balloons swaying above the town and harbour. The depot was wrecked in the explosion, seriously injuring two personnel. An RAF sergeant later died in hospital. There were no civilian casualties.

Saturday 26 April
14.07 TO 15.03 – SHELLS

The shell warning went off just after 14.00. One fell in the harbour and the next exploded at the entrance to the Trevanion Caves. Military opinion refuted the suggestion that the caves had been the target. Shells fired on the town could not be placed with such accuracy. Nevertheless, two soldiers were killed and a further eight were injured. More shells fell on Connaught Park, and very close to the castle.

Tuesday 29 April
09.45 – SHELLS

Although this was the longest period of shelling since last summer, only one airburst type exploded over the town. It had burst over Mayfield Avenue and slightly injured two people.

Shells fell at the gun sites east of the town, bracketing Guston, East Langdon, Martin Mill, Swingate radar masts and the Wanstone Battery. There were as many as six shells exploding within seconds of each other and all of them were of the air-burst type, sending shrapnel out in all directions. Visibility was extremely clear and the French coast plainly seen. Considerable damage occurred at the gun emplacements and several military personnel were injured, along with three civilians working there – Dennis Keeler, William Irving and James Rogers.

★ ★ ★

TEAR GAS IN DOVER

The Dover ARP arranged for the public release of tear gas exercises in Dover on Monday 5 May at 15.00 to 19.00. The object of these exercises was to bring home to the public the need for always having a gas mask with them.

In the afternoon, tear gas containers were opened in the main street between Beaconsfield Road and the Town Hall. Most people had their gas masks with them and walked through the area, but some were caught without respirators. The concentration of gas, however, was not large enough to cause any serious inconvenience.

As people came to the area affected, they were warned of the gas by the police. They carried placards announcing that the gas had been released and wardens used rattles. Buses stopped while the drivers put their gas masks on and the passengers did the same. Another test in the evening occurred at the junction of Worthington Street and Biggin Street, and also in the Market Square. More gas was used here and many people ran away as fast as they could, for few carried masks in the evening. In addition, the decontamination squads dealt with oily patches of a substance similar to mustard gas put down in Peter Street and Queen's Gardens.

Wednesday 7 May
19.33 TO 20.57 – SHELLS

Although sporadic bombing of our industrial cities continued for another two years, May 1941 saw the last of Germany's night saturation bombing techniques. Sirens continued to wail – they were never silent. Shells continued to come over and there was little respite.

The shell warning sounded after 39 Leyburne Road, fortunately unoccupied, suddenly fell into the street at about 19.30. The next explosion was in Market Square, outside the Westminster Bank. It overturned a Ford V8 motor car. The occupants, Mr Hare, general manager of Tillmanstone Colliery, and a naval officer, were taken to hospital suffering from shock and minor injuries. An East Kent bus was severely damaged and both the driver and conductor were cut by flying glass. Eighteen-year-old Louie Pritchard, just arrived for fire-watching duty, was killed instantly by a large jagged piece of plate glass, when the window of Igglesden & Graves, the baker's, was blown out. Joseph Eley lost his life while standing on the pavement, and twenty-one-year-old Ethel May succumbed to her terrible injuries long before she reached the hospital. She was not identified until the following day because she lived at Hougham Lodge Farm.

Other shells exploded in Priory Road, where there were three serious casualties, and Norman Street, and a workshop collapsed behind the Co-operative Grocery Department. Two more reached Green Lane, Glenfield Road and Buckland Valley Farm.

★ ★ ★

Reginald Foster, the *Daily Herald* front line reporter at Dover, who later wrote *Dover Front*, decided to re-form a cricket club at Capel le Ferne. The original club had been closed in 1940. The new club was called Capel Civvies Cricket Club. Reg Foster was secretary and Tom Moor, licensee of the Royal Oak public house, was the treasurer. The first fixture was played against a Royal Artillery XI on 10 May 1941 and, during the season, with sufficient support and enemy action permitting, games were arranged with just about every service unit in the area, including the police and Civil Defence.

Farmer Tom Mount's field, close to the Royal Oak, was reasonably flat, except for a few undulations, rabbit holes and bomb craters. Reg Foster recalled: 'It was a very desirable site. The boundary wire coincided with the boundary of the Royal Oak. Every cricket ground should have a pub within a ball throw. White being thought too conspicuous from the air, after all, Messerschmitts were still flying around at low level, it was decided to play in either grey flannel or uniform.'

In that war-defying season Capel put village cricket back on record, although it is doubtful *Wisden's Cricket Almanack* ever recorded it. Many to whom the war was very near – minesweeper men, airmen, coastal battery teams – enjoyed briefly, the best that Capel could offer. Cricket and beer. There may have been better cricket, possibly even better beer, but no combination just like the two, at that particular time.

Spectators included many journalists, both British and American. One, a pianist-photographer, who did not play cricket but helped with the social life afterwards, eventually went to the Middle East and his action pictures were his last. Ben Robertson, the American writer, later killed in a Lisbon Clipper crash, was an interested by slightly puzzled spectator.

The rough and ready ground became a meeting place for thwarted sportsmen. Privates and captains, seamen and lieutenants, were all glad to find an enduring corner of embattled England. Mrs Moor, Tom's wife, happily performed the miracle of laying on tea and cakes at every match. Later she even managed to put on a cricket supper at the Royal Oak. Reg Foster said, 'If Goering had come across we could have given him a pint, some steak-and-kidney pudding and some useful background material about the state of England. It might have helped a lot.'

Saturday 10 May
03.25 TO 06.35 – HEs – *FLAMMENBOMBE*

It was a full moon and the Channel waters glistened and shimmered. Above the huge, mountainous clouds, heavily laden bombers were heading towards London. Searchlights probed the sky looking for victims and, occasionally, the ack-ack fired a lethal round or two when the enemy was caught in a beam.

It was almost 03.30 when a lone Heinkel 111 appeared over the town. Its course would have taken it out over the gleaming Channel and back to its French airfield. Bomb doors open, it released a shower of SC250s and one *flammenbombe* over the castle area.

Cliff James, Royal Signal Regiment recalls:

> One bomb hit the castle, one damaged the sergeants' mess and another failed
> to explode. The latter knocked over a pole carrying most of the telephone
> lines leaving the castle. We were instructed to mend all the lines that had
> snapped when the pole toppled over. There were about six of us linesmen, all
> frightened out of our wits, trying to be as quick as we could in case the bomb
> exploded with us on the pole right above the thing. In a way it was funny.
> Our NCO in charge was at a safe distance from us, anxiously peering from
> behind a bank, while us poor signalmen were doing the repair. The lines were
> all of the same colour and indistinguishable, so we had to test each pair of
> wires before repairing and reconnecting. We spent over an hour on this fiddly
> job but at last every line worked. Later that day the Royal Engineer Bomb
> Disposal Squad excavated the bomb. I watched it leaving the castle. Talk
> about living on your nerves! I was shattered at the end of that job.

★ ★ ★

DOVER WAR WEAPONS WEEK

The Dover War Weapons Week, which began on Wednesday 21 May, and
which ended on Wednesday 28 May, was a big success, £209,105 was the
final total. This was almost double the target aimed at – £110,000, the
price of two Motor Torpedo Boats, and reflects credit, not only on the
organizers, but on the people of Dover who remain here. With such a
reduced population, and many businesses and industries gone, there were
not a few people who considered that even the target of £110,000 was too
high. When the first day brought in £42,000, opinions changed quickly,
and by the end of the fourth day the question was by how much the
amount would be exceeded.

★ ★ ★

On Wednesday 28 May the Mayor received an ambulance sent from North
America by the British American Ambulance Corps. The ambulance was given
by Henry, Charles and Jack Misner, of Port Dover, Ontario in Canada, and the
Corps wrote to the Mayor stating that they thought it fitting that the ambulance
should be given to Dover.

The ambulance, a khaki-coloured Chevrolet, was driven to Dover by a member of FANY, who was received by the Mayor and Mayoress, members of the

First Aid Post personnel at the Winchelsea Caves, photographed in 1941, are from left to right (standing): Mrs Glass, Kathlene Bland, Sylvia Anscombe, Mr Watts, Bridget Willis, Vera Willis; (seated): Mrs Holborn, Florence Lamoon, Gwendoline Curd, Dr Waugh, Sister Craft, Francis Kemp amd Mrs Betts

Council, the Town Clerk, the Chief Constable and other officers, and Mrs Beeston WVS.

★ ★ ★

A letter sent to the *Dover Express* stated:

Owing to my being totally incapacitated by blindness through shell shock, I am compelled to CLOSE MY BUSINESS, which I established forty-three years ago. This will take place on 31 May 1941. Any accounts due from me should be sent as soon as possible to 35 High Street. I will esteem it a courtesy if any accounts due to me could be treated in a like manner. I am sorry to have to shut down after all these years, but in my present condition of being unable to see, no other course is open.

Signed C.E. Beaufoy
Builder & Undertaker

★ ★ ★

SENTRY SHOOTS CIVILIANS

Three Dover men travelling in a car from Deal to Dover, on Sunday 1 June, were shot at by a sentry. The weather was misty and it was suggested the driver of the vehicle had mistaken the road leading to Dover and must have turned into a military area. The sentry challenged but could not be heard over the noise of the engine. He opened fire and two of the men were struck by bullets. They were taken to hospital suffering from thigh wounds.

Thursday 12 June
00.26 TO 05.13 – *LUFTMINE*, LM1000

The *Luftwaffe* progressively intensified its aerial mine operations in the British shipping lanes. At the same time, however, the British civilian population was on the receiving end of many reprisal raids. The incident at Dover on 12 June 1941 was one of the worst experienced by the town so far, resulting in fifteen fatalities and over twenty seriously injured.

The ALERT had sounded at 00.26, but it was another three hours before a lone Heinkel 111 was approaching the town with a sinister *Luftmine* (LM1000)

When the LM1000 aerial mine floated down on its parachute to explode on Randolph Road, in the early hours of 12 June 1941, it caused fifteen deaths and over twenty more were seriously injured. It also demolished forty houses and seriously damaged a further 150

beneath its fuselage. Its target, presumably, was the gasworks in Union Road.

The mine was released from about 1500 feet, and floated down on its parachute to explode on the unsuspecting, sleeping occupants of Randolph Road. The explosion demolished 40 houses, seriously damaged 150, and partly damaged a further 420 in adjacent streets. Over one hundred people were evacuated from shattered homes. Three of the gasometers had their iron plating blown in, releasing thousands of gallons of water which lay between the two skins protecting the gas.

Within a short space of time soldiers had joined ARP rescue teams. They toiled for many hours, in relays, to dig out those people trapped beneath tons of rubble. Before dawn broke upon the devastated scene there was already a pitiful row of lifeless, blanket-clad bodies, lying beside the kerb in Union Road.

The Salvation Army mobile canteen was serving tea to the dust-covered rescuers, who stood in silence, their hands cut and bruised by the jagged, sharp edges of tile and brick. Most of them had never before experienced such carnage. They were bewildered by it all. Beholding dismembered bodies, still warm to the touch, was unnerving, to say the least.

Four complete families had been wiped from the face of the earth in the time taken to blink an eye. At No. 8, brothers George and Harold Cock were found alive but their parents had died. Five of the Castle family were quickly, and unceremoniously, dragged from their wrecked home feet first, even three-year-old Malcolm. They were among the first to be carried away to hospital. At No. 14 there was intense activity where the whole Willis family had been buried. Small tunnels appeared like magic in the debris, through which rescuers made slow progress towards cries for help. Agonizing minutes passed before sixteen-year-old Vera was found, still alive. Her multiple injuries, however, proved fatal, even before she reached hospital. Four-year-old Brian was found about an hour later but there were no signs of life in this little warm body. Twenty-five-year-old Horace had been crushed against a wall, beneath which lay his mother and father. All had died.

As the sun rose in the sky so more victims were found. Some had already succumbed to their terrible injuries, while others were given life-saving emergency treatment. Doctors and nurses were frantically fighting against time.

Among the rescuers were many volunteers who, without a moment's delay or thought of their own safety, joined in to swarm over the piles of bricks and masonry. Albert Minter was one, another was Jonathan Mills, who had been invalided out of the Seaforth Highlanders soon after Dunkirk. He ran from his home and was among the debris before anyone knew he was there. He heard a muffled cry for help coming from a pile of rubble at the rear of No. 10. He recalled:

I dug a tunnel through the wreckage, propping up debris with pieces of wood. As I crawled through I came across the handle of a pram sticking out of a pile of bricks. I tore away the bricks and uncovered the pram in which I felt a kiddy's leg. There was a baby about a year old in the pram, and before I pulled it out I remembered to put my fingers into its mouth and draw out the dirt and dust to save it from suffocating. After carrying the baby to safety, I crawled back through the tunnel and came across a wrecked bed, which had been overturned. I broke off the back of the bed, chopped through the springs, then slit up the mattress to pull the feathers out. There was a woman in the bed and one of her legs was pinned down by a length of piping. This I cut with a hacksaw handed down to me by Albert Minter. Now I reached down to the woman's head and managed to get a bottle of water to her mouth and let her have a wee drop. She said, 'There's another baby there.' I smelt gas escaping and shouted to get it turned off, and then, after I had given her another drop, they got the woman out. Going forward, I found the other kiddy's cot, and as soon as I got the child free a bit, I sucked at its mouth and blew back again to see if there was any life in it. But unfortunately there wasn't.

Mills and Minter had been working in the rubble at what was No. 10 and had been responsible for the rescue of Ella Smith, seriously injured, and her five-year-old daughter Daphne. Three-year-old Doris had died in her cot. The bodies of Minnie and Charles Talbot were eventually recovered from No. 12 but Annie and Harold were found alive, although seriously injured. When the Kent Mobile Unit arrived in convoy most of the injured had been found. Other casualties included Douglas Wills, Mary Chapman, George Castle, Dorothy Oliver, Gertrude Goldsack, Mr and Mrs Dove and a Mr Reed. A man and woman were later dug out of the wreckage but remained unidentified.

Saturday 18 June
SPITFIRE CRASH

When returning from a 'Wing Sweep' over Cap Gris Nez, 609 squadron was bounced by Messerschmitts. Plt. Off. S.J. Hill's Spitfire was heavily damaged in the ensuing combat and was forced to break off the engagement. He managed to avoid 'ditching' in the sea but, too low to bale out of his stricken machine, decided to crash-land at RAF Hawkinge. Ack-ack gunners anxiously watched his slow progress. The Spitfire left a trail of black smoke in its wake. Then without warning, it plunged into the side of the hill beside the Folkestone Road near Capel le Ferne. Bursting into flames on impact the pilot perished in the cockpit. He was later buried at Hawkinge Cemetery.

Monday 30 June
BLENHEIM CRASH

Blenheims of 59 squadron, based at Detling, had been bombing German military installations on the French coast around midnight. One of them returned at low level making for Dover. Perhaps it had been damaged. We will never know. It hit a barrage balloon cable above Admiralty Pier. The aircraft swung round like a top and spiralled into the sea. Only the pilot, Plt. Off. J.N. Whitmore, was found and was later buried with full military honours at Hawkinge Cemetery. Sergeants Dulley and Truman were never found.

★ ★ ★

A limited number of 'Morrison' steel table shelters will be available for free distribution to householders within the Borough of Dover, whose income is below £350 per annum (to which may be added £50 for each child of school age in excess of two), or who are compulsorily insured under the National Health Insurance Act. A limited number of these shelters may also be available for sale at approximately £7 each to householders with a greater income than that stated above. Persons who wish to register for a table shelter must fill in a form, which may be obtained at my office at Brook House. Applicants for these forms must state whether they propose to apply for a free table shelter, or whether they desire to buy one.

Signed S.R.H. Loxton
Town Clerk
Brook House Dover

Thursday 10 July
13.40 – MESSERSCHMITT CRASH

The RAF was to learn the secrets of the latest Messerschmitt Bf 109F fighter of 1/JG26, when *Hauptmann* Rolf Peter Pingel, too low to bale out, made a forced landing in a corn field near St Margaret's Bay. Close to the cliff edge, he scrambled out of the cockpit, pistol in hand, ready to set his aircraft on fire. But a burst of machine-gun fire from a sentry persuaded him otherwise. Pingel dropped his pistol and put his hands above his head. A *Gruppenkommandeur* with twenty-two victories to his credit and holder of the *Ritterkreuz* decoration, he was taken prisoner of war.

The RAF were to learn the secrets of the latest Messerschmitt BF109F fighter, when *Hauptmann* Rolf Peter Pingel, of 1/JG26, made a forced landing in a cornfield at St Margarets on 10 July 1941

Wednesday 25 July
00.45 TO 01.22 – SHELLS

The Prime Minister made a quick visit to Dover in June. Determined to press on with installing the latest gun batteries, he was informed that completion was delayed because of unsuitable gun mountings, lack of materials and a labour force, and further learned of the deficiencies of ammunition fuses and charges.

In spite of heavy bombing raids made on German installations in France, they were not similarly inconvenienced it seems. They fired a salvo of ten shells at Dover on this day, eight fell in the harbour area and only one exploded on the town. Barwick's Yard, Market Street, was the recipient where a large shed was demolished and a further twenty houses were damaged. There was one female casualty, hurt by flying debris.

★ ★ ★

Dover was always in the news, both national and international, but the latest press release mentioned a new song which became one of the most popular of the war period. It was published by Shapiro, Bernstein and Co. New York, with words by Nat Burton and music by Walter Kent, and the song called 'There'll be blue birds over the white cliffs of Dover', took the music world by storm and was sung in just about every theatre in England, not to mention the Dover Hippodrome. Over fifty years later, it is still among the most nostalgic songs associated with the Second World War, both in the UK and abroad.

★ ★ ★

The Reverend W.E. Purcell, vicar of St Mary's Church, still made entries in his leather-bound vestry book. 'Evensong – shelling during service', is a typical example. In the remarks column for the last Easter Day appeared the comment, 'Service attended by the Mayor and Corporation – heavy machine gunning of balloons during service.'

As the vicar climbed the steps to the pulpit to make his sermon, two Bren guns near the church opened fire on Messerschmitts. There was no comment from the congregation – nobody went out. He asked them to sing a hymn and by the time it was over the raiders had gone.

On another occasion, ten minutes before a wedding was to take place, a shell warning sounded. The vicar, an air raid warden, reported to his post. The bridegroom, a sailor, seemed puzzled at finding the church empty. The bride came along 20 minutes later, having donned her trousseau in a near-by shelter.

Tuesday 19 August
21.35 TO 22.15 – HEs

A Heinkel 111 drew attention to itself by circling the town before releasing bombs. Ack-ack opened fire just as the bombs fell. Tapley's Garage in Cambridge Road was hit. The explosion brought down most of the building and blocked the road. Then three bombs exploded on the shipwright's workshops at the end of Snargate Street, where there were three casualties. Another fell behind the Hippodrome theatre, in the Wellington Dock. Hal Monty's revue had already finished by then and all the artistes had returned to their lodgings. Most of the rear windows were smashed, once again, and Mr Clements, on fire watch, was blown off his feet and struck by a large piece of masonry that came through the roof. Mrs Havers was just leaving the theatre when the explosion occurred. She was unceremoniously thrown flat to the ground by a passing sailor. The sailor vehemently protested his innocence when the bruised and shaken lady managed to crawl out from beneath him.

Enemy action was less intense now although bombers continued to hit targets further inland. Main objectives were laying mines in our coastal waters.

The first week of this month was peaceful enough, but on this particular night a lone JU88 dropped bombs below the castle escarpment. The already battered Burlington Hotel took three direct hits, killing the caretakers, Mr and Mrs Turner, instantly. William Horn, special constable and also manager of Peppin's the tailor's, Biggin Street, was killed at 43a Burlington Mansions. In the same building the Decorts had the fright of their lives when the floors of their flat disappeared beneath them. Fortunately Mrs Decort had run out into the corridor, which saved her life. Her husband was in the lavatory and just managed to grab a water pipe as the lavatory pan fell into a deep void.

The unoccupied Marine Garage in Woolcomber Street also received a direct hit. Rubble blocked the roads and the rescue teams were unsure if any one was buried there. They toiled for hours before giving up. It was a different story at

The towering Burlington Hotel complex near the seafront was systematically pounded by bomb and shell. On 7 September 1941 it took three bombs when a JU88 bomber released its missiles over the town, killing three people, including the caretakers Mr and Mrs Turner

the Burlington. Hurricane lamps and heavy-duty torches were used to penetrate the darkness, where successive floors had fallen upon the one below until there was one huge mass of broken timber and masonry. It was frustrating for the men trying to locate those trapped, not knowing whether they were alive or dead. Joseph and Rosa Turner, however, were not recovered until the following afternoon.

★ ★ ★

The Chief Constable of Dover, Mr Marshall H. Bolt, OBE, left the town to take up a new job as Chief Regional Fire Officer at No. 12 NFS Region, Tunbridge Wells. He relinquished his job as ARP Sub-Controller. The new Sub-Controller was now a former Chief Inspector of Police, Mr A.E. Scutt, who had been in charge of the Dover Control Centre since its inception. Chief Inspector H. Saddleton was appointed acting Chief Constable.

★ ★ ★

Two German merchant ships, escorted by armed trawlers and E-boats, were attempting to pass through the Dover Strait on the night of 8–9 September. Coastal forces were still short of boats and those based at Dover were slow – unable to exceed 24 knots.

Lt. Cdr. E.N. Pumphrey, RN, was in command of a small force of MTBs. The crews, having been at sea for the past five nights, were at 'long notice' – one hour. Most of them were enjoying a 'leg show' at the Hippodrome, which included such acts as Laughter & Lovelies, Ten Adorables, Gypsy Romano and her accordian, Cyraldo and his six Mysterious Maids and Hylda Baker, the comedienne.

The theatre manager received an urgent phone call, and in seconds the crews rushed out. Boats 35 and 218 got away from the Camber quickly but 54 had developed engine trouble. The enemy vessels had, by this time, already left Boulogne on a northbound course, and Pumphrey was ordered to intercept them at Blanc Nez. Two other MTBs were known to be at sea near the Varne. What followed was the first successful torpedo attack made by Dover-based MTBs.

It was a flat calm night, moonless – ideal conditions for Coastal Forces. Two 3,000-ton vessels were plotted about two miles distant. The MTBs closed in unseen, getting nearer and nearer to their targets. Pumphrey, apprehensive about the trawlers and E-boats, passed through the outer screen of E-boats at reduced speed. He then rung-up for full power. The terrific noise generated by the three engines alerted the enemy.

Motor gun boats in Dover harbour were used to attack German E-boats and R-boats in the close confines of the English Channel throughout World War II, and led to some of the most heavily fought engagements in naval history

Tracer shells curved towards the MTBs; nevertheless, No. 35 ran-in to less than 800 yards and fired a torpedo. There was a blinding flash – an underwater explosion. MTB 218 had fired her two 'tin fish' but her target had altered course at the last moment. Pumphrey had one torpedo left – it had misfired. Dover-based MGBs also joined in the action but the story is too long to record here.

Wednesday 17 September
20.10 TO 21.24 – HES

Another night intruder sortie was made by a JU88. The siren went off when the message was received from the castle operations room. Other JU88s were on similar missions crossing our coast at about 10-minute intervals.

The sky was bright and the bomber clearly seen. Its bombs, fitted to wing-racks, were released simultaneously. The ack-ack opened fire but were too late to make the raider alter course. Bombs straddled the streets and demolished ten houses, seriously damaging a further seventy-six, including the Red Lion public house at Charlton Green. No. 25 Bartholomew Street erupted, killing Edward Dive and his fourteen-year-old son Frederick. They were found pinned together by crushing forces. John Hatton's lifeless body was recovered after many hours searching among the rubble of his home at 26 Granville Street. Total casualties were 27, adults seriously injured numbered 11 male and 2 female, with 7 female slightly injured, and 4 children.

Rescue squads found difficulty in reaching Granville Street because the roads were blocked by rubble. Wardens, police and soldiers scrambled over the piles of bricks and masonry, hastily flinging everything to one side in a frantic effort to reach those buried before they succumbed either to the enormous pressures or the escaping gas which rapidly filled basement areas.

★ ★ ★

FIRE GUARDS

A further step forward in the development of the Dover Fire Prevention Service had been taken. Mr John H. Mowll, as Chief Warden, was entrusted with the responsibility to the Dover Corporation for the organization of the Fire Guard, and Mr H.W. Andrews, Group Warden, would now act as his deputy. The Emergency Committee had agreed to the following appointments: Fire Guard Staff Officer, Inspector Fenn; Head Fire Guard, Warden E. Lawrence; and five senior Fire Guards: Wardens S.H. Bailey, S.H. Davey, C. Dunkling, H.W. Pritchard and W.H. Smith. Headquarters was at the Civil Defence HQ Bridge Street.

★ ★ ★

The announcement that the Prime Minister had been appointed Lord Warden of the Cinque Ports at the personal wish of the King, was considered a great honour. 'May the fact that Mr Winston Churchill has become Lord Warden of the V Ports be a timely and auspicious omen of Victory,' ran an article in the *Dover Express*.

★ ★ ★

ESCAPE FROM BELGIUM

After drifting for three nights and two days in a 9-foot motor dinghy, described as a 'tub' with an outboard engine, four Belgian men and one elderly English woman, mother of one of the men, were brought to safety by a Dover launch. They had left the Belgian coast at night, and had almost given up hope of rescue when they were spotted by a reconnaissance Spitfire 20 miles from the English coast. The refugees had lost all sense of direction and were drifting back towards the enemy-held coast. The English woman was the wife of a Belgian business-man. Three months had been spent in organizing their escape. They had suc-ceeded in securing petrol from enemy supplies and also scraped together brandy and food for the trip. The Spitfire had dived low over the boat when the pilot saw something white fluttering at the end of an oar. The letters SOS had been written on it with lipstick.

Wednesday 1 October
23.48 – HES

The sirens went off just before midnight when a JU88 came in to drop bombs on the town. The ancient Archcliffe Fort was hit, an army lorry was set alight and there were three serious military casualties. Packed with trawlers and motor launches the Granville Dock was also hit, but there were no reports of either damage or casualties. Another bomb exploded just behind Adrian Street, dam-aging properties in Albany Place and Cow Gate Hill. Two more fell on Military Hill North, just above Selbourne Terrace, where a night-watchman Frederick Bexill was killed. The York Inn, Snargate Street, was seriously damaged by another bomb. There were no other casualties.

★ ★ ★

When Dover Council discussed cross-Channel shelling, Major John Martin, one of the members, said the town had had its 1,500th ALERT of the war. He opposed a request from the Board of Education that schooling should be given without delay to the 1,200 children remaining in the place. The schools had been closed since June 1940. Captain F.R. Powell, chairman of the Education Committee, said arrangements had been made to provide 825 children above the age of seven with an hour-and-a-half's tuition each day. Alderman F.H. Morecroft said neighbouring towns which Dover was asked to copy had not had shells dropping on them. 'We live right under the muzzles of the guns, yet chil-dren play about in the streets,' he said. He went on, 'If some of the education officials had the courage to come and live in Dover for a few weeks perhaps they would go away with a different view.'

Thursday 2 October
19.40 TO 23.30 – HES – UXBS

Three Heinkel 111s were identified heading for the town as the ALERT sounded at about 19.45. The 3.7-in ack-ack guns at Farthingloe were already loaded – their barrels traversing towards the raiders.

Six SC250s fell close to the docks exploding on Archcliffe Road and Limekiln Street, demolishing a row of houses and rendering over forty people homeless immediately. Two public houses were badly damaged by blast – the Archcliffe Fort and the Granville Arms. William Stacey had been walking home to the Rope Walk area and was killed instantly.

When the rescue squads arrived it was some hours before they found Alfred Court at 122 Limekiln Street, where he had died. There were quite a few customers in the Archcliffe pub when all the windows and doors suddenly blew in. The landlord ducked behind the counter but the mirrors and bottles just smashed to smithereens. George Manton, licensee of the Granville, heard the first bomb explode and rushed out to take his children to the shelter. His premises were similarly wrecked. John Greer was killed when his home collapsed in Snargate Street.

Clarendon Street erupted when Nos 135 and 139 were demolished. A number of people were trapped in the debris. Mary Dyer was found alive but terribly injured at 37 Military Road. She died two days later. WRNS and airmen at Dover College had narrow escapes when bombs fell in the grounds.

Bombs straddled the dock area causing serious damage to vital installations and equipment. One failed to explode and naval personnel were hastily evacuated. MGBs lying in the Ferry Dock were already fuelled and their ammunition boxes full to the brim with bullets, cannon shells and depth charges. The MLs were similarly equipped and ready for the night's foray in the Strait, also the MTBs which were ready to sail in two hours' time. Skippers ordered engines to be started up. One by one they slipped their moorings at the quayside and slowly moved out into the outer harbour area. More than half their crews were among the audience at the Hippodrome, watching Andrée, the daring exotic beauty, billed as the 'Darling of the Forces'.

The Wesley Chapel in Folkestone Road was severely damaged, also surrounding properties, including the Red Cow public house. Another unexploded bomb was discovered sticking out of the ground in the Packet Yard. Small fires were started in a number of shops. James and Annie Tapsell were missing when their house had collapsed on them. Once again the rescuers faced the ordeal of finding them before more masonry came down. Eighty-three-year-old Patrick Carberry was found in the ruins of 6 Dour Street, right next door to the missing Tapsells. Up the street Frank Field was later discovered at No. 49. Both Carberry and Field were taken to hospital with severe wounds. Frank was dead

on arrival, but Patrick was to survive another 24 hours before he died. Then the
Tapsells were found, both dead.

Three bombs exploded in Folkestone Road, at the junction with Malvern
Road. The roads were blocked with bricks, tiles and rafters. Thirteen people suffered injuries of one type or another. Gunner W.J. Carpenter of the Royal
Artillery, was walking in Folkestone Road, when he heard the familiar sound of
bombs falling. On the other side of the road he saw Doreen Hart, unaware of the
imminent danger. Instead of taking cover, and with complete disregard for his
own safety, he ran across the road and threw himself on the young girl, knocking
her to the ground. Carpenter was severely wounded when the bomb exploded.

The GOC-in-C of the Royal Artillery published a commendation in the AA
Command Orders for 6 November 1941. It said, 'The GOC-in-C. wishes to
congratulate Gunner W.J. Carpenter on his fine example and his prompt and
courageous action, and directs that his action be inscribed on his regimental

Children would recall, in sharp focus, the house that had collapsed . . . the smell of escaping gas . . .
the grey air and stench of explosives, the damp brickwork and plaster, the body of a small child
wrapped in a grubby sheet

conduct sheet.' Both Doreen Hart and Carpenter eventually ended up in hospital at Epsom. Carpenter had his left leg amputated.

★ ★ ★

Audiences at the Hippodrome had seen some first-class performances in recent weeks. One of the most popular of the music-hall stars was Miss Evelyn Laye, billed as 'Britain's Queen of Musical Comedy', accompanied by Albert Whelan. At the conclusion of Miss Laye's performance at the second house one Saturday night, Mr Armstrong, on behalf of the management, thanked her for her kindness and unselfishness in coming down to Dover. Later that same evening the Mayor attended and Miss Laye presented to him a cheque for £100 on behalf of herself and Albert Whelan, to be used by him for any deserving cause, at his discretion.

The following week there was a play in three scenes, by Arnold Ridley, called *The Ghost Train*. A NAAFI show organized by ENSA, it starred Arnold Ridley as the station-master, and readers will no doubt remember him as Godfrey in the BBC series 'Dad's Army'.

★ ★ ★

NOTICE IS HEREBY GIVEN – ran an advertisement in the *Dover Express*:

The Town Council of the Borough of Dover have decided to provide education for certain children who are still living in the Borough, and that the following Schools will be opened on Monday 13 October 1941, for part-time education:

PIER (C) – Archcliffe Road
CHRISTCHURCH (C.E.) – Military Road
ST. MARTIN'S (C) – Markland Road
ASTOR AVENUE (C) – Astor Avenue
BARTON ROAD (C) – Barton Road
BUCKLAND (C) – London Road
RIVER (C) – Common Lane, River

Only school children above the age of 8 years will be admitted in the first instance, and parents must register them at the schools nearest their homes on Monday 13 October, 1941, between 9.00 a.m. and 12 (noon) or between 2.00 p.m. and 4.30 p.m., when further instructions will be given as to the

Dover Borough Council decided that children above the age of eight years should have part-time education from 13 October 1941. This is Buckland Sunday School group on Palm Sunday, 29 March 1942

days and times the children are to attend. As the number of children at any one time must be restricted, all classes will be composed of boys and girls. Parents are warned that all school children above the age mentioned must be registered and will be required to attend the schools regularly.

Signed S.R.H. Loxton
Town Clerk
Dover
3 October 1941

Inevitably the national newspapers had a field-day. 'Cave Kids Sent Back To School' wrote Vivien Batchelor in the *Daily Express*; 'Children Get Cave Drill Before School', said the headlines in the *Daily Sketch*. 'Hell Fire Corner' children they were called. One estimated there were 825 children going back to school, many for the first time in eighteen months, those who were never evacuated and those who had returned to the town. Before lessons began at the Pier School, under the cliffs, the children went through cave drill. Their cave was only 10 yards from the school entrance.

The chairman of the Education Committee, Alderman F.R. Powell, had strongly opposed the re-opening of schools. He said:

I have done my best to persuade the mothers to send their children away. Until a month ago I even had powers to prosecute them for keeping their children in Dover. I did not use my powers, and now, of course, parents can only be prosecuted if they fail to send them to school. But if a shell falls on one of the schools while the children are at lessons, parents will have no one to blame but themselves.

After the controversy had died down, five children were found gassed in a cave on Thursday 23 October. The tragic discovery was made by a mother of four children. Bombed out of their home some weeks before, Mr and Mrs Benn had been re-housed at No. 2 New Cottages, Finnis Hill, off Limekiln Street. In the cliffs behind their new home was a chalk cave. It was here that William aged four, Bertram aged three-and-a-half, Francis aged two-and-a-half, Sylvia aged fifteen months and a neighbour's child Kenneth Duggen aged three years, were tucked up in their cots. Heating was supplied by an oil stove, and a piece of tarpaulin covered the entrance. Mrs Benn visited the cave at 23.00 that night to see that the children were safe. Thick fumes met her. Inside she discovered William dead and the rest of the children in varying stages of asphyxia. The others survived after hospital treatment.

★ ★ ★

The British Empire Medal was awarded to Miss Winifred Mary Scanlon, assistant supervisor at Dover's post office. The announcement appeared in the *London Gazette* on 10 October. Miss Scanlon had served thirty-two years with the post office, and by her courage and devotion to duty set a fine example to her staff of women telephonists. Through air raids the women maintained an efficient telephone service while in constant danger. Miss Scanlon refused to leave her switchboard while bombs were falling and she was, therefore, known as the 'Stick-it Girl'. She lived on the seafront at the Shalimar Hotel, managed by her sister, a favourite haunt of off duty WRNS .

Tuesday 21 October
18.40 TO 19.56 – HES – IBS – UXBS

Enemy action in the Dover area was now considerably reduced. Shelling continued, however, mostly aimed towards convoys and the coastal guns. It was a respite eagerly seized by local authorities to clear up bomb- and shell-damaged sites.

On this Tuesday, however, a bomber, chased by a night-fighter, came over the town. This resulted in two people losing their lives with another five injured. Stanhope Road received most of the bombs. Nos 36 to 42 were demolished while another bomb took out the rear of Nos 44 and 46.

Six houses lay in ruins and in minutes soldiers were assisting in the rescue of those who had suddenly become victims. Mrs Pelham and her daughter were extricated from the wreckage, then Mr and Mrs Cave and their son were found. The search continued to locate Sidney and Elsie Davis at No. 38. Sidney was found during the night, but it was not until the following afternoon that Elsie was discovered.

The death toll would have risen had it not been for the fact that the occupants of No. 40 were visiting a neighbouring town. They returned to find their home in ruins. In an adjoining house two women and a little girl were rescued just before a wall collapsed. The south-west wing of a large house called Chaldercot in Leyburne Road, fell into the roadway, but it was fortunately unoccupied. Two other bombs failed to explode when they fell in the grounds of Castlemount School. Incendiaries had been scattered over open ground at Hougham and Capel. There were no further casualties.

★ ★ ★

The well-known London journalist Collie Knox, after visiting Dover, wrote in the *Star Evening News*:

Hell's Corner is proud of its scars – Alderman J.R. Cairns, who has been elected Mayor of Dover for the fifth year in succession, was hardly more eloquent. When I tracked him down I found a burly figure, a man with a downright manner and a 'I've-got-my-foot-in-the-door' look in his eye. 'Can't tell you much', he said, '. . . you know it all. We carry on here. The people of Dover are brave, wonderfully brave. Can't say too much for them. Wish people would take their children away. Some of them are bringing them back. But we carry on. Am single-handed today. Excuse me. Good morning.'

Dover, like its mayor, is very monosyllabic. So would any town be in a district which, during the last twelve months was shelled on 76 separate days, with hundreds of shells crashing into the area. . . .

The sight of this beaming Postmaster was like a privilege. He revels in shells. One night a shell fell 30 yards away from the front door of his office. Another burst on the pavement. During the war [so far] the telephone operators have only gone down to the emergency switchboard seven times. 'Our supervisor,' said the postmaster, while he was showing me a drawer full of bits of bombs and shells, 'has just been awarded the BEM.'

Saturday 1 November
14.50 TO 15.52 – SHELLS

Winston Churchill had once remarked, 'There is nothing more exhilarating than being shot at and missed.' At 14.30 a ranging shot fell in the harbour near the Camber. Two minutes later another exploded on the football ground at the Boys' County School, where a game was in progress between the Army and Navy. The result – one sailor and one soldier killed, plus fifty-two-year-old William Norley, who was working in his allotment at Astor Avenue. The ambulance arrived, then went, but the game was abandoned.

★ ★ ★

Lt. Cdr. Pumphrey's MTB was in action on the night of 3 November, accompanied by another commanded by Lt. P.A. Berthon, RNVR. Between them, ably assisted by MGBs led by Lt. P.F.S. Gould, RN, sank a 5,000-ton German ship. Coastal Force boats were steering a parallel course with the enemy ships. With their Oerlikon guns they pounded the enemy escorts until they turned away under cover of smoke-screens. They engaged an armed trawler, designated a T Class torpedo boat, the equivalent of a small destroyer. Lt. Fowke's MGB sustained too much damage, and was forced to break off the fight. Fowke only had one engine intact, and Gould's boat was severely damaged also. Gould's boat was badly holed, the wireless mast had been shot away and one of the propeller shafts was useless.

The First Lieutenant and two of the crew were wounded. Unable to send a distress signal for fear of being detected, Gould calmly stopped within sight of Cap Gris Nez, and began to bail out his waterlogged boat. At daybreak they were fortunately spotted by a reconnaissance Spitfire pilot who radioed for assistance. They were later towed back to Dover.

Friday 7 November
22.59 TO 23.57 – HES – IBS

The siren went off just before 23.00. An unidentified aircraft dropped eight bombs and one canister of incendiaries. No. 12 Leyburne Road was demolished completely and effectively wrecked the house next door. Nos 10 to 14 Harold Road were the next to be wrecked and were later rendered useless for further habitation. There were no fatalities but seven people suffered various injuries. Four bombs fell close to the Grand Shaft Barracks, wrecking the Military Police NCOs' mess in Archcliffe Road. All the incendiaries fell along the Folkestone

Although incendiaries and one or two 'fire-pots' fell on Dover, fire-fighting was not a major problem. High explosives – bombs or shells – did not usually cause serious outbreaks. The AFS crew at the Finnis Hill Cave Depot was often in the forefront of rescue work and repairing damaged properties

Road and were promptly tackled by police, wardens and members of the Home Guard. No serious fires developed.

Saturday 8 November
17.56 TO 23.39 – HES – IBS

Moonlight was reflecting from the railway lines running into the Shakespeare Tunnel, when a JU88 pilot decided to make them his target. Bombs exploded in the sea and also near the Archcliffe Fort, where the occupants of Z4 ARP Post were shaken and distressed by the blast effect in their little sandbagged room.

At 23.00 the siren went off again. Another JU88 came to repeat the performance. Bombs exploded across King Lear Way, wrecking Nos. 1 and 3, while incendiaries spluttered in the Rope Walk area. Thirty-nine-year-old Arthur Skelton was about to leave home for firewatching duties when the bomb struck. He was killed on his own doorstep. The rest of his family escaped because they were in the Anderson shelter. Eighty-year-old Albert Keyton was living on his own at No. 3, when it collapsed. Although found seriously injured he died nine days later. The railway lines remained undamaged. But unbeknown to the

German pilot, wagons containing torpedoes and boxes of ammunition for Coastal Force boats were in the sidings.

★ ★ ★

The gallantry of Kent Home Guard officer, Lt. A.J. Whittingstall, of the Capel le Ferne platoon B Company, 8th (Cinque Ports) Battalion, had been cited in orders by Lt. General B.L. Montgomery, C-in-C South-East Command on 14 December. When a man slipped and dropped a live hand grenade, Lt. Whittingstall ordered his platoon to lie down. He then threw himself down with his feet towards the grenade, hoping to limit the danger area. When the grenade exploded he was wounded by his action. He was later awarded the MBE.

★ ★ ★

In the first week of December MTBs had made, unsuccessfully, an attack upon a small merchant ship. MTB No. 218, commanded by Lt. H.P. Granlund, RNVR, had been holed below the waterline by a large calibre shell, and most of the equipment had been damaged. While the boat was rapidly becoming waterlogged, the leading telegraphist stood on blankets and pillows to help stem the flow of water. Setting course for Dover, stern first, and with water up to the wheelhouse decking, 218 came into harbour five and half hours after the ordeal started. Vice-Admiral Ramsey wrote, 'His [Granlund's] skill and resolution on this occasion were of a high order, and his leadership was reflected in the admirable behaviour of his ship's company.'

Monday 15 December
16.14 TO 18.30 – SHELLS

November had passed by without anyone really noticing. One of the balloons had broken away on 22 November and, in spite of all the machine guns opening fire on it, drifted away to the north and out of sight. December opened quietly. America entered the war after the infamous attack on Pearl Harbour. There were few ALERTS in Dover until this particular day. Four shells came over from France to hit the town, while many more exploded on the gun sites near St Margaret's. No information has been recorded about the latter. In the town, 30 George Street and 33 Stanhope Road were extensively damaged and one soldier killed. Bunkers Hill and Balfour Road also received shells.

Tuesday 16 December
17.25 TO 18.04 – HES – IBS – UXBS

A German aircraft dropped a flare over the town before it released bombs. About 400 incendiaries were spluttering in Biggin Street, in front of the post office, outside the Co-operative grocery shop and near the Prince Louis public house. Others fell in Biggin Court where the upper storeys caught alight.

The comedian Wally Patch was about to start his act at the Hippodrome, when suddenly the siren sounded. On the same 'bill' was Kala Hari, 'The Exotic Cuban Contortionist', who recalled:

> My agent asked me to go down to the Dover theatre at short notice. I said no they are bombing it. But he said, 'Oh – its all quiet there now. I'll give you an extra fiver'. I was singing a Carmen Miranda song when the ack-ack guns opened fire. It was a terrifying noise. The gas lamps began to flicker just as I was doing my contortions. I heard Wally say from the 'wings' – 'Go it gel!' Above the faltering strains of the orchestra, I shouted back, 'I don't want to be caught with my legs round my neck!' Later, sipping a gin and lime in the stage bar, to calm my frayed nerves, the whole theatre shook to its foundations.

The high explosives detonated at Vale View Road and the Grand Shaft Barracks. Six people were made homeless when twenty houses were seriously damaged, a further forty slightly damaged in Folkestone Road and Monins Road. A bomb failed to explode when it buried itself under No. 41 Council House Street. The area was immediately evacuated. Other incidents occurred at the Camber, Priory Hill, Pencester Road and Saxon Street.

Wednesday 24 December
20.16 TO 21.37 – SHELLS

Since the 16th there had been few incidents to talk about. It was a convoy of British ships passing Dover that caused German shells to fall off the harbour. Not one hit the town.

On Monday of this week the Hippodrome opened with Ted and Barbara Andrews (parents of the film star, Julie Andrews), who were billed as 'The Canadian Singing Troubadours'. The comedian Billy Shakespeare extolled the prowess and virtues of the soldiers, sailors and airmen in the audience. They all looked slightly embarrassed by it. Behind the manager's desk was a large poster that proclaimed:

To Hell With Hitler
And His Unexploded Bombs
The Hippodrome Is Still Open

Only on two nights was the theatre closed because of danger. Except for one week when a revue company could not get through to Dover because of a railway dislocation, the old music hall had kept open through air raids and shelling.

In the early days of the Blitz, it was sometimes hard to book artistes but usually a programme was made up from local service units, or anyone else for that matter. Inevitably, some of the jokes uttered on stage were too Rabelaisian to be printed here.

There were some top artistes who considered a week at the Dover Hippodrome too dangerous and there were many others whose fees were astronomical. On the other hand, there were those who considered it an honour to be engaged at a music hall well within sight of the enemy. The eleven girl attendants and four barmaids always turned up whatever happened. There was never an occasion when an artiste stopped his or her act because of enemy action. The 580-seater theatre, like the town itself, was probably better known throughout the world than it was in England.

American journalists who had stayed behind waiting for Hitler's invasion, that never came, were so impressed with the music hall that their cables, printed right across the United States, told how, even though air raids and shelling raged, the people of Dover, and especially the servicemen, thought a striptease show much more interesting!

The Lagoon Cave was decorated with paper chains, which helped to create an illusion of festivity in the sombre surroundings where over fifty children were entertained to tea and afterwards to a concert party on Christmas Day. After tea, each child received a present from a large tree festooned with silver paper, and at the hands of Mr Wildish who was dressed as Santa. A similar party was held at the Athol Terrace Caves, where a naval officer, suitably attired as Father Christmas, gave out presents to over thirty children. The NFS gave a film show afterwards.

CHAPTER FOUR

1942

'It was a Silly Thing to do Billy!'

January opened quietly for Dover, although there were a number of shell warnings. It was not until Sunday 11 January that one shell fell on allotments behind Westbury Road. On Thursday the 22nd a shell exploded in the rear garden of 5 Maison Dieu Road, damaging properties, but there were no casualties reported. Only one person was slightly injured when a shell demolished 16 Liverpool Street, just after 10.00, severely wrecking another five dwellings. The casualty was found in 14 Liverpool Street, an old boarding house, used by the naval police.

Searchlights were being directed to illuminate the barrage balloons on most nights, a sure indication that RAF aircraft were in the vicinity. Cold, icy winds blew on most days in January, sleet showers added to the discomfort of sentries and those manning the coastal gun batteries. In February came the freezing fog and sea mists.

In the New Year's Honours List were Mrs A.M. Beeston, Centre Organizer of the Dover WVS; Mr J.H. Mowll, Chief Warden; and Mr A.W.B. Mowbray, Head Postmaster, all receiving the MBE.

Thursday 12 February
THE CHANNEL DASH

While the fog and sea mists were protecting our forces, so this natural phenomena aided the enemy also. Thick fog covered the Dover Strait when, under cover of darkness, the German battle-cruisers *Scharnhorst* and *Gneisenau* and the heavy cruiser *Prinz Eugen*, sailed out of Brest harbour where they had been sheltering for many months. By dawn, screened by six destroyers and ten torpedo-boats, and above them the indomitable Messerschmitt fighters, they were steaming up Channel in poor visibility.

The enemy force was sighted off Le Touquet by an RAF fighter patrol. Almost immediately afterwards the radar picked them up from Fairlight, east of Hastings. At 11.45 the warships were passing Boulogue, and were entering the narrowest section of the Strait. Led by Lt. Cdr. Pumphrey, five MTBs passed out of Dover Harbour, just 20 minutes after receiving a telephone call.

The MTB attacks were neutralized by the dense smoke-screen laid around the warships by the attendant E-boats, which maintained an excellent defensive barrier. The jubilant Pumphrey, on the bridge of MTB 221, realized he was hopelessly out of range when he fired his torpedoes. Unable to penetrate the defensive screen the MTBs reluctantly retired.

Brigadier C.W. Raw, 12 Corps Commander, decided to engage the warships with his four 9.2-in South Foreland Battery. Visibility down to 5 miles the targets were at extreme range and could not be seen with the naked eye. Using the South Foreland radar the battery opened fire at approximately 30,000 yards range for just over 15 minutes until the warships passed out of range completely.

The Coastal Artillery HQ plotting room in a casemate beneath Dover Castle. Personnel under 12 Corps Commander Brigadier C.W. Raw were responsible for the bombardment of enemy shipping in the Strait. Townspeople objected strenuously when they became victims of retaliatory shelling by the German long-range guns

Seldom has it fallen to the lot of the civil population to suffer bomb and shell but the man and woman in the streets of Dover conquered them

As soon as the 'cease fire' had been given the warships were attacked by six Swordfish torpedo-bombers of the Fleet Air Arm, who had flown in to RAF Manston earlier. Despite the courageous gallantry of those airmen their attack failed. None of the torpedoes found their mark and all six aircraft were lost in the most deplorable conditions imaginable.

The new 15-in guns, 'Jane' and 'Clem', at Wanstone Farm, were still being installed during this particular Dover battle. If they had been ready there is little doubt they would have inflicted considerable damage on the German warships. So ended the first important action of the Dover counter-bombardment batteries. Greater successes were achieved later when more targets offered themselves.

★ ★ ★

A new member of Coastal Forces was Lt. Peter Scott, RNVR, artist, writer and ornithologist, who arrived at Dover on 3 March 1942, for MTB experience.

A new arrival at Dover on 3 March 1942 was Lt. Peter Scott, RNVR, artist, writer and orinthologist, who joined the Dover Coastal Force for light-craft experience. Later as Lt. Cdr. his adventures in the English Channel and beyond became legendary, and gained him the MBE, DSC and Bt

His arrival coincided with the rescue of an MTB in trouble. Within just half an hour of his train pulling into Priory Station, he was a passenger on a C Class MGB No. 322, commanded by Lt. J.H. Hodder, RNVR, followed by MGB No. 330, with Lt. D.C. Sidebottom, RNVR on the bridge.

The burning wreck of MTB No. 31 was laying off the North-East Varne buoy in bright moonlight. One crew member had been killed, and others were on a life raft close by. The MTB was eventually salvaged and towed back to Dover where it was beached in the entrance to the Wellington Dock.

Coastal Force operations in the summer and autumn of 1942 were to prove successful in sinking an increasing number of German merchant ships. The German reaction was to strengthen quite considerably escorts of shipping.

In good weather conditions, Coastal Force COs continued a series of running battles with E- and R-boats, and their achievements, over vastly superior enemy forces, often were awarded with the highest decorations.

★ ★ ★

SENTRY SHOOTS NAVAL OFFICER

A well-known naval officer at Dover was seriously injured on Monday 16 March, by a rifle shot fired by a sentry. Lt. William Grenville Worthington, RNVR, aged thirty-nine, was an authority on the nineteenth century, and his bibliography of the Waverley novels was a standard work. He had also broadcast talks on early history of the gramophone and on the development of jazz music. Lt. Worthington was driving his car from Temple Ewell, where he had dined with Sonja Findlay. It was after midnight, raining hard and very dark, when he approached a road block showing a red light. A Royal Marine sentry challenged the car. When it failed to stop the sentry fired a shot, and the bullet entered the car and seriously wounded the lieutenant in the stomach. He was taken to hospital and an emergency operation was performed by Dr T.J. Cobbe. The irony of this episode was that Lt. Worthington died of shock on Thursday 26 March during Dover's Warship Week.

Three weeks later there was another inquest at Dover's Town Hall. MISHAP WITH A REVOLVER ran the headline in the *Dover Express*. Arthur Herbert Groombridge, a corporation employee, had been accidentally shot by a naval sentry in Union Road. The coroner expressed concern that young men were being ordered to stand sentry at military establishments without any preliminary knowledge of firearms. During the inquest it was revealed in evidence that the young naval rating was being shown how to unload the revolver when the shot

Veiled in a dense mist, commandos led by the legendary Major Lord Lovat waded ashore from Dover-based motor launches just west of Boulogne on the night of 22–3 March 1942, to test the German defences. Lord Lovat is chatting with Admiral Ramsey on the quayside at Dover

was fired. The unfortunate Groombridge happened to be passing the entrance of the naval establishment at the time and received the fatal injury.

★ ★ ★

Boulogne was raided by a small party of Commandoes on the night of 22–3 March. Veiled in dense mists, motor launches of the Dover ML flotilla silently approached the sand dunes west of the French port. Led by Major Lord Lovat, the raiding party waded ashore in shallow water. While they were carrying out their reconnaissance to test out German coastal defences, searchlights came on when their crews were suspicious of the launches laying off the sands. Since Dunkirk there had been numerous raiding sorties made by commando units from Dover. They all returned safely this night but was this the reason for the bombing raid made on the town on the following night?

Monday 23 March
20.54 TO 21.47 – HES

It was a brilliant moonlit night. The sirens went off just before 21.00. Four
JU88s were identified in silhouette, against the silver clouds. Ack-ack guns
opened fire. The cacophony of sound burst upon the ear-dums as exploding
bombs straddled Plum Pudding Hill.

Windows and doors blew in and roof tiles cut through the night air like
knives. When a JU88 released its bombs so another followed in a shallow dive
towards the town. Bombs hurtled into the Market Square, taking out the back
of the Carlton Club, demolishing the East Kent Road Car Company office, the
International Stores, and several other shops.

Mrs Lilian Cleak, the stewardess of the club, was not released from her tomb
for thirteen hours. She had remained conscious throughout her ordeal. A tunnel
was made, only large enough for one person to get through. An officer in the
Buffs and a Salvation Army officer no doubt saved her life as they passed rubble
back from one to the other and eventually reached her in time to find that the
gradual subsidence of tons of wreckage was threatening to crush her to death.
Heavy lifting gear was brought to shore-up the beams and rafters. For five hours
the army officer stayed by her side and was able to give her an injection of morphia when the pain became unbearable. She was finally released about 10.00 the
following morning. Her two children, Pauline and Ivan, were in the billiards
room. They were rescued unhurt by soldiers.

The club was a venue for many of Dover's leading citizens, and among those
killed was Councillor William Austen, who had been deputy mayor three years
before, Percy Sneller a well-known local haulage contractor, and Donald
McKenzie, manager of the Co-op Bakery and Charles Banks who had been
employed by the Royal Engineers. Both Austen and Sneller were Special Police
War Reservists. Two teenagers had been killed outside the club – Ella Dixon
and Jack Graves.

Perhaps the worst incident happened at the East Kent Road Car Company
garage in St James's Street, where an armour-piercing bomb penetrated the air-
raid shelter, situated inside the garage, killing most of those taking shelter. Nine
members of the East Kent staff died that day. Brian Taylor, local manager of the
company, and a lieutenant in the Home Guard, died instantly when his office
was demolished.

While the rescue squad, soldiers and many volunteers, swarmed over the rubble to reach the dying and injured, so the basements were filling up with water
from fractured mains. Shattered bodies, some still alive, were passed through a
hole in the shelter roof. Ambulances, nurses and doctors, ran a shuttle service to

ROYAL
HIPPODROME
Managing Director—H. R. Armstrong   Telephone 999

5.10 **CONTINUOUS PERFORMANCE** 7.0
Week commencing Mon. Dec. 6

The Radio and Film Star
BABS DUDLEY
The Golden Voice and a Piano

RAY and RAYFORD	DeBEAR & DuBRAY
Gay Deceiver & the Nitwit	The Delightful Deceptionists

The Fascinating Nude
:: GLORIA ::
In her
Dance of the Seven Veils & Fan Dance

SYD BESSON	THE FIELD SISTERS
Monarch of the Bells	
Marimba–Xylophonist	Dancers-De-Luxe

JIM NOLAN
A Real Enemy of Gloom

Stalls 3/-, 2/-, 1/6   Circle 2/6   Box Seats 4/-   Pit 1/-
Gallery 8d.

H. G. Wright, Printer, 19b High Street, Dover.

Twice-nightly shows at the theatre must have performed infinite war service not only to the packed houses but to the world-wide audiences who saw through the eyes of visiting journalists

The museum and covered market in Dover's Market Square was first damaged by a bomb on 21 October 1940, hit again by another on 23 March 1942, then further damaged by a shell on 4 October 1943

When an armour-piercing bomb struck the air-raid shelter at the East Kent Bus Co. Garage, St James Street, on 23 March 1942, it killed nine people inside

and from the hospital. Bodies, some terribly dismembered, were eventually laid together in one small area to await identification.

Inspector William Pearson was one of the first hauled through the gaping hole in the concrete. Then followed Minnie Hawkins, William Ford, Frederick Hogben, Robert Lynch, Frederick Mische and Walter Sherward. Victor Pilcher was found still alive but died four days later from many internal injuries.

Other bombs exploded at the top of Stanhope Road, demolishing Nos. 74 and 76, then two more fell on Barton Road, where Nos. 61 and 63 were wrecked. Another rescue took place at the corner of Barton Road and Nightingale Road. The Reverend T.A. Roberts and his wife were trapped in their Morrison shelter. Although the house was on fire PC Ewer and Captain Cole, an ARP warden, tunnelled through the rubble and got them out. Unexploded bombs were later found at Edred Road and behind No. 90 Maison Dieu Road.

In spite of the disaster in March 1942, demolishing the East Kent Road Car Company's garage and offices in Russel Street, and killing nine staff, the remainder elected to stay in the town. The double-decker bus to and from Canterbury stops in St James's Street – or what was left of it

Friday 3 April
00.27 TO 02.12 – HEs – IBs – UXBs

Bombs had been dropped on the town on Wednesday 25 March, but fortunately each of them fell on open ground. There were no casualties. But on this Good Friday there was another moonlight raid, similar to that of two weeks before. Casualties were again heavy, including a number of fatalities, the majority being women. Many houses were either demolished or seriously damaged. For about three-quarters of an hour there was the unceasing noise of a very fierce ack-ack barrage and explosions of bombs.

Most people had been killed when a bomb made a direct hit on an underground shelter in Union Road. About thirty people were sleeping there when one end of it collapsed, killing nine people outright. Many others were injured, and the proximity of the casualty hospital helped to save a number of lives.

Among those killed were four members of the same family: Ernest and Queenie Revell, and their two daughters, Gladys aged sixteen, and Joyce aged

Top row, left to right: Watson, Kemp, Deverson, Holmes, Special Constable, Lawrence, Eades. Middle row: Heffon, Lillicrap, Gillespie, Mason, Beets, King, Norman, Parish, Sgt. Smith Special Con. Front row: Vine, Vine, Fenner, Fenner, Philpott, Ellen, Ellen, Bailey, Cameron. Bottom row: Mrs Tugwell, ARP messenger, A. McVey

thirteen. William Warman, a coal merchant, and his wife Ethel also died instantly.

Rescuers worked for many hours releasing people trapped beneath the rubble of two semi-detached houses. Here, two sisters, Beatrice and Winnie Goodwin were brought out alive after being buried for over fourteen hours. Unfortunately Beatrice later died. In the same house, two other women, Margaret and Mary Flynn, were found dead. While they were being dug out at 11 Pencester Road, the Goodwins were able to talk with their rescuers and were passed cups of tea. Their neighbours at No. 9 were also buried. Maud Finnis was rescued alive after ten hours, but her sisters, Annie and Elsie Robson, both in a Morrison shelter, died before they could be reached. Two days later, in the same house, the body of a naval doctor was discovered.

Eight people were discovered trapped in debris after two houses in Priory Gate Road were partly demolished. Several were brought out alive, including members of two families, one a child of seven. It was dawn and rescue work had been slowly progressing during the previous six hours. Martha Abbott was found just as dawn broke on the horizon. She was rushed to hospital but died of

The moonlight raid on Good Friday 3 April 1942 demolished and severely damaged many prop-erties in the town. Nine people were killed in just one incident in Union Road. This was the scene in Priory Gate Road, between the Priory Station and Dover College

terrible injuries. Later her husband Alfred was found dead in the basement at No. 8.

There were several RAF casualties when a bomb exploded at the corner of Church Road and 190 Folkestone Road. Warden Warren was injured here, and a number of small fires developed in Hardwick Road and Shakespeare Road. Three bombs fell in the Dover College grounds, and two failed to explode at Bunkers Hill.

Ambulances were standing by as the morning's rescue attempts were proceed-ing in a sensible, methodical way. Lord Monsell, the Regional Commissioner, visited the town that morning, and was impressed with the Rescue Squads and their leaders. He called for the Kent County Mobile Rescue Reserve Party to assist. The convoy of lorries and men from neighbouring towns arrived two hours later.

The commendable piece of work by Warden J. Warren, was brought to the notice of the Regional Commissioner. One bomb had almost flattened his ARP Post. Telephone wires were down all over the town and small fires had started in several places in his particular area. Although injured, he cycled to Central Control with a message although bombs were still falling. He finally collapsed, having cycled back to his post, or what was left of it, and when taken to hospital, doctors discovered he was suffering from a broken shoulder blade.

Another warden seriously injured was Edward Gandy. He had been on duty in the B2 Post, which had been built on top of the underground shelter in Union Road. When the bomb exploded on the shelter the blast had lifted the concrete structure several feet and toppled it into the crater. Gandy was still inside.

The Mayor was so impressed with the determined and courageous rescue work, achieved in so many different locations, that he wrote to the *Dover Express*:

I desire, on behalf of the Town Council, to express most sincerely, my thanks for, and appreciation of the splendid work performed by all Civil Defence Services, police, and the National Fire Service on the occasions of recent enemy attacks on the town, and also to all others who assisted. The capable, energetic and courageous manner in which the various incidents were dealt with, was instrumental in saving many lives, and the gratitude of the whole town is due to all those who carried out their arduous duties under such difficult and trying circumstances.

Signed J.R. Cairns
Mayor
9 April 1942

★ ★ ★

TOMMY-GUN ARREST AT DOVER

On Monday 27 April, the Dover Police arrested a seventeen-year-old Home Guard from Suffolk. He was carrying a tommy-gun and ammunition, and said that he hoped to cross the Channel and use it. In court he told magistrates:

I knew it was no good going with a rifle, so I took the tommy-gun. I put it in a sack and went to London first, and then on to Dover. I got to Dover about five minutes to eight, and went into a small inn until ten o'clock. I intended taking a small boat across the Channel, and I was only 150 yards from the boats when I was picked up by the police. I have never fired a tommy-gun, but I have read the instructions. I planned this, hoping it would get me in the army. I tried last year, but I was too young. I intended to make for Paris and find Laval and Darlan. I was going to kill them and return to

England. They are traitors. I should have shot up a few Germans on the way, and destroyed as much stuff as I could.

The misguided youth was put on probation and ordered to pay a fine of £2. 8s. 6d. (£2.42), on the charge of stealing the gun and the ammunition.

★ ★ ★

'At a recent Investiture held at Buckingham Palace, Mr E. Penfold received the BEM awarded him in the New Year's Honours List by H.M. the King, in recognition of services rendered. Mr Penfold was in charge of the engineering staff at the Telephone Exchange Dover, and has put in much hard work in restoring vital communications which have been damaged by air raids and shells.'

May was another reasonably quiet month for Dover. The incident reports were as follows:

Wednesday 6 May – 20.50 TO 21.00 2 HEs in harbour. No casualties.
Thursday 7 May – 20.49 TO 21.15 2 HEs Northfall Meadow. Army M.T.
   sheds damaged. No. 9 Castle Avenue damaged. 1 slight casualty.
Saturday 23 May – 14.48 TO 17.00 16 shells in sea off harbour.
Saturday 30 May – 04.03 TO 05.32 HEs. 8 bombs dropped in Dock Yard. In
   sea and Camber. No reports of damage or casualties.

There are no incidents recorded for June 1942. During the first half of the month the RAF was making night attacks on targets in Germany. There were actions in the Strait by our Coastal Forces' MTBs and MGBs, with sea battles on 19, 20, 21 and 23 June.

★ ★ ★

Dover Educational Committee's returns for May 1942 showed that in Wales there were 978 children on the books. In Dover, the number on the books was 1,206. Children in Dover were now able to attend school for two and a half hours per day, and children from six years of age were admitted from January. It was hoped that children would be able to attend full-time classes as soon as the authorities considered it practicable.

★ ★ ★

The George Medal had been awarded to Gilbert Mitchell, a farmer, of Reach Court Farm, St Margaret's Bay, near Dover, and the BEM to his wife, Kathleen Mary Mitchell, and her sister, Miss Grace Lillian Harrison, a member of the Women's Land Army. The *London Gazette*, in announcing the awards, said:

> Mr and Mrs Mitchell and Miss Harrison have made an unexampled effort and shown sustained bravery and devotion to duty in carrying on farming under the gunfire and air attacks of the enemy. The farm is at the nearest point to the Continent, and is scarred with filled-in shell craters. The farm buildings are probably the most vulnerable in the country, yet work was carried on throughout the Battle of Britain and ever since. During intense air raids the German pilots machine gunned the farm, and work on the land stopped. But in spite of all the difficulties and dangers there was no change in the routine of milking and attending to stock. They not only saved their own crops but also those of other farms which had been evacuated.

Mary Twyman, who joined the Womens Land Army in 1942, recalled in *A Land Girl's Memories of Hell Fire Corner*, written after re-visiting Appleton Manor Farm, forty years later:

> Tented rows of corn shocks waited to be piled high on the creaking wagon; the harness clinked gently and a tractor clattered noisily. A dozen or so Green Howards from the nearby Army camp, khaki sleeves rolled up and pitchforks at the ready, moved towards the half-built straw stack on which I stood, ready to pass the sheaves to the boss. I was wearing my new dungarees and aertex shirt for the first time. The tender palms of my hands were beginning to blister with the rough twine. Working in the open countryside so close to the coast made it necessary to keep a weather eye open for hedge-hopping Messerschmitts. They could be in and out, popping away with their machine guns before any warning siren. No portable 'loos' were provided, so it was necessary to find a secluded spot in various places when the need arose and which also served as a 'bolt-hole' in case of enemy action.

The year before, the Royal Norwegian Navy had taken over eight motor launches whose crews were mainly from the Norwegian Merchant Service. Now part of the British Navy, No. 52 ML flotilla arrived in Dover in July 1942, with four MLs earlier converted as minelayers. A special feature of these MLs was the Dumbflow silencer, which enabled the launches to operate very close to the enemy-held coast.

The Norwegians joined up with the Royal Navy's 50 ML flotilla to operate at night during moonless periods, laying mines in German convoy routes and blocking enemy port entrances between Zeebrugge and Boulogne.

Finn-Christian M. Stumoen recalls:

When we were not laying mines, we went out on E-boat patrols. The worst enemy we had was the fast German E-boats. They had speeds of 40 knots, and with heavy armament. In addition, there was always the threat from shore batteries. The ML's speed was 17 knots for a short while, and then reduced to 15 knots. We did not have much armament. The boats were a defensive weapon which could operate secretly so as not to engage the enemy. We would creep up on the French coast, lay our mines, and creep out again. Nobody should know we existed. Nothing was released about our work until after the war.

The mines came aboard during the day. The depths were set and safety-pins placed. WRNS did this, under the command of Lt. Pengborne. From this moment, a tense atmosphere rested over the crew, since we always expected shelling from France. In the cliffs we had the bomb-proof shelters,

Norwegian wireless operator Leif Tangen was thrown into the sea when ML 210 struck a mine. 'Somebody shouted in English "swim for it". They hauled me alongside . . . then I heard gunfire closeby . . . I screamed in fear.' Norwegian crewed ML 213 returning to Dover at first light

where the civilians could take cover. In addition mines and fuel were stored there.

The minelaying could at times be very exciting. We went out at dusk so we could have the darkest time for minelaying. When we got to the point where the mines should be laid, the cox'n had to remove all the safety-pins to prove that the mines were laid alive. They had to be returned to Lt. Pengborne on return to harbour.

When approaching the enemy coast, the ships had to be in close contact. Signal lamps and radio could not be used. We actually had to talk to each other – ship to ship. At this point we were going at slow speed, Dumflows on, hardly a sound could be heard from our ships. To find the accurate position for laying the minefield, we had reels of thin wire on the aft-deck. The wire was dropped at No. 1 buoy, and on a meter we could see how many yards we had sailed.

The order could be either to lay mines in enemy convoy routes, or to block port entrances. When we came inside the range of German hydrophones the searchlights came on, and they would open fire on us. We were never hit from shore batteries. At this moment we knew that E-boats would be alerted, and ordered to intercept. Many times we laid a smoke-screen and disappeared in a hurry. Coded signals were transmitted from VAD (Vice-Admiral Dover), to tell us to steer a certain course to avoid the enemy track. What we did not know, however, was the position of enemy minefields.

Friday 24 July
09.17 TO 10.26 – SHELLS

British convoys were shelled during the first week of July and our heavy guns replied. People took shelter as this was the first shelling to occur since 23 May. There were no casualties or damage reported.

On this day, however, just one shell exploded in the front garden of 100 Maison Dieu Road, seriously injuring Mr Castle, a road-sweeper. About an hour later an MTB caught fire in Wellington Dock. Both Dover's fire engines attended but the crews were unable to approach the burning boat for fear of being struck by exploding ammunition. Cannon shells and bullets ripped into buildings along Snargate Street and Northampton Street. The fire spread to depth charges which instantly exploded, causing even more chaos. Other boats had managed to start engines and move away from the inferno, but even so, there were several naval casualties.

'Jane', one of the Wanstone Battery's two 15-inch guns, with an extreme range of 42,000 yards, was not ready for 'action' until June 1942. The number of rounds fired by the guns during the period of engagements were 1,243

Saturday 25 July
23.48 TO 01.43 – SHELLS

In line astern, without lights showing, MTBs and MGBs slowly passed through the boom at the eastern entrance of the harbour. Once clear of the harbour the engines erupted into a roar. The little boats of the Coastal Force smartly disappeared into the darkness, their mission to cause as much mayhem as possible among enemy ships daring to sneak along the French coast. German observation posts, however, were vigilant. Eight shells straddled the harbour, sending people to their shelters and the caves. There were no casualties reported.

Sunday 26 July
05.05 TO 06.14 – SHELLS

The Coastal Force boats were already at sea when two ranging shots fell in the sea before the next salvo hit the Ferry Dock. The next exploded on allotments behind Prospect Place. Telephone wires were stripped from their poles and sheds were demolished in the blast. There was little damage and no casualties. Wardens, policemen, Home Guard sentries and gunners, waited patiently for the

The Dover Company 8th (Cinque Ports) Battalion Local Defence Volunteers first went on night-duty patrols on the hills and cliffs around the town. Renamed the Home Guard in August 1940, the Capel Le Ferne platoon parades outside the Royal Oak public house in 1941

next salvo. All was quiet. They stood to watch a beautiful sunrise – shafts of yellow brightness, piercing the dark cloud-mass over the Channel.

During the day the demolition of damaged buildings in Townwall Street, and adjacent streets, became a priority. Every time a shell exploded in the town huge chunks of masonry fell into the roads, frightening people passing below. The Round House and the Dover Patrol Hostel were the first to come down.

There was considerable activity during the month of August, and yet there were few incidents to affect the town. Coastal- and long-range guns were in action most days and MTBs and MGBs, not forgetting the MLs, were out in the Strait almost every night.

There were three incidents on 8 August. Dover balloons had got off lightly since losing two balloons and some of their equipment on 2 October 1941. On this occasion they lost one balloon at Granville Gardens when Messerschmitts came in just after 08.00. The cable fell across an MTB in the repair depot at Wellington Dock.

There were six separate ALERTS on the 11th when enemy aircraft flew in to bomb Deal, where eight people lost their lives. The next day shells were exploding between Dover and St Margaret's, some straddled the radar masts at Swingate. Our heavy gun emplacements to the east of the castle came in for another intensive barrage on the following day as seventy shells fell in the area.

On Saturday 15 August, at about 01.00, seventeen shells came over, one salvo falling on the Langdon battery site. While that was going on a fierce engagement was taking place between our small craft and enemy shipping. Naval engagements in the Strait on the following Sunday brought an instant shelling response. When Coastal Force boats returned to Dover early in the morning they brought with them fifteen German prisoners of war. They were kept temporarily in the castle.

Shelling continued throughout the remainder of the month, and was largely concentrated on the heavy artillery sites. On 27 August Dover had received its 2,000th ALERT. It was also the day a film called *21 miles*, made by an Army Film Unit, was shown in local cinemas. The film had been produced for the United States and the famous American broadcaster Edward Murrow was the commentator. In the film the Mayor and several townspeople had been interviewed, among them a Mrs Swatheridge, who said, 'We've been shelled, dive-bombed, high-level bombed, and machine-gunned. The last lot we had, we had the house down about our ears. But we are still sticking it, and we are going to stick it until the boys go over the other side.'

On the night of 23–4 August, Norwegian ML 210, with the British ML 103, were on E-boat patrol in the Dover Strait. Finn-Christian M. Stumoen recalls:

Lots of radio traffic on the air. I was just decoding a signal from VAD, when an explosion shook the whole ship. I knew immediately that one of us had struck a mine. A few minutes later I had the signal ready as follows, 'Return base clear of enemy track.' If we had received this signal a little earlier, we might have been able to avoid this position. When I came on deck, my eyes met a sight which I shall never forget. Mines were floating all around us, and the crew were trying to keep them away from the side of the ship, with oars and whatever they could get hold of. The British ML 103, burning in the background, did not make the scene any better.

As she struck the mine and caught fire, one of the ratings on ML 210, Arne Fjerstad, ran aft towards the bridge shouting, 'ML 103 has exploded. You must stop! You must stop!' It did not take long before we were alongside, and most of the crew could walk onboard ML 210. Some had severe burns. We went alongside a trawler for medical help.

★ ★ ★

Captain Arthur Reginald Harvey, of the Salvation Army, who was in charge of the Red Shield canteen, Snargate Street, had recently been awarded the BEM for his gallantry during the air raid on Dover on 23 March 1942, when the Carlton Club was partially demolished. It was Captain Harvey who had tunnelled under the debris with an Army officer to comfort Mrs Cleak for about five hours until she was rescued. During this time he had supported a mass of rubble which threatened to crush the woman.

During August a number of loudspeakers had been installed in the main streets of Dover. People were to be urged to take cover when serious enemy action was in progress. Councillor Ryland said that he had been struck by the failure of people to take cover when there was a shell warning. 'If there was a serious attack on the town,' he had said, during his original proposal on 26 May, '. . . many would be killed before they realized that they should take cover.' The work of installing the loudspeakers was carried out by the Tannoy Electrical Company Ltd.

So violent was a thunder storm on 31 August that sixteen balloons were set alight by lightening. Burning fabric fell on houses and streets for nearly two hours, leaving just six balloons intact. RAF crews worked furiously to clear up the mess in the town but by 22.00 all twenty-two sites were flying their 'jumbos' again.

Friday 4 September
21.12 TO 22.29 – SHELLS – HES

The town had been spared from shells bursting among the streets and buildings during the past month. It was, therefore, something of a surprise when the first shell of a salvo hit the town instead of falling in the sea. Everyone expected the first shell to be the usual ranging shot. Nevertheless, the cliff face above Limekiln Street suddenly erupted in a huge shower of chalk. The NFS Depot in Finnis Cave was only slightly damaged by blast, although the crew had the fright of their lives. One sailor was injured by flying shrapnel. The next landed at the junction of Northbourne Avenue and Noah's Ark Road, where an ambulance was almost wrecked outside the Isolation Hospital. Fifteen minutes later a bomber released a few SC250s in Union Road and on the Ferry Dock. Damage was minimal and there were just two naval casualties.

Saturday 5 September
13.09 TO 13.26 – HES

Since 1941 Hitler's bomber force had been committed to the Russian Front. Thus an effective striking force in the west was considerably reduced. This meant that some of the *Luftwaffe's* fighters in northern France were modified to carry a single bomb beneath the fuselage. This modification resulted in a number of surprise attacks on our coastal towns in the south and south-east of England. They became known as 'tip-and-run' raids.

By the end of June 1942 the Messerschmitt Bf 109s were gradually being strengthened by the introduction of the new and formidable Focke-Wulf FW190, a high-speed monoplane fighter with an outstanding performance. The 'tip-and-run' raids made by the FW190s were just as effective as their counterparts.

It was exactly an hour after midday when four FW190s made their debut in the skies over Dover. The raiders kept to a respectful height because of the concentration of ack-ack guns in this sensitive area. Even so, they came down in a shallow dive and released their bombs on the town. Nos 1 and 2 Albert Road received a direct hit and were demolished. A further sixteen dwellings received severe damage, and upwards of one hundred were slightly damaged. Several people were trapped in the debris. Casualties were two females killed, three females and two males seriously injured, with a further three females and one male slightly injured.

Mrs Laura Austen, aged forty, and the wife of an East Kent bus inspector, was rescued with fatal injuries at 2 Albert Road, and in the rubble of No. 1 they found the mutilated body of Marketa Sadler. The Austens' four children, Patricia, May, Sheila and John, were extricated with some difficulty. They all survived the explosion. Robert Sadler, son of the family living at No. 1, was also found injured. Rescuers continued to work in the wreckage hoping to find Robert's father, and when hope of finding him alive was being discussed by the team, he walked up the road to see his house in ruins and his wife dead.

Another bomb took out the back of 341 Folkestone Road, then one exploded at the rear of the Ordnance Depot in Folkestone Road, causing slight injuries among workers inside. The last missile exploded over Barwick's Cave, on the cliff face above Snargate Street. Troops billeted at the Grand Shaft Barracks thought it was a shell.

Sunday 6 September
10.21 TO 22.43 – HES – SHELLS

The sirens wailed again when another four FW190s were heading for Dover. Within minutes the first bomb had exploded near the RAF balloon site at Broadlees Meadow, quickly followed by another which hit the roadway near the entrance to the harbour. The third bomb exploded in Castlemount Grounds, just below the Castle Keep, and the last one almost completely demolished the

disused Jewish synagogue in Northampton Street, damaging Wood's shop opposite and the Hart's storeroom. There were no casualties.

More serious was the shelling which occurred in the evening, when it was
estimated that over one hundred shells were fired by the German batteries,
falling east of the town. Seven shells fell on non-military targets.

The first to hit Dover was an air-burst type, which exploded over the town
centre. The next, an armour-piercing type, cratered Swains Yard, opposite 21
Pioneer Road. The blast damaged adjacent properties and seriously injured
Lance Corporal Leonard White of the Home Guard. He died later in hospital.
Two females and one male were seriously injured.

A salvo fell in Castle Street and St James's Street, demolishing Hawkesfield's
offices, and damaging Fremlin's Brewery. The Grenada Cinema, Castle Street,
received serious structural damage. The evening's film was stopped and the audience filed out of the building. There was no panic or casualties.

When a shell exploded close to Mannering's Mill, London Road, William
Decort, a butcher of Bench Street, was cycling home from River. He had
already been told to take cover by a policeman. Decort had been rescued from
Burlington Mansions just a year before. A large piece of masonry struck Decort,
knocking him off his cycle. Not badly injured, he was taken to hospital. There
were three more casualties when shells demolished two houses in Charlton
Avenue and behind Priory Hill. Although damage was severe there were no further fatal casualties.

★ ★ ★

The award of the George Medal to 2nd Lieutenant J.L.G. Warren, of the
Buffs Regiment, was announced in the *London Gazette* on 18 September. The
citation stated:

In March 1942, at Dover, a woman was imprisoned under the debris of a
bombed house. 2nd Lt. Warren tunnelled under the debris some 100 feet to
reach the woman. With the aid of two small motor-car jacks he eased the
weight on the woman's chest, and prevented further settlement of timber
baulk. Lying in the tunnel, and with the risk that the debris might collapse
further at any moment, Warren remained with the woman for five hours,
speaking encouraging words to her and keeping her face and mouth clear of
dust and rubble. Twice he gave her morphia injections, on the instructions of
a doctor. It was, undoubtably, due to his courageous and perservering action
that at great and constant risk to himself, the woman's life was ultimately
saved.

It will be remembered that Captain Harvey, Salvation Army, received the BEM for his participation in the rescue of Mrs Cleak from the Carlton Club.

★ ★ ★

High speed ASR launches from Dover were attacked by about twelve FW190s in mid-Channel. The skipper of one launch Flg. Off. J.R.L. Hill, an Australian, was killed in the attack. When the fighters left the scene the launch was burning furiously and only one crew member remained alive. Attracted by the smoke another launch raced to the rescue. Just as it arrived the FW190s came back to attack again and the second launch was set on fire, the crew jumping into the sea. Then two more launches arrived at considerable risk to themselves. Several men were picked up, but the dead went down with the burning boats. Corporal Banks of launch No. 10 swam around the men in the water seeing to their safety, and on at least one occasion inflated the Mae-West life jacket of a man who was too exhausted to do it himself. Over six feet tall, Flg. Off. Hill had been at Dover since the first arrival of the ASR launches and had seen much action.

Dover's air-sea rescue launches meet in mid-Channel to recover a pilot from a RAF rescue buoy, several of which were moored at intervals in the Strait of Dover

Monday 5 October
19.47 TO 21.28 – SHELLS

'All members of H.M. Forces are to return to their place of duty forthwith', read a slide, hastily superimposed over the screen at the local cinemas. This recall, not unfamiliar, emptied the cinemas and the Hippodrome theatre immediately.

The Hippodrome had just closed its doors when the first salvo from France struck Northampton Street, opposite the ASR boats. The theatre lost most of its windows and shrapnel wrecked dressing-rooms and also the stage bar. The staff had already left for the nearest cave. Five minutes later houses were wrecked in Queen Street. Steven's Dye Works and St Mary's Infants School were also severely damaged by blast. There were three minor casualties when another shell exploded on 21 Priory Road, demolishing the front of the building completely, blocking off Norman Street. A huge explosion at Pioneer Road, which demolished No. 12, removed every roof tile from adjacent houses. There were no casualties.

Buckland Avenue received the next shell which badly damaged Nos. 43 and 45, and rendered many other houses useless, including the Scottish Laundry. Then Nos. 58 and 60 Priory Hill erupted in a shower of bricks and tiles, causing severe damage to all surrounding properties. Victoria Street lost Nos. 12 and 13, and the Shalimar Hotel on the seafront had all its windows and doors blown in yet again.

WRNS billeted at Dover College were promptly evacuated when shells exploded in the grounds, seriously damaging the chapel and old tuck shop. But the most serious incident occurred in Adrian Street, where Nos. 26 and 28 collapsed and many more properties were badly damaged.

Dover's Heavy Rescue Squad had recently formed with Reginald Leppard as their Staff Officer. Their depot was at Lewisham Road, River, where six squads formed, each squad consisting of six men and one leader. Open lorries were used, containing ropes, ladders, pick-axes and shovels. Training was carried out at the ruined Burlington Mansions and a small depot was later added at the Trevanion Caves.

At Adrian Street there were four fatalities and twelve others injured. Mr Page happened to be walking through Last Lane and had his foot blown off. Rescuers began their long search for victims. Mr and Mrs Marsh at No. 28 were buried deep in the wreckage. They were completely oblivious of the systematic activity going on above them. Tunnelling through the debris rescuers found Mrs Marsh with a severe thigh wound. Her husband was found later minus one ear. William, their thirty-six-year-old son, had died before they could reach him. At

No. 22 they found eighty-six-year-old Emma Odell. They could detect no signs of life in her frail body. Henry Gatehouse was also found dead. Doctors could only find superficial wounds on the twisted body of thirty-five-year-old Agnes Terry recovered from No. 34. On the label attached to her clothing were the words, 'Died of Shock'.

The labelling of the unfortunate victims at any incident was not only to assist doctors and nurses, but also to assist the town's Chief Mortician 'Baggs' Baggaley, who had accepted the job at the outbreak of war. Near the mortuary at Tower Hamlets, he built a small chapel, frequented by many bereaved families.

★ ★ ★

An inquest was held at the Royal Victoria Hospital (now moved to Waldershare Park) on Saturday 17 October, on the death of William Frederick Smith, aged ten years, who was killed when a live mortar bomb exploded. His mother, giving evidence, said she visited her son in hospital and told him, 'It was a silly thing to do Billy.' Billy had joined three boys pushing a barrow who were collecting mortar bombs from a field, used by the army for field training purposes. A live mortar bomb was found lying near a hedge, and the boys took turns to throw it at a gate post. Several attempts were made to hit the post. The last and fatal throw, succeeded in an explosion which cost Billy his life.

The Coronor remarked, '. . . surely something could be done to put the possibility of danger out of reach of the children?' A verdict of death by misadventure was returned by the jury.

★ ★ ★

Field Marshal Smuts visited Dover on Friday 23 October, accompanied by the Prime Minister, the Chancellor of the Exchequer, the Turkish Ambassador, Mr Morganthau, and Mr Averell Harriman, the US Ambassador. They were met at the Priory Station by the Mayor, the Admiral, Dover Command, and the Brigadier commanding Dover Garrison. The entourage was conveyed by cars to an area immediately behind the police station at Ladywell, where they inspected over 130 representatives of the Civil Defence Services.

★ ★ ★

Vice-Admiral Sir Henry Daniel Pridham-Wippell, KCB, CVO, was now the new Flag Officer commanding Dover. Vice-Admiral Sir Bertram Ramsey, CB,

Mrs Eleanor Roosevelt, wife of the President of the United States, inspects the WRNS at Dover College on 30 October 1942. On her right is the Director of the WRNS Mrs Lawton Mathews, with Chief Officer Mrs Malschinger on the left

MVO, who had held the command since the war began, had left Dover to undertake other duties, and eventually was nominated Commander-in-Chief of the Naval Forces for Operation Overlord, the allied invasion of France.

On 2–3 November 1942 the Norwegian ML 125 struck a German mine. Finn-Christian M. Stumoen recalls:

> Everyone looked forward to the days when the moon appeared. Then we would have a few nights in peace, if the Germans did not start shelling Dover. The wireless operator on ML 125 and I had been to fetch the mail from HMS *Wasp* in the morning. We had sat down on the seafront in the nice sunshine, and looked over to the enemy coast, where we would be sneaking in when night fell. My friend Mortensen told me he would be getting married, and related excitedly about all the arrangements which had been made.
>
> As usual, by dusk, we went out fully loaded with mines. The weather was calm and clear. I sat in the wireless office in ML 210 and listened to the Dover

radio traffic. As we approached the position where we were to lay mines all hands were on station. The speed had already been reduced. The cox'n had removed all the safety-pins, and we were ready to begin minelaying.

Suddenly there was a terrific explosion. I thought we had been hit. The whole ship shuddered. ML 125 had struck a German mine. The bow was blown off, just in front of the bridge. The stern was floating intact, with all the mines, which had now to be thrown overboard. A dinghy was lowered from ML 213 and manned by Sub. Lt. Rolf Berntzen and cox'n Knut Johannessen. Four men were floating around in the water. One of them was dead. As they picked up survivors, the dinghy capsized, and now they were all in the water. A British ML put in an appearance and a searchlight lit up the area. They picked up all the Norwegians. One of the British sailors, and the cook on ML 210, jumped into the water to help Rolf Berntzen secure a line around the wounded. The Number One had been killed, they tried to get his body onboard, but he fell back into the water and struck Berntzen on the head. ML 125 was towed back to Dover harbour, where ambulances and doctors were standing on the jetty. One of the engine crew died later in hospital.

None of us slept much the rest of the night. The remains of ML 125 were taken into Wellington Dock. The next morning, on my usual trip to fetch the mail, I went to see the remains of ML 125. A sad sight met me. The mine had hit the wireless room. There, on the table in the little room, over the morse-key, I saw a white sweater sticking out of the water. My friend Mortensen had died on duty.

Thursday 5 November
TYPHOON HITS BALLOON

Rocket-carrying Typhoon fighters were shooting-up all sorts of targets on the French coast – military installations, troop concentrations, railway systems and *Luftwaffe* airfields, in fact anything that presented itself. Flt. Sgt. S.H. Spallin, of 609 squadron, was returning from one of these intruder sorties and, unfortunately, struck a balloon cable suspended over Admiralty Pier. The aircraft spun round like a top to crash into the harbour. The pilot was unable to extricate himself from his spinning cockpit and died when the Typhoon sank.

Monday 9 November
19.56 TO 22.35 – SHELLS

Military observers on the cliffs spotted gun flashes on the French coast. Telephoned messages were being received in the plotting room beneath the castle when the first salvo plopped into the sea. The next exploded at the rear of 22 Pencester Road, causing damage to over fifty houses in Maison Dieu Road and The Paddock. There were no casualties. Ten minutes later another salvo struck Woolcomber Street and Wellesley road, where the road was blocked by rolls of barbed wire blown over from the beach defences. Clarence Lawn received the last shell, shattering houses already severely damaged.

On the following day only one shell reached the town. It fell on Marine Parade and destroyed a kiosk. One shell hit Dour Street the day after, stripping off roof tiles and causing blast damage, and on the 12th another exploded opposite 14 East Cliff. No casualties were reported.

The Duke of York's School was suddenly attacked by four FW190s on Wednesday 2 December. It was just before 11.00. No warning had been given. Ack-ack gunners could not find a target to aim at because of the sharp, low-level hedge-hopping flight-path. Cannon shells ripped into buildings but there were no casualties.

Thursday 10 December
20.59 TO 23.26 – SHELLS

There had not been a shell warning for four weeks. The first shell exploded in the Drop Redoubt, part of the Western Heights complex. As this occurred on military ground there were no reports of either damage or casualties. Another exploded on 121 Snargate Street, seriously damaging properties on either side of Gander's newsagents shop, where two people suffered injuries. The next was an air-burst type which exploded over Priory Station, puncturing the water tower. The King William public house, Tower Hill, just fell into the street when hit. A fire started and began to spread to adjacent properties but there were no casualties. The one fatality occurred at 79 Folkestone Road, where David Burns, a Company Sergeant Major in the Home Guard, and a taxi driver for Sawyer's Taxis, was killed instantly by the blast.

Friday 11 December
00.15 TO 03.05 – SHELLS

Sirens wailed just after midnight when two shells exploded near the gasworks in Union Road. Shrapnel punctured the gas holders which resulted in the gas supply being turned off in the town until mid-morning. Another exploded on the bank beside the railway at Crabble Meadow, damaging houses in Bunkers Hill and St Radigund's Road. The last shell took out 31 Victoria Street, where sixteen-year-old Doris Moore was fatally injured. She died in hospital the next day.

This YMCA mobile library van, provided by the British War Relief Society, USA, made weekly visits to anti-aircraft gun sites, coastal defence guns and the heavy long-range guns in the Dover area

In spite of shortages local shops were trying to fill up their windows with Christmas fayre. Those without windows of any kind put up notices saying BUSINESS AS USUAL. But war-time austerity was taking its toll. Bakers had not the raw materials to produce the traditional Christmas cake. Paper chains appeared hanging up in the caves and shelters. Everyone did their best to pre-serve the essential ingredients of a typical English Christmas. But no one knew, for certain, where the next shell would strike. There was no guaranteed immu-nity from sudden death.

CHAPTER FIVE

1943

'Look, There's been People Killed'

The first weeks of January were uneventful but in spite of a depleted bomber force in the west, Germany managed to bomb London on the night of 17–18 January, the heaviest bombing since July 1941.

Since New Year's Day the weather, predictably, was a mixture of cold east winds, sleet, freezing rain and snow showers. The sirens wailed and people reluctantly left their warm beds to take shelter. Bleary-eyed shivering Dovorians listened to the bombers passing overhead.

Monday 18 January
19.29 TO 20.35 – HES – IBS

It was 19.30 when JU88s approached the town at about 8,000 feet. Searchlights stabbed the pitch-black, overcast sky, unable to penetrate with their beams. The heavy ack-ack guns opened fire and shrapnel fell in the area, hitting the roof tiles and chimneys.

A shower of incendiaries fell on the town with a couple of oil bombs and high explosives. Buckland Farm received one whole canister of incendiaries but they were allowed to burn out where they fell. Those which fell in built-up areas set alight roofs and lofts in Clarendon Street, Clarendon Place and Folkestone Road, where Pickford's Depository and also the Girls' Orphanage were damaged by fire. Others were tackled at Winchelsea Street, the Citadel Barracks and Percival Terrace, where a Mr Foad was seriously injured. There were no other casualties.

The Control Centre incident board gradually filled with chalked messages. Telephones rang incessantly as the wardens discovered fires in their own particular areas. The NFS was hard pressed to attend every fire and relied heavily upon the Fire Watch parties. Unoccupied premises were the most difficult to tackle. Doors and windows were broken to gain access to extinguish the missiles.

Two bombs fell at the junction of Lower Road and Common Lane, River, but neither exploded. Several RAF lorries in the vicinity were quickly moved out of harm's way, just in case they suddenly, and without warning, exploded. Over fifty people were immediately evacuated. An oil bomb, which fell near the Esplanade Hotel on the seafront next to the clock tower, lit up the whole area and could quite easily be seen from ships at sea.

There were no further incidents in January, although on the last day there was a thunderstorm which brought down the balloons. One of them careered along Biggin Street, dragging its cable and breaking the loud-speaker wires.

German long-range guns fired about eighteen shells at a convoy on 9 February. On the following day they shelled the coastal gun batteries near St Margaret's. The 540 Coast Regiment, RA, at Wanstone Farm, was heavily bracketed and suffered several casualties. One gunner, and thirty-nine-year-old Edith Burville, working in the NAAFI at Fan Bay, were killed.

Tuesday 2 March
21.05 TO 00.02 – SHELLS

The first shell demolished 6 Beaconsfield Road, at the junction with Granville Street. Several properties were damaged but there were no casualties. The next exploded in the chalk pit at Tower Hamlets and to the rear of 71 High Street, where the telephone wires collapsed into a jumbled heap. Another exploded in the old cemetery at Cowgate. The most serious incident occurred beside the Prince of Wales Pier, where a number of minesweepers were tied up. HMT *Opossum* took a direct hit and sank at her moorings. Naval casualties are unknown.

Friday 12 March
02.24 TO 04.45 – SHELLS

A large enemy merchant vessel, with escort ships, was observed leaving Boulogne harbour. Dover guns had already opened fire upon the convoy. Three MTBs, lying at 'short notice' in the Ferry Dock, quickly prepared for sea action. Aldis lamps blinked their coded messages across the choppy waters of the harbour, as the boats, in line astern, roared through the eastern entrance, quickly followed by a supporting force of MGBs.

Star shells lit up the night sky as aircraft of the Fleet Air Arm made their

ALL CLEAR – Ivy
Sheppard of 1 Atholl
Terrace leads the way home
from her local cave shelter,
carrying Edwin over her
shoulder with Maureen
holding on to the pram in
which lay Terry. Fifty years
on the cave entrance is still
there

attacks. So intense was the ack-ack from the escorts the aircraft were driven off.
The MTBs were soon within range. Lt. M.A. Forster, DSC, RNVR, in MTB
No. 38, at 700 yards range fired two torpedoes at the large vessel. Struck amidships the merchantman began to list. Both the MTBs and MGBs were attacked
with ferocious gunfire. The Coastal Force boats returned licking their wounds,
having sustained damage both above and below the water-line. Some crew
members had been wounded in the sea battle but there were no fatalities on this
occasion.

While the sea action was hotting up, the town came under fire from the
German guns. The first shell exploded close to B4 ARP Post, in Maison Dieu
Road, where all the occupants were treated for shock. An important underground electric cable was severed, and the NFS sub-station was almost wrecked.
The next exploded opposite Norman Street but damage was insignificant. It just
brought down masonry from buildings already shattered beyond repair. The last
shell extensively damaged a house in Brookfield Avenue, used by Fire Watch

Parties. The fire watch team had a lucky escape. They were playing cards in a garden shelter a few doors away. Their own shelter was completely demolished.

Monday 5 April
00.20 TO 03.15 – SHELLS

Another German convoy with escort was spotted on radar. The 15-in guns 'Jane' and 'Clem' at Wanstone began a barrage which lasted for 106 minutes. They used seventy-five rounds, and thirteen hits were recorded in the battery log book. The South Foreland batteries' 9.2-in guns joined in. They fired fifteen rounds, recorded later in their log book as twelve straddles. In the 'remarks' column for that entry it states: 'Large vessel damaged 1000-ton vessel sunk.'

The German long-range guns fired on Dover. Two shells came over just before 01.00, one struck the rear of 60 Leybourne Road, damaging houses in Harold Terrace, while the other failed to explode on impact in the garden of St Ursula's Convent School, Castle Avenue. Fifteen minutes later another shell took out the back of 15 Park Avenue. Then one exploded on the foreshore at East Cliff. Half an hour went by before the next exploded in The Paddock, off Maison Dieu Road, partially demolishing Nos 6 and 7, and injuring Miss Watson.

The shelling was intermittent. The next salvo arrived about two hours later, wrecking the Mail Packet public house in Woolcomber Street, and also Hopper's Bakery. A small group of army personnel in vehicles had just arrived in Woolcomber Street when a shell exploded on the already-battered St James's Church. There were four military and two civilian casualties. The last shell for the day arrived in the afternoon, wrecking Whyam House in Maison Dieu Road, and blocking Ashen Tree Lane.

Saturday 1 May
22.12 TO 00.47 (2 MAY) – SHELLS

The 15-in guns opened fire on a small German convoy. They used fifty rounds in 56 minutes, and scored four hits. The 9.2-in guns joined in with twelve rounds. One vessel was damaged.

German guns retaliated with three shells. One exploded in Northampton Street, blowing a huge crater in the roadway and damaging several properties. The next hit the approach to Prince of Wales Pier, where there was one slight casualty. The last shell reached Union Road, damaging houses from Nos. 13 to 25. Fortunately most people had taken to their shelters. There were only two slight casualties.

St James church, seen here in 1943, was first hit by a shell on 20 October 1940, again on 5 April 1943, and suffered further damage in 1944. The Duke of Wellington used to hold court here for the Cinque Ports Pilots

Sunday 9 May
17.40 TO 18.46 – SHELLS

It was just after 17.30 when two shells hit the town. Mr and Mrs Knights were shunted into the basement when their home at 13 Maison Dieu Road collapsed on top of them. Thirty-four-year-old Cyril was later found to have died, while his wife was only slightly injured. The other shell exploded beside the already-wrecked Burlington Hotel.

Saturday 22 May
02.21 TO 04.04 – HES

The *Luftwaffe* in the previous month began to use a newly designed Dornier 217 light bomber. Its only attribute was a slight speed advantage over the earlier machines. They were being used on small-scale night attacks on a variety of targets, mostly coastal towns, and usually made by single aircraft.

The sirens went off just before 02.30. A cluster of small calibre bombs was dropped demolishing seven houses in Mayfield Avenue and extensively damaging others in the vicinity. There were four fatal casualties, one seriously injured and eleven slightly.

At No. 126, Charles and Louisa Chapman, and their seventeen-year-old daughter Doris, were killed, while the other daughter was seriously injured. Forty-nine-year-old Ivy Fussell, a laundry worker, was found dead at No. 118. In another badly wrecked house sixteen-year-old Joyce Doolin was trapped in her bed by a fallen rafter which pinned her legs. She was unable to move. While the rescue teams toiled among the rubble, War Reserve Constable Minter remained with the terrified girl for two hours and prevented more rubble falling on the unfortunate victim. Joyce was eventually released and only then did the constable come out of the tunnel. He was taken to hospital in a collapsed state. A total of thirteen were hospitalized. So severe was the damage that eventually fourteen houses were taken down by the authorities.

According to an ARP report, exactly one month later a bomb sank HMS *Adam*, while tied up beside the Prince of Wales Pier.

★ ★ ★

Dover's 'Wings For Victory' week began on Saturday 5 June, with a target of £160,000 – the price of two Lancaster bombers. Exhibitions, parades, dances and many other activities, held in the town and in the rural areas, were started off by Air Vice-Marshal Basil Embry, who asked the town to 'lend the money to buy the tools.' The final total for Dover Rural District came to £41,429 and the total for the town was £170,729. On Saturday 12 June, the Mayor sent a telegram to Emby saying 'Dover has smashed its target and gained its Wings. Many thanks for your inspiring support.' *Signed* Cairns, *Mayor.*

★ ★ ★

Sunday 27 June
16.29 TO 19.17 – SHELLS

Shells falling among convoys was an every-day occurrence. People were becoming complacent because the last shell to hit the town had been on 9 May. But this incident claimed many lives.

The shell warning sounded at 16.30. Several people were out walking in the streets and parks, among them servicemen and servicewomen. It was a glorious day, warm and sunny.

On Sunday 27 June 1943, civilians and service personnel were walking in the streets. It was a gloriously sunny afternoon. Then a shell exploded. within seconds the street looked like a battlefield

Ride 'em Cowboy, a 'slap-stick' comedy starring Bud Abbott and Lou Costello, was showing at the Plaza Cinema when the siren went off. The projector shut down, and everyone was asked to leave. Biggin Street filled with people blinking their eyes in the bright sunlight. Some moved off in groups towards the Market Square.

Then the catastrophe happened. A shell burst in Cannon Street, outside the premises of Montague Burton's. Within seconds, as the acrid fumes of exploding cordite hung in the still, evening air, like some huge shroud, the street looked like a battlefield.

Frank Young had been an ARP messenger before joining the Royal Navy. He was home on leave. He remembers:

We heard this big explosion in the town, so we went with the other wardens to have a look, and decided that we had better follow them down on our bikes with a first aid kit on our backs. So we went cycling down there and met one of the wardens coming back in a panic. 'Look, there's been people killed down there . . .!' We got into the Market Square, and apparently what had happened, and why there were quite a few killed and injured, was that there were quite a lot of people in the Plaza Cinema and when the shell warning went they were sent out. The Germans dropped a 'sneaky one' just as the people had started to go back into the cinema.

I always used to wear my old gauntlet gloves because they were handy when picking up all sorts of odds and ends – bodies and that. There was a couple of squaddies who had a bloke with his ankle badly damaged. I couldn't do anything about it. I told them to wait for the ambulance. I went up a bit further and opposite there was a butcher's shop, and just beyond that, some houses had fallen down in a big heap. We didn't know if anybody was under the rubble. But laying in the middle of the road was a WRN. She looked absolutely dead. We just happened to look back at this girl when she gave a gasp. So I rushed over to have a look. We turned her over and a piece of shrapnel had entered her back and just blown everything out the front. That was her last gasp. It was such a shame.

Down in the Market Square there was a squaddie laying there, and from his back you could not see anything wrong with him. I put my hands under his armpits and turned him over. It was not a pretty sight. There was a squad of other bodies laying up and down the street which we couldn't do anything with because they were all dead – poor souls.

One WRN, eleven servicemen, and a young girl, Rubina Streeter, had been killed. Ten civilians and twenty-one servicemen were injured. They were taken to damaged shops to await an ambulance. Eight of the servicemen killed were in the Dorsetshire Regiment.

It was several weeks before the crater was filled in. It remained a sort of *aide-mémoire*, not only for those who had lost their lives so tragically, but as a poignant reminder to take cover when the warning sounded.

Monday 28 June
22.43 TO 02.29 – SHELLS

A large German convoy near the French coast was spotted by the Dover Coastal Force flotilla. Radio messages plied between the little boats and the plotting rooms. The MTBs and MGBs scattered out of range before Wanstone's 15-in guns opened fire in their direction. The first to fire was the Fan Bay 6-in guns. Although they were unable to reach the enemy ships the flash of the gun barrels, called 'flash-fire', was to make the enemy ships alter their course to a predictable zig-zag pattern. This gave the plotters time to estimate range and course of each individual vessel. Wanstone Battery fired fourteen shells, quickly followed by the South Foreland Battery firing a further thirty-eight shells. In the 56-minute engagement only one hit was recorded.

At 23.30 the German guns replied with a neat salvo of three shells. The first hit the GPO building in Priory Street, wrecking part of the structure and

The lifeless bodies of three telephone operators were recovered from the wreckage, after the first of three shells hit the town on 28 June 1943, partially demolishing the telephone exchange in Priory Street

destroying all telephone communications. Rescue squads were quick on the scene. Meticulously searching the debris they found three telephone operators had died: John Parfitt, George Kerry and Walter Garrett.

The second shell hit houses in Priory Road, where three of them collapsed into the street, killing ambulance driver William Golding, seriously injuring two soldiers and slightly injuring four others. Another shell exploded at the rear of the National Provincial Bank in Market Square. The Red Lion lodging house, St James's Street, was partially demolished, and 3 Effingham Crescent, used by the naval authorities, was also damaged.

Monday 5 July
02.17 TO 04.42 – SHELLS

Two German destroyers were plotted on the Dover radar near Dunkirk. This resulted in Wanstone and South Foreland batteries opening up a bombardment lasting 52 minutes. Between them they fired sixty shells, at a range of 32,000 yards, and the whole action was a close co-operation with six MTBs.

Three German shells fell on the town. One hit the ruined Burlington Hotel, the next exploded in St James's Street, and the last hit Russell Place, where six unoccupied houses were damaged beyond repair. Part of Leney's Mineral Water factory and garage were also badly damaged by blast. There were no casualties reported at either incident.

Wednesday 4 August
22.18 TO 23.57 – SHELLS

The Prime Minister visited Dover with the US Secretary of State for War H.L. Stimson to see the result of shell damage. This had been triggered by complaints brought up in Parliament by the MP for Dover. According to townspeople, not least the Councillors, the long-suffering citizens were

Winston Churchill visited Dover on 4 August 1943 with US Secretary of War H.L. Stimson. They were to view the damage in the town that was triggered by complaints brought up in Parliament. At 10.30 p.m. a shell exploded on the YMCA in Effingham Crescent

becoming fed up with constant shelling as a reprisal for the Dover guns indulging in artillery duels. Of course, Dovorians were unaware of the precise reasons for British gun actions.

It was almost 20.30 – the Prime Minister had already left the town – when the first shell came over to explode at the rear of Dover College. There were no casualties, as the WRNS had been evacuated to the Dover Boys' County School as a safety measure some weeks before. The next shell fell at the entrance to the college, in Effingham Crescent, and the last one exploded in Granville Dock, resulting in two fatal naval casualties.

Tuesday 24 August
10.50 TO 13.43 – SHELLS

Three shells had hit the town on the previous day resulting in blast damage at Hillside Road, Bunkers Hill and near the RAF balloon site in Broadlees Meadow. There was only one female casualty.

A convoy had been passing through the Strait the day before and another came through this Tuesday. Shells bracketed the ships while motor launches laid smoke-screens. The first shell to hit the town exploded in the college grounds, close to the balloon site. There was one WAAF casualty. The next hit Prospect Place, and at 11.30 a large-calibre shell exploded in East Street, wrecking eighteen houses and killing fifty-year-old Dorothy Gregory at No. 11.

At midday three shells arrived at the same time, two exploding in the allotments near Edred Road, seriously injuring Edward Austen, while the other hit 18 Edred Road, practically wrecking a further six dwellings. In fact, damage was so severe that more than twelve houses were rendered uninhabitable. The last shell wrecked Bicknell's newsagents and tobacconist shop in Priory Road. There were no casualties there.

★ ★ ★

Civil Defence arrangements were suddenly overhauled in August, the Fire Service strengthened, stocks of food and fuel were increased, and there was a military presence in Dover Rural District, never before seen. Some of the country lanes were widened, new telegraph poles erected, and light ack-ack guns appeared in fields overnight. Increased road traffic meant more accidents. People were being bowled over in the streets at an alarming rate. The words 'Second Front' were on everyone's lips.

In the first week of September a full-scale amphibious exercise took place

The South Foreland Battery of four 9.2-inch guns was not ready for 'action' until October 1941. The first action was against the German battle-cruisers *Scharnhorst* and *Gneisenau* and the heavy cruiser *Prince Eugen* on 12 February 1942. A gun is inspected by some distinguished Americans on 25 August 1943

with the code name Harlequin – part of Operation Starkey, an attempt to convince Hitler and his generals that the proposed invasion of the Continent would come from the south-east of England.

At a number of strategic points troops assembled to try out embarkation in various types of invasion craft and put to sea. Some of them got within a few miles of the French coast. Hundreds of fighters and bombers of the RAF and the USAAF crossed the Channel over a period lasting three hours.

Military and civilian police, ever vigilant, were, more than ever, stopping people in the streets asking for identity cards and special permits. All vehicles were being stopped at fixed barriers on roads leading into the town and many passengers were subjected to long interrogation at railway stations.

Operation Starkey was a resounding success. It not only convinced the German Military Command of the Allies' intention to strike by way of the Pas de Calais, it also convinced the civilians.

Disgruntled troops made long route marches around the Dover countryside. They fought each other in mock battles and skirmishes, and unwittingly left behind deadly hand grenades and mortar-bombs. Three Dover boys found a hand grenade on Plum Pudding Hill. It exploded and the eldest lost a hand while the others suffered severe facial injuries.

During the early morning of 1 September, a passing convoy was shelled but none hit the town. The following day a similar action took place. On 4 September, in a 46-minute bombardment, Wanstone and South Foreland batteries opened fire on German shipping off Calais. One large vessel was sunk and another set on fire. Only one German shell reached the town to explode against the Prince of Wales Pier. No casualties were recorded.

Saturday 25 September
04.25 TO 05.44 – SHELLS

Two shells hit the town during a German bombardment of one of our convoys. The first damaged the beer storage yard of Fremlin's Brewery, just behind Market Square, setting a lorry alight, while another exploded on 11 Pencester Road, fortunately unoccupied since it was bombed in 1942. The Lord Nelson public house was also blast damaged on this occasion but there were no casualties.

Sunday 3 October
22.05 TO 23.00 – SHELLS

Fan Bay Battery fired its usual 'flash-fire' sequence and an enemy medium-sized vessel took violent evasive action. Wanstone fired fifteen shells and South Foreland sixty-eight during the 49-minute engagement. Three shells reached the town from France. The first exploded in Pencester Gardens blowing out shop windows, and the next took out the rear part of the Dover Technical College, demolishing the Corporation Baths and damaging the police station. The last one hit 20–21 Park Street. The building collapsed into the street. There were no casualties reported.

Dover Castle – 'The Key of England' – stands reassuringly as a backdrop to this photograph, taken through a gap in a demolished wall of the Ladywell Technical College, when it was hit by a shell on Sunday 3 October 1943

Monday 4 October
00.26 TO 01.05 – SHELLS

A 40-minute engagement by the 'big guns' sent thirty-five 15-in and fifty-six 9.2-in shells bracketing a German convoy off Cap Griz Nez. One large vessel was sunk and two other craft were observed to beach. It was just after midnight when four German shells came over. Tolputt's Yard, at the rear of Pencester Road, received the first, then the next exploded on the Guildhall Vaults public house on the corner of Queen Street and Bench Street. Severe damage was caused to many shops in the area. Flashman's Depository in Dieu Stone Lane was hit for the second time, and the final shell exploded on the seafront opposite the Yacht Club. One naval casualty was reported.

Depending on the type of cross-Channel gun being fired, and the calibre of shell and charge used, the delay before the shell fell on Dover was usually between eighty and ninety seconds. This is Bench Street, Dover, on 4 October 1943

Flashman's Depository, Dieu Stone Lane, was first hit by a shell on 4 October 1943, destroying furniture in store from damaged dwellings. Struck again a year later the fragile building was demolished as unsafe

British coastal guns had engaged a German convoy near Cap Griz Nez, firing ninety-one shells and sinking one large vessel. The Guildhall Vaults, on the corner of Queen Street and Bench Street, was wrecked just after midnight on 4 October 1943 during the German reply

Monday 18 October
AMERICAN FORTRESS CRASH

Almost every week incidents concerning damaged American Flying Fortresses and Liberators, returning to England from their bombing missions, occurred in the rural areas behind Dover. Bert Danson recalls:

> My father and I were returning to Dover along the A2 Canterbury Road, with a van full of apples collected from a farm at Acrise. Shortly after passing the Halfway House, we spotted a Flying Fortress flying in the direction of Canterbury. Smoke was pouring from one of the engines. The bomber then swung round as though to head back towards the sea. Several of the crew baled out. No parachutes were seen to open. Most of them landed in nearby fields. We had just reached the Shepherdswell crossroads near Lydden Hill, when the bomber veered towards us.
>
> Dad, who owned a greengrocer's shop in Tower Hamlets, was faced with

the decision to either accelerate under the monster or slam on the brakes. Both options were tried but the fully loaded van refused to speed up. The B17, belonging to the 94th Bomber Group, by now well alight, lumbered straight up the A2 at hedgerow height, neatly slicing telegraph poles in half, to eventually slam down onto the roadway. It then veered left through a hedge and ploughed into a field. We ran towards it and the pilot came up to us, asking if we were okay. Joined by other members of the crew they went off to find their colleagues.

Monday 25 October
20.25 TO 23.50 – SHELLS

Dover radar picked up a German vessel heavily escorted by five armed trawlers, known as R-boats. The bombardment by our guns lasted about 104 minutes, resulting in the large vessel and one of the escorts being sunk. The 540 Coast Regiment log book records that eighty shells were fired.

The German guns replied. Ranging shots fell in the sea then the first to reach the town exploded on 79 London Road, used by H.M. Customs as an office. Four serious casualties occurred when another shell exploded between houses in Heathfield Avenue and the Scottish Laundry.

The most serious incident happened at Glenfield Road, where Nos. 20 and 22 were almost completely demolished. Adjacent houses were so badly damaged by blast that most of the unfortunate residents were evacuated, their homes declared uninhabitable.

Thirty-eight-year-old Alice Shearn, and her daughters, fifteen-year-old Alice, thirteen-year-old Joan and four-year-old Brenda were all killed in the explosion. Nine-year-old Margaret was found seriously injured. Many hours later the body of fifty-eight-year-old Phoebe Payne was recovered from the debris. Mrs Payne and the Shearn family were all buried in the same grave at the Charlton Cemetery a week later. Each coffin was covered by the Union Jack.

The shell which hit Lewis's Garage in Cherry Tree, set alight petrol and oil tanks, and wrecked adjacent premises. Another exploded at the rear of Coleman's Convalescent Home, near the devastated Glenfield Road. An ATS driver was seriously injured when her army lorry caught fire. Other incidents occurred at Waterloo Crescent, Parsons Way, Pardoners Way and Drop Redoubt. There were no further casualties.

Wednesday 3 November
22.05 TO 23.00 – SHELLS

Two enemy destroyers were seen steaming up Channel by one of our reconnaissance aircraft. Dover's gun plotting room was able to confirm the signal by radar.

Wanstone and South Foreland Batteries anxiously waited for their targets to come within range. Fan Bay guns fired their usual rounds but the destroyers failed to alter course. Wanstone immediately opened fire. Thirty-eight rounds were used and one of the destroyers was later observed on fire. The action lasted just 33 minutes.

The Germans replied almost at once. Ten shells hit the town. Several exploded without causing much damage, while others badly damaged houses in Minerva Avenue, Heathfield Avenue, Cherry Tree, Lorne Road and Brookfield Avenue. The Z4 ARP Post at the Archcliffe Fort was blast damaged, and the Coleman's Home was damaged once again. Seventy-two-year-old Margaret License, widow of a former cycle dealer, lost her life when a shell demolished 8 Northampton Street. A few minutes later another shell exploded on 78 and 80 Glenfield Road, killing Alfred Jenkins. Four other people were injured. These incidents were the last recorded for November.

★ ★ ★

One of the biggest West End variety shows ever to entertain Dover audiences appeared at the Royal Hippodrome, on Sunday 19 December, 1943. It happened quite by chance, when the Royal Artillery was to put on a show in aid of the RA Prisoners of War Fund. The Lord's Day Observance Society intervened and the show was cancelled.

This action was given wide publicity in the national newspapers. The well-known comedian Tommy Trinder immediately offered to bring a first-class show to Dover which would not contravene any Sunday laws. The cast included Tommy Trinder, Sonnie Hale, Tessie O'Shea, Derek Roy, Cherry Lind, Morton Frazer and the Jerry Allen Trio. They all gave their services free. They played to a packed house, many standing, while others were turned away because the theatre was full to overflowing. During the three-hour performance, and with the help of raffles and collection boxes, the show raised £130 for the POW Fund.

★ ★ ★

Although there was little absence among the ack-ack units then defending Dover, unit commanders were instructed to warn their troops of the severe penalties they could expect in every case of avoidable absence.

Major Percy Ross, CO of 390 HAA Battery, chose to add a rider of his own. He would dismiss any case where an accused produced a reasonable excuse for absence which he had not heard before.

A few weeks later, Major Ross found himself viewing across his desk six of his most reliable personnel, including a highly regarded Bombardier. His heart sank. There seemed no option other than to remand them to the Commanding Officer. The Bombardier was appointed to speak for them all and was asked what he had to say. He replied, 'Sir, we were trapped under a billiard table,' and after a short pause, added, 'Is that the excuse you haven't heard before, Sir?'

The six gunners had been playing snooker in the basement of the Dover YMCA, in Effingham Crescent, when a shell demolished part of it. Rescued some hours later they were returned to camp in police cars. The case was dismissed.

Thursday 23 December
19.50 TO 22.30 – SHELLS

A 60-minute bombardment of a large enemy tanker in the Strait prompted a one-shell retaliation from the French coast. It exploded on the Congregational Church, Russell Street, and partly demolished Leney's Garage. Three lorries were buried beneath the rubble. Previously damaged houses in the area were again wrecked. As they were in a much-shelled part of the town they were all fortunately unoccupied. There were no casualties.

★ ★ ★

Entertainments centred around small orchestras and dance bands regularly appeared at Dover Town Hall. Squadron Leader Blakeney with his RAF Embassy Band often made appearances outside Dover; they are seen here at the Leas Cliff Hall, Folkestone

On Christmas Eve about 130 children, whose fathers were either prisoners of war or missing in action, were entertained by Woodlands Ambulance Depot and Fire Guards, at Peter Street Hall. The hall was suitably decorated in the time-honoured tradition of the festive season, and for a few hours it became a magical wonderland. Snow White and the Seven Dwarfs had gathered round a gaily lit Christmas tree festooned with tinsel, snow and bon-bons.

The party began with a grand sing-song, and gathered strength as the children became used to their surroundings. PC Ewer and PC Punter, as Popeye and a clown, fooled around and played party tricks to the children's delight. Some children entered a talent contest. The prize was won by Violet Mills, who sang 'You'll Never Know, Dear, How Much I Love You', in the approved Vera Lynn style.

Tea and cakes followed, then jingle bells were heard and Father Christmas made his entry on a sleigh drawn by reindeer. Each child received a present, most of them toys made by ambulance men in their spare time.

For the time being, in those few precious hours, some semblance of normality had returned to Dover.

CHAPTER SIX

1944
'It Will Not be Long Now'

On Thursday 20 January, for the first time, the sinking of an enemy ship by fire from British guns was officially notified for publication. The Prime Minister sent a message of congratulations addressed to the Commander, Coast Artillery. It read, 'Hearty congratulations on the good shooting of the Dover guns.'

As dawn broke RAF Typhoon fighters went out to search for the attacked ship and found it already in a sinking condition a mile offshore from Sandgatte, near Calais. The funnel and superstructure were sticking out of the water and the ship had settled evenly without showing any list. It was later identified as the 7000-ton *Munsterland*.

★ ★ ★

FIRE GUARD NOTES

Once again I would like to appeal to everybody to give an eye to the Street Fire Equipment Points as an epidemic seems to have broken out again of destroying the stirrup pumps at these points. Nozzels are cut away, and one pump has been taken away altogether. I am sure it doesn't need me to stress what a serious thing this is; it may even cause the loss of life of a Fire Guard who goes to use a defective pump in an emergency. Parents and school teachers could very usefully put it over to the children, and anybody, seeing these pumps being tampered with at any time, could notify the police and help cut down this sabotage – for that is sabotage after all.

Dover Express 7 January 1944

Friday 21 January
JU88 CRASH

After a period of inactivity lasting several months, the *Luftwaffe* suddenly appeared over England in some strength. This offensive was known to the British as the 'Little Blitz' and in Germany it had been code-named Operation *Steinbock*. It was an offensive ordered by Goering as a reprisal for the devastating bombing raids made by the RAF and the USAAF on German cities.

Seven of the fourteen German bombers shot down over Britain were claimed by the ack-ack gunners. Lt. J. White, a plotting officer with the Dover ack-ack, said afterwards:

> It was the biggest concentration of flak we have seen for some time – just like the Battle of Britain, except that this time it was at night. There was enemy traffic in the sky all the time and one raider came screaming down over our heads and crashed on a gun site. The plane was shot down by the guns of a sister regiment not far away, though we did not learn this until the raid was over.

The aircraft mentioned in Lt. White's account was a JU88 A-4 of 4/KG6, which crashed in flames on the gymnasium at the Citadel Barracks, at 21.10. Three crew members were killed, *Uffz*. K. Dorschner, *Obergefr*. H. Neumann and *Obergefr*. H. Waterkamp. Another crew member *Obergefr*. H. Grun, although seriously injured, had managed to bale out and landed near a farm-house at Hougham. Despite exploding petrol tanks and ammunition, soldiers fought the flames until the arrival of Dover's NFS. 'The battery thought they were being dive-bombed,' said Lt. J.D. MacMillan, 'but they were old hands and stood to their guns. When our boys went down to the town at the weekend, people were slapping them on the back for the show they put up.'

Saturday 22 January
04.16 TO 06.00 – HES

The target for *Steinbock*, which started the previous evening, was London. Although it was the heaviest attack since the raid on Birmingham in July 1942, it fell far short of its intended purpose. Most of the bombs fell over the south-east of England when the ack-ack barrage and RAF night fighters met the onslaught.

In the early hours of Saturday morning a stick of bombs fell on Stanhope Road, demolishing nearly twelve houses but only killing one man. Of the five

Former Dover ATS girl Elizabeth Owen joined the 42nd Kent Company Platoon in 1939. Husband Captain J.E.D. Owen was a radar officer and, being the youngest, was depicted in this 1944 caricature sitting in a cot (bottom left). The commercial artist – a soldier – is unknown

people taken to hospital with a variety of injuries, one was a baby of nine months who died the next day.

Several lives were saved by the Morrison and Anderson shelters. Wardens arrived quickly at the scene and were searching the wreckage when the Heavy Rescue Squad arrived. The first persons rescued were Mrs Pedley and her two young daughters who had been sleeping in their Morrison. They were not injured. But next door at No. 8, the body of sixty-four-year-old Thomas Godmark, a former warden and shelter marshall, was later recovered. He had died of shock; the Morrison had saved him from any injury. His wife Caroline, and their daughter Violet Hemmings, aged twenty-one, with her nine-month-old baby Valerie, were rushed to hospital.

On the other side of the road, ex-policeman Albert Nunns was rescued injured from his bedroom. In the garden of No. 3 was an Anderson shelter, in which were his wife, Mrs Tugwell, his married daughter, and an elderly lady from the house next door. Although one bomb had exploded close to the shelter, only Mrs Tugwell was injured – she was badly bruised. The shelter had been severely damaged by blast, leaving the corrugated sections buckled. There was widespread blast damage in the area.

This incident was the last made on Dover by piloted aircraft. Stanhope Road, where many houses were demolished or wrecked, had probably suffered more damage, for its size, than any other road in Dover.

★ ★ ★

On Friday 18 February, at the Town Hall, Alderman E.G. Oak-Rhind, CBE, Chairman of the Kent County Council Civil Defence Committee, on behalf of the Kent County Council, presented to the Dover Civil Defence Services its CD flag. He was accompanied by Mr P.M. MacGrath, Col. J.H. Campbell, DSO, OBE, County ARP Controller. With them on the platform was the Mayor, J.R. Cairns, and members of the Dover Emergency Committee and of the Town Council, together with the Reverend A.S. Cooper (Chaplain to the Corporation) who carried out the consecration. About one hundred members of Dover's Civil Defence were present under their Sub-Controller Inspector Fenn.

Monday 20 March
00.03 TO 23.20 – SHELLS

It had been a hectic month in the Dover Strait when long-range guns were in action on most days. Our guns were firing on enemy shipping and the Germans replied. A feature of the German shelling was the firing of an increasing number of guns simultaneously. The War Office issued a statement which said our guns had hit an enemy tanker of some 4,000 tons. It had disappeared from the radar screens completely. Subsequent air reconnaissance reported the tanker missing and it was presumed sunk. It was later identified as the *Rekum*.

The long-suffering townspeople were already in their iron-clad shelters when the first salvo came over at 00.30. The first of twenty shells struck Nos 12 and 13 Prioress Walk. Here the rescue squads found five-year-old Maureen Smillie and her seven-year-old brother Donald, dead in the rubble of their home, and their parents seriously injured.

The next hit Lewis's Yard in Eric Road, did considerable damage to a baker's shop and a confectionery shop, but there were no casualties at either premises. No. 11 Cambridge Road was hit, then another shell exploded harmlessly on Chitty's Sports Ground.

There were more casualties at the Grand Shaft Barracks. An army captain and a regimental quartermaster sergeant of the South Staffordshire Regiment lost their lives. Two shells exploded simultaneously on the Crabble Rag Mill, demolishing several buildings, then another hit the top of De Burgh Hill.

Two RAF personnel were seriously injured when the annexe of HMS *Wasp* was hit.

Shelling ceased until 21.30. Then it started again. Citadel Barracks received the first shell. The military did not reveal either damage or casualties. The New Mogul Inn was badly damaged in Adrian Street and also the Dover Express office in Snargate Street, when two shells struck half an hour later. But within five minutes the Wheelwrights' Arms, at the junction of Granville Street and Bridge Street, erupted into a shower of bricks and tiles. Brook's grocery store was set alight and burned out completely.

Stanhope Road received the next shell which took out the rear of Nos 7, 9 and 11, bringing down the brickwork in three separate piles. Other shells damaged Edred Road, Meadway River, where a house called Langdale was partially demolished; No. 16 Maison Dieu Road, where a 6,000-volt electric cable was severed causing a complete black-out over half the town, and the last hit 6 Camden Crescent. There were no further casualties.

For more than two hours the explosions of shells and our guns being fired were heard almost without a break. The night sky was illuminated by the flashes. After the initial period it was less intense. Official sources stated our guns had fired 140 rounds.

The third bout of shelling, which began at 21.30 on the following night, was not so fierce, and lasted only 40 minutes. Two-gun salvoes from our guns brought a German reply in under five minutes. Almost all of the shells either bracketed the gun sites or fell in the sea.

On 31 March the Secretary of State for War made a further order under the Regulation 13 of the Defence (General) Regulation Act (1939), declaring that certain areas were to be protected which were to come into force on 1 April. Dover had always been in a Protected Area; although townspeople had been able to walk along the seafront, sentries barred their way to more sensitive areas. The new orders prevented anyone without a special pass from being anywhere near the seafront. Large boards were erected, sealing off all roads leading to the harbour.

The gradual build-up to what became the Second Front for the proposed invasion of northern France, code-named Operation Overlord, gave rise to massive troop concentrations in an already-overcrowded garrison town. The big hoax which had begun the year before, now reached a new 'high' in outwitting Hitler's High Command. Under the code-name Operation Fortitude, fictitious American and British units were formed and known as 'Fusag', allowing exaggerated radio traffic to filter through to the enemy listening posts.

Troop movements of the Canadian 2 Corps and the British 12 Corps increased around Dover, bringing with them all the paraphernalia associated with a military campaign of some magnitude. Special stencilled signposts appeared at road junctions and some were nailed to trees. Even the harbour

Spies and deception. A naval officer thought it odd that the Post Packet Boat, delivering mail around the harbour, never called on the landing craft. Perhaps the low-grade enemy agents also thought it odd. Nevertheless, Hans Hanson signalled their presence to his *Abwehr* controllers in Hamburg. This is a rare photograph of the dummy landing craft in Dover harbour, taken in July 1944

became part of the hoax. In it there grew a fleet of small landing craft, moored in pairs, each of them measuring approximately 130 feet long by 30 feet at the beam, and weighing almost 13 tons. Under the code-name Bigbobs, Captain R. Hugh Clark, MC, helped to construct these dummy craft. He recalled:

> They were constructed from pre-formed sections made from scaffolding tube, the sections being pinned together. The frame included a large number of castor wheels to enable the craft to be moved on land. The frame was covered with canvas and buoyancy was provided by a large number of 40-gallon oil drums. Below decks were duck-boards – walkways for easy maintenance, and the whole was covered with camouflage netting. The dummies were built at night. A team of thirty men would commence work as soon as it was dark. They were built, launched and moored before first light. To bring some authenticity and life into the scheme of things we used to spill oil on the water around them, hanging washing out on a line from time to time, and even burned oily rags below deck to simulate smoke coming from a galley stove. A naval officer once remarked that he thought it odd the Post Packet Boat never delivered mail to the landing craft!

Thursday 20 April
23.00 TO 23.44 – SHELLS

Four shells were fired at Dover just after 23.00. The first demolished 22 Godwyne Road, Clyde House next door, and a doctor's surgery was badly damaged. The next one landed on the pavement outside 106 Maison Dieu Road, causing an awkward crater which blocked the road. Fifteen minutes later there was a direct hit on George Thomas's ironmonger's shop in King Street, which was completely wrecked, while other properties were shattered by blast. There were no casualties reported. The Lord Nelson and the Cause Is Altered public houses were also damaged.

★ ★ ★

Tuesday 6 June
12.12 TO 13.15 – SHELLS (D-DAY)

When General Eisenhower, Supreme Allied Commander of Operation Overlord, had said in the dead of a June night 'Go!', there was not one man in any of the services, both American and British, who was less than confident of success. This colossal undertaking – the biggest invasion force ever assembled in the history of warfare – moved off with absolute precision.

By midday several British and American convoys began steaming down the English Channel, to bolster the invasion beach-heads on the Normandy coast. Minesweepers and light coastal craft from Dover were busy every hour of the day, laying smoke-screens, looking out for mines and E-boats.

With so much activity going on in the Strait, the German guns opened fire, the shells bracketing the ships until they had steamed out of range. SS *Sambut* was hit. A fire was started onboard. A crew member had been killed together with eighteen soldiers, before she was brought close in-shore to Shakespeare Cliff.

Thursday 7 June
13.28 TO 19.20 – SHELLS

The results of months of research and design culminated in the production of two prefabricated harbours, known by their code-name as Mulberry 'A' and Mulberry 'B'. Each of them, when fixed in position off the coast of Normandy, would be the size of Dover Harbour, complete with a floating breakwater. The components were made in England and towed across the Channel and sunk or moored in position.

Segments of these huge concrete and steel caissons and floating piers, when towed past Dover, were a fascinating sight to jubilant Dovorians. It is still an unexplained mystery how they got through the Strait quite unmolested.

Nevertheless, twelve shells came over to explode on the town. It was almost

Twelve shells came hurtling over the Channel on 7 June 1944, and caused considerable damage in the town. At Christ Church School, Military Hill, there were five casualties recorded but no deaths

13.30 when the first one hit Westmount YMCA in Folkestone Road, seriously injuring four females and one male. Henry Whitewood was seriously injured at the Southern Railway Loco Sheds, near Snargate Street, when they received a direct hit. He died a week later. No. 38 Queen's Avenue had the front demolished, then Malmains Road was shattered by blast damage. Further blast damage occurred at Clarendon Place, when a shell exploded behind Nos. 25 and 27. Seventy-two-year-old Stephen Jenkins was found beneath the rubble of his home. Rescuers could not revive him and he died of shock.

Kitchener Road received a shell which partially demolished Nos 27 and 29, injuring three people. Ambulances were out the whole time. A further five casualties were dealt with at Christchurch School on the Western Heights. Further up the hill a shell exploded close to an ack-ack site, and then another struck a house nearby. All these latter incidents were on War Department land. Damage and casualties were not revealed. Two other shells exploded within two minutes of each other. One of them partially demolished 41 Albany Place, where sixty-four-year-old John Mullane was killed. There were fourteen other casualties here, including a child.

Sunday 25 June
03.55 TO 05.36 – SHELLS

Shells falling around convoys was an every-day occurrence, both during the day and night. The constant detonations of the German guns firing, coupled with shell explosions, had quite a traumatic effect upon the townspeople. Huddled together in the caves and shelters they were remarkably composed, and sang the latest songs to keep their spirits up. But even so, they were conscious of the fact that this could be their last day on earth.

The *Empire Lough* was hit. Loaded with cans of petrol *en route* to the invasion beaches, they exploded, flying into the air like flaming missiles. The Dover tug *Lady Brassey* towed her out of the convoy and beached her beneath Abbott's Cliff.

Wednesday 28 June
16.30 TO 20.33 – SHELLS

The old Drill Hall on the seafront was hit. The Royal Army Medical Corps personnel were billeted there, ready to receive emergency casualties taken off the

Each night, at dusk, little processions would make their way to the caves and shelters, for there at least they might get some sleep. The next morning, however, as they went to their daily tasks the unannounced shell or bomb might fall

damaged ships. Three soldiers were killed and a further thirteen injured. The collier *Dalegarth Force* lost three of its crew when a shell made a direct hit. Three hours later a shell exploded at the rear of the Salvation Army Citadel in the High Street, blasting properties in Priory Hill. There were two seriously injured here. Godwin's Bakery, 67 London Road, was severely damaged and fire started, but there were no further casualties.

★ ★ ★

The *London Gazette* published the names of two men for having received an expression of Commendation for Brave Conduct. They were John William Arnold, of Clarendon Place, Dover, and William Henry Shingleton, of Lowther Road, Dover. The citation read:

> For bravery following a land-mine explosion. On observing smoke rising from a deep moat following the explosion and seeing a soldier nearby gesticulating and calling for help, Shingleton and Arnold with other employees of the Dover Harbour Board, went to the site. With the full knowledge that there had been a land-mine explosion, and that other mines were probably in the moat, Shingleton and Arnold then lowered themselves into the moat some 20 to 30 feet below, by means of a rope, where they discovered one soldier fatally injured and a second badly injured, and unconscious. By means of ropes and a stretcher, which was lowered to them, the injured soldier was raised.

★ ★ ★

Shelling had increased since D-day, and Dover, Deal and Folkestone took the full force of these reprisal actions. After the invasion of Europe, the townspeople were more optimistic of the outcome when reading newspaper reports and listening to the wireless broadcasts. But their growing sense of relief was short-lived. Hitler unleashed his new weapon – the V1, a pilotless flying machine, which soon began to appear over the countryside, and carrying a 1-ton warhead propelled by a rocket motor.

Soon after Bomber Command raided Lubeck in March 1942, Hitler ordered retaliatory attacks on non-military targets. Those living in Dover at the time would not have noticed the difference. Bombing and shelling incidents seemed largely indiscriminate.

On a remote island in the Baltic in 1936, at a place called Peenemunde, a secret research establishment was built, where Werner von Braun, a leading authority on rocket propulsion was the director. One of the products developed there was the V1 – *Vergeltungswaffen* (Weapon of Revenge), better known to the British as the flying bomb, doodlebug or buzz-bomb.

By 1944 dozens of launching ramps had been built by slave labour, which ran from Dunkirk to Abbeville. Photo reconnaissance indicated ramps at Siracourt, Watten, Wizernes, Marquise and Mimoyecques. The Pas de Calais area was the most obvious choice of site, ideally suited to launch flying bombs at London, on a pre-set height, range and speed.

The first V1 sighted, one of four launched, was seen by the Royal Observer Corps Post at Dymchurch, at 04.08 on 13 June. By mid-August the V1 menace brought a heavy concentration of light and heavy ack-ack guns into the coastal areas which, together with RAF fighter aircraft patrolling selected areas, accounted for 80 per cent of all bombs destroyed.

★ ★ ★

Inspector A.J. Fenn, head of Dover's Civil Defence Services, was asked to accompany a Canadian journalist around the town during August. The Canadian later wrote:

> I went with the Inspector to a huge bowl behind the cliffs which was scooped out years ago to supply ballast for ships returning light to Continental ports. Now this bowl marks the entrance to the catacombs in which are found the bunk beds of those who seek air-raid shelter, and in which a complete emergency hospital has been established. The whole region is honey-combed with tunnels in which is complete equipment for emergency and even siege. Nursing Sister Banks is in charge of the hospital and she showed me the various places which in an ordinary hospital would correspond to the wards, operating room, kitchen and the dispensary. Beyond the hospital are the public shelters. A minimum of 800 Dover residents sleep here each night. In the days of frequent ALERTS there were many more. The centre of the maze of tunnels is called 'Piccadilly Circus', and from it the tunnels radiate in all directions. There is complete equipment for the shelters both for routine nightly visits and for emergency conditions. If needs be, the whole population underground could be maintained in health and reasonable comfort for many days. Food supplies for two weeks are also maintained, and in addition sanitary facilities for all purposes. The kitchens can provide 200 hot meals within half and hour.

In late July 1944 the American 127th AAA Gun Battalion arrived at Liverpool aboard HMS *Scythia*. It took only three weeks before they were assigned to

'Civilian spirit is high too . . . kids – "Any gum chum?" . . . from the cliff we watch MTBs lay a smoke screen for a convoy. Jerry played cat and mouse bracketing the patrol boats now and then.' (Above) Irvin and McCulloch of 'B' Battery 127th AAA Gun Battalion

ack-ack defence against the flying bomb, arriving at Dover to be located on the old aerodrome site at Swingate. The battalion had A, B, C and D batteries, each equipped with four 90-mm guns, remote-controlled and linked to radar and a computer.

The Americans were using the latest proximity fuse, code-named Bonzo, and were in action almost as soon as they had arrived. Being so close to the Swingate radar masts and also the 15-in guns, they were unfortunately in one of the most exposed positions imaginable. Their battalion area was hit on many occasions by the German long-range shells. The first time this happened over a dozen shells exploded. D battery lost most of its equipment. Lt. Clarence Ash recalls:

As battalion motor-pool officer, I was responsible to see that the vehicles of the 127th were properly serviced. On one particular fine, sunny morning, the siren had blown, and all our maintenance crew had taken cover in a zig-zag trench some distance from the old hangar in which we worked. I was becoming extremely nervous since we were not taking advantage of such a nice

'Shells now come over as they pleased . . . projectiles bursting in unison . . . a cold funny tingling went up and down my spine . . . everyone prayed that night . . . I'll call anyone a liar who wasn't scared . . . there are no atheists in foxholes. . . . ' Corporal Allan J. English, 'C' Battery, 127 AAA Gun Battalion, United States Army

morning. I grumbled about not getting anything done. I walked 40 to 50 feet towards the trench in which my men had taken cover, and shouted, 'Hey! You bunch of yellow bellies, how about coming in here and doing some work?' There was a short pause. It was followed by a most deafening explosion as a shell landed between where I was standing and the trench. When the smoke had cleared Cpl. Charles Dilday stood up and yelled, 'Sir! You go straight to hell!' Since I realized what might have happened if they had climbed out of the trench, I threw my cap down and said, 'I guess you are smarter than me.'

Sunday 13 August
00.19 – V1 (FLYING BOMB)

The first flying bomb mentioned in the Record of Incidents appears on this day. One of them was hit by ack-ack fire, and at such close range that it blew up directly over a gun site at Lydden Spout. Two Nissen huts were wrecked, seriously injuring a gunner and causing four others slight wounds.

Tuesday 15 August
14.00 – V1 (FLYING BOMB)

Hit by ack-ack this flying bomb exploded on Fairview Terrace at Hougham, severely damaging the Three Horse Shoes public house. There were two casualties.

Wednesday 16 August
05.20 – V1 (FLYING BOMB)

Ray Pidgeon, who ran the Sunny Corner shop immediately above the railway entrance to Shakespeare Cliff, had just returned from Z4 ARP Post, having been on fire watch duty. He went to bed hoping to get some sleep before opening his shop. Then he heard the sound of a flying bomb. Looking through his bedroom window he saw it heading towards the shop. He quickly rolled under the bed with his dog. Hit by ack-ack the V1 dived into the cliff face to explode on impact. The shop was wrecked. Furniture and stock were removed the next day. Ray returned to the shop eight weeks later. Nine other V1s were brought down to explode in the sea but one exploded near the Farthingloe gun site.

On the following day the sleepy village of Alkham was roused from its slumbers when a V1 exploded early in the morning. Another arrived just after 15.00, and a further seven were shot down over the sea.

The heaviest concentration of flying bombs flew in over our coast to the west of Dover during the initial stages of the campaign. When the launching sites were overrun by allied forces, however, the sites were quickly re-sited further east. Anti-aircraft guns and patrolling fighters were given strict areas, within which they were to engage the robots. Fighters sometimes encroached upon these selected areas for the ack-ack and were in danger of being shot down by our guns. Some of them were – especially those from the naval gunners on ships in the Channel who blazed away at the first sign of a target.

Tuesday 29 August
18.50 TO 22.35 – SHELLS – V1

Since Friday 18 August flying bombs were being brought down by ack-ack off Dover every day, and most of them fell into the sea. The exception was on Saturday, when a Tempest fighter shot down one of them which dived and exploded on impact at Bell Farm, Lydden. There were no casualties.

Shells added to the danger. The first exploded on a house called Braeside in London Road, River, damaging several adjacent properties and injuring an Army Chaplain. The next demolished 35 St Radigund's Road, where there were six people injured, one seriously. Two other shells fell just after 09.00, one damaging the railway track at the entrance to Widrid Tunnel, while the other fell on Marine Parade.

The naval vehicle repair depot at Tapley's Garage, Cambridge Road, was the next to be hit, where a Petty Officer was injured. Then an armour-piercing type made a huge crater outside 20 St Andrew's Terrace, overturning an army lorry and bringing half the house down. Sixty-one-year-old Alice Marjoram, living next door, was later found dead in her home.

A V1 had exploded over Admiralty Pier, and another, carrying leaflets, had exploded over Hougham. On the last day of the month another flying bomb exploded over the Lydden Spout gun site.

Friday 1 September
01.55 TO 07.18 – SHELLS

As the allied armies advanced along the French coast the V1 launching sites were overrun. This caused a lull in flying-bomb activity. However, there was increased cross-Channel shelling. The German commanders made special efforts to use up their ammunition before they, too, were overrun. The last V1 launched from the Pas de Calais was in the early afternoon of 1 September, when it was shot down by ack-ack off Hythe. But in the early morning, just before 02.00, the first of twenty-six shells fell on the town. The rear of 29 Maison Dieu Road collapsed, slightly injuring two people, then the rear of Whyam House, East Brook Place, tumbled to the ground. Five minutes later a shell demolished 5 Military Hill, killing William Cook, then another erupted in the back garden of 59 Salisbury Road. The next salvo straddled Norman Street, and Saxon Street, demolishing dwellings already shattered beyond recognition.

The Heavy Rescue Squads were out in force – now totalling ten squads. Reg Leppard supervised his squads as each incident occurred, only to be called away to attend the next one. When a shell exploded at the entrance to the Lagoon Cave, High Street, the second time it had been hit, he was met with heaps of rubble, glass splinters and shop wreckage. Buried deep in the debris were many people who had taken shelter, long before the first shells came over. The body of Charles Tyler Benbow, a well-known local character, was the first brought out. Then followed Mabel Hubbard of the Globe Inn, Peter Street. The last two fatalities at this incident were thirty-nine-year-old Ellen Mills, and her four-year-old daughter Yvonne.

Another two seriously injured casualties happened when 8 and 10 Odo Road were demolished. Gas, water and electric services were fractured in so many different places that the whole town suffered. There followed a one-hour lull.

Fifty-five-year-old Special Constable Robert Wheeler had just telephoned into the police station from the police box in Lower Road, River. A shell exploded beside Pavilion Cottage. Robert was killed by blast which violently threw him up the road. Six-year-old Sheila Hare was found under the debris, in what had been her bedroom at 17 Lowther Road. Sadly, rescuers found no signs of life in her little body.

An ambulance was sent to receive casualties from the rear entrance of the Lagoon Cave, in Tower Hamlets. A shell exploded and wrecked it completely. Woolworth's store was extensively damaged, and the blast effect removed large chunks of masonry from the top of the buildings in Worthington Street and Biggin Street. There were more casualties when the frail Dickensian dwellings in Stembrook were no match for an 18-in armour-piercing shell.

Further shells hit the town and the damage was becoming more widespread. The constant detonations sent shivers down the spine. When 18 Wyndham

It was just after 2 a.m. when the first of twenty-six shells fell on the town on 1 September 1944. The Canadian Army was gradually approaching the German long-range guns at Cap Griz Nez. These were the shattered remains of buildings in the Stembrook area after a shell burst

Road was partially demolished there were no rescue squads available. Additional squads were sent for from neighbouring towns. Before they arrived, however, people in the street began searching the debris and found the twisted body of forty-three-year-old Lydia Ricketts. Other shells fell at Bunkers Hill, Hillside Road, London Road, Dolphin Yard, Tolputt's Yard, Selbourne Terrace, Lower Road, River, Waterloo Crescent and Liverpool Street.

Throughout the shelling, Gwendoline Curd and a companion nurse visited the caves to check for anyone who might need medical treatment. She recalls: 'We went by taxi, as at times, it was a hazardous business. I vividly recall walking through Market Square on my way to the Oil Mill Cave when a shell exploded at the corner of Market Street and Cannon Street. I sheltered under Hart's Furniture Store, until two soldiers escorted me down Snargate Street.'

Dover, it seems, waiting patiently for its liberation, was still a symbol of Britain's resistance to the fury of Hitler's Naval Coast Battalions. Townspeople were unaware that their liberation was a matter of days away or perhaps hours. There was to be no rejoicing yet for, after all, the month had only just begun.

The solid, reassuring castle, standing above the town, had been a symbol of Britain's history for centuries. They had taken everything Hitler could throw at them, but always it had been borne with the same defiant pride and patience that was immortalized in London's ordeal during the Blitz. There was, however, a difference between London and Dover, for since the first enemy action of 1940, the town and port had known no respite from German hostility. It could not be forgotten how close together were the front lines that ran through the middle of the English Channel.

Saturday 2 September
01.08 TO 01.15 – SHELLS

British guns opened fire first, they were bombarding enemy ships escaping from the ports of Calais and Boulogne. Just after 01.00 the first shell exploded on Chitty's Mill. The old flour mill was destroyed by fire. Ten minutes later the minesweeper HMT *Lois* took a direct hit and sank at her berth beside the Prince of Wales Pier. There were a number of naval casualties. De Burgh House, in De Burgh Street, collapsed into the street soon afterwards.

The NFS battled with the blaze at Chitty's Mill but could not save it from complete destruction. A large quantity of grain and all the machinery was lost as was nearly one hundred jobs. The mill never re-opened.

Sunday 3 September
12.53 TO 17.13 – SHELLS

In spite of the intense shelling, townspeople carried on, preserving corporate life in all essentials, when hell itself, it seemed, was all around them. Children were playing on the swings in Pencester Gardens when the first shell exploded in the afternoon. Several buildings were damaged, including the Woolton Restaurant. Ray Benjamin recalls:

> The nearest I got to a shell was on a Sunday when our boat was one of those off duty. Two of us decided to go to Canterbury, but unfortunately the siren went and all buses were stopped. So we contented ourselves with a walk around Dover. We just meandered until we ran into a few more of our lads. At a loose end we went into a park nearby to sit in the sun. The women all seemed to be occupied with Yanks so we avoided them. The park was fairly full and there was quite a bunch of children having a whale of a time in one corner. We had been sitting there watching them and generally relaxing when out of the blue a shell burst almost directly overhead. Everyone raced for the air-raid shelter that was in a corner of the park and we were ready to run with them when we heard the children screaming. I must say, I was never so proud of being a member of that crew than I was on that day. Not a word was said but every one of us turned and chased across to the children. We finished up carrying a child each or more apiece, whilst a couple of us pushed prams, or pushchairs, as well. We made it to the shelter safely but not long afterwards a shell landed outside the shelter, making quite a large crater. That was the closest I ever wanted to be to a shell!

There were casualties at Horton's Yard, Charlton Green, when a number of ARP cars were buried in the garage. Fremlin's Brewery in Dolphin Place received another shell damaging the bottling machinery. Then the back entrance to the Grenada Cinema was badly damaged by blast. On inspection the following day it was considered too dangerous to open. Crundall's Saw Mills, Dour Street, was also damaged, along with Hewitt's Bakery, which had been almost rebuilt from earlier damage. A number of air-burst shells shattered roofs in St Radigund's Road, Cowgate Hill, Strond Street, Waterloo Crescent and the Ferry Dock. There was one fatal naval casualty with four others seriously injured in the dock area.

Tuesday 5 September
00.05 TO 00.16 – SHELLS

Each day the powerful rumble of the allied army's heavy guns were heard across the water. Great tongues of flame from burning storehouses reached up into the

The fragile Dickensian-type buildings, largely constructed of inferior brickwork supported by timber, were no match for an armour-piercing 18-inch shell which exploded in Dolphin Lane

night sky. But the truculent German gunners at Cap Griz Nez would not give up. Their shells still flared across the Strait.

At 00.05 the first shell demolished 8 Castle Hill Road, on the corner of St Laurenston Place. Then eight air-burst type shells bracketed the American ack-ack site at Swingate. Military vehicles were wrecked and a fire started in the garage. A few minutes later the chapel in St Mary's Cemetery collapsed. The Admiralty Repair Ship *Moorfowl*, tied up in the Camber, received severe damage, and William Hutchings was killed when white-hot shrapnel seared through the air.

★ ★ ★

In the *Nota Bene* column of the *Dover Express* on Friday 8 September, there was a long tirade from the editor. It is too long to be included here but the gist of it really concerns his animosity towards the London newspapers. He was especially angry with some of the headlines, and I will quote some of the more glaring: CHANNEL GUNS BOOM OUT LAST HYMN OF HATE – DOVER LISTENS TO

Each day the powerful rumble of heavy guns could be heard. Just after midnight on 5 September 1944, eight air-burst type shells exploded over the British and American gun sites behind the Castle. Military vehicles were severely damaged when a fire started in a garage

THE DEFEAT OF AN ARMY – BIG GUNS ARE SILENT ACROSS THE CHANNEL – PEACE COMES TO HELL FIRE CORNER – and this last, in the *Daily Sketch*, said, 'It was Liberation Day yesterday for men, women and children of Hell Fire Corner.' The editor followed this with, 'How nice to read this in your morning paper among the ruins of your home brought down during the night!'

The spate of cross-Channel shelling provided one of the bitterest gun duels of the war in that area. Our guns were busy firing on enemy shipping trying to get through the Dover Strait away from our oncoming troops. There was just one huge cacophony of noise and yet there was more going on than people realized.

An Admiralty report said that several groups of enemy vessels had attempted to break out of French Channel ports and were being intercepted by our Coastal Force boats. MTBs under the command of Lt. C.A. Law, RCNVR, which engaged a number of E-boats in the vicinity of Boulogne, obtained numerous strikes before the enemy escaped in the darkness. Lt. Cdr. B.C. Ward, DSO,

RN, sank one enemy vessel with torpedoes, while several escort boats were also sunk when a group of ships was engaged near Calais.

Wednesday 6 September
13.54 TO 23.35 – SHELLS

There were three serious casualties in Snargate Street when a shell burst caused severe damage to the entrance to Barwick's Cave. All the casualties were sailors who were dealt with by naval medical teams. Woolcomber Street, already battered beyond recognition, lost dwellings from Nos. 12 to 18, then another exploded behind the Bull Inn, London Road. Blast caused considerable damage to a newsagent's shop, a grocer's, a dairy and the post office.

★ ★ ★

During D-day, and afterwards, the launches based in the harbour were engaged in laying smoke-screens around our convoys. At night they kept up their usual E-boat patrols and assisted with the MTB patrols. But the war operations of the MLs were drawing to a close.

From Flag Officer Commanding Dover
Admiral Pridham-Wippel
7 September 1944

All ships and vessels in Dover Command.
Now that the activities of Dover forces are drawing to a close, at any rate so far as enemy seagoing action is concerned, I wish to congratulate all in the Command on their highly successful discharge of their responsibilities assigned to them.

Sunday 10 September
08.18 TO 16.54 – SHELLS

Two shells came over without warning. The first exploded in London Road, opposite Haywards & Paramor, seriously damaging Gores, Lloyds Bank, Jenners, Makey, Fittalls and Turnpenny's. Eighteen-year-old George Locke and fifty-three-year-old Fred Mead were killed outright while another seven people became casualties with various wounds. The only other shell to hit the town fell on open land above Castle Hill. But a further nine shells were observed falling around a convoy passing Dover in the afternoon.

The men of the American 127th Battalion were still in their original positions behind the castle, and had effectively discharged their duties with regard to the V1 campaign. They were now awaiting orders to move out to join their colleagues on the Continent. But their experiences at Dover had not ended with the suspension of the flying bombs.

Private Robert Niesewonger was on guard outside the old aircraft hangar, in which were stored thousands of 90-mm AA shells. Fifteen air-burst shells exploded above the battalion area. Robert was killed by flying shrapnel. Damage sustained included three brick-block buildings, two water towers, ammunition dumps, five 2¹/₂-ton trucks, two tractors, five 1-ton trucks and trailers, tents and equipment. The Wanstone 15-in gun site also received air-burst type shells. British gunners wounded by blast and shrapnel were quickly treated by the American medical personnel.

Monday 11 September
03.10 TO 16.43 – SHELLS

Allied armies had surged towards Antwerp. They had also taken Le Havre, Dieppe, Paris, Lille and Abbeville. The list grew longer each day, but Dover remained 'besieged'. Every BBC broadcast was listened to with avid interest. The people watched, listened and speculated, 'It will not be long now.'

It was almost 04.00 when a shell hit 2 Dodds Lane, killing seventy-three-year-old Agnes Hart while she slept. The next series of dwellings demolished were Nos. 1, 2 and 3 St John's Place, then came 2 Trevanion Street, Stokes Yard, Templar Street, and the railway cutting at Green Lane. Nine shells fell in the sea outside the harbour.

Tuesday 12 September
17.54 TO 22.40 – SHELLS

It was 18.00 when 8 Folkestone Road was demolished. There were no casualties. The next shell exploded opposite Christ Church Vicarage, Folkestone Road. Three people were walking home and lost their lives: fifteen-year-old Ernest McGuire, an NFS man Herbert Dowdell and Christopher Wade. Albert Bussey, the church verger, was seriously injured in the chest and he died later that day in hospital.

There was a lull of one hour. Then the shells came over again. The first salvo did little damage when the shells fell on open land at Whitfield Hill and Crabble Lane. The next took three lives. Nos. 42 and 44 Dickson Road were completely wrecked and the blast also damaged properties in Tower Street. Rescuers were told that thirty-six-year-old Kathleen Hogben and her sixteen-year-old son Harold had been at home when the shell struck. They were recovered from their flattened Anderson shelter. While their lifeless bodies were being removed, sixty-year-old Rosalyn Staveley was found in the rubble at No. 44. She had died, hideously injured, by a multitude of death-dealing wounds. Other shells fell at Mangers Lane, and behind the Ordnance Depot, Folkestone Road. There were more casualties during this evening's shelling but added to the fatalities were one airman and one soldier.

Wednesday 13 September
16.03 TO 23.59 – SHELLS

While the allied armies were driving towards the German frontier, General Crerar's First Canadian Army, consisting of six Canadian and British divisions, was strung out along the French coast preparing to assault Boulogne, Calais and Dunkirk. Hitler had left a formidable garrison of troops under orders to fight to the last man in these Channel ports. Le Havre held out for just 48 hours, but Boulogne and Calais were to resist for another six days.

The undercurrent of tension in Dover was almost palpable. There were some people in the town who scarcely believed that relief was at hand. 'I shan't believe it until I hear it on the wireless,' one woman remarked to a journalist.

At 16.03, when all the shops had closed for their half day, a shell exploded at Clarke's Nursery, Barton Road. Then a train arrived at Priory Station. At the barrier was the ticket inspector, a Special Constable and two military policemen. People were leaving the station when a shell exploded near the entrance. Two servicemen and an ATS girl were killed instantly, also nine-year-old Frederick Spinner, sixty-one-year-old Julie Green and the forty-nine-year-old constable Alfred Langley.

A shell took out 8 Granville Street, opposite Chitty's Mill, where fifty-two-year-old Thomas Doherty lost his life. Charlton School and Cooks Cottages, Charlton Green, were demolished by the next one. There was severe damage to surrounding properties, where William Champion was seriously injured; he died later in hospital. Nos 28 and 30 Cooks Cottages had already fallen into the road when another shell wrecked No. 1 Victoria Street.

Few telephone wires remained intact, and gas, water and electricity services were fractured in so many places it caused quite a dilemma. Casualties were mounting alarmingly. The next death was at 15 Kearsney Avenue, where forty-year-old John Price was on duty in the Home Guard.

ARP messengers were dashing about on bicycles with reports for the Control Centre because there was a lack of communications. One of them tumbled into the gutter in Dour Street when No. 38 collapsed into the street in a cloud of dust. Just after 20.30 shells exploded at Bunkers Hill, Salisbury Road, the bowling green at Crabble Court, and in Charlton churchyard, where a 30-foot crater appeared.

One family at Charlton Green had a lucky escape when their house was partially demolished. Suffering from shock they were persuaded to attend hospital. While they were away another shell blew their Anderson shelter out into the road. Two other shells exploded simultaneously bringing down the chimney stack at Chitty's Mill.

Three minutes after midnight on the following day fourteen shells rained down on the town. After the chaos of the previous day it was prudent to take cover. Any hope of a speedy deliverance must have seemed only a dream and yet there was only one slight injury reported. Shells fell at Godwyn Road, Connaught Road, and Biggin Street, where Boots the Chemist had the lower half blown out into the street. Just after midday another shell blew out the rear of the Angel Inn, High Street, then a house called Binfield, Ethelbert Road, was partially demolished.

There was a lull lasting three hours. Then the first salvo exploded on the cooling ponds at the waterworks. Slip Passage received another along with Cambridge Road and Northampton Street. A 40-foot crater appeared in St Mary's Cemetery, and the explosion blew out all the windows in the lower chapel. Vehicles were buried under debris at the Co-op Garage, Maison Dieu Road, then shops in Snargate Street were shattered yet again. Barwick's offices in Market Square were wrecked in the evening, then the Clarendon Hotel had a near miss. Two more shells fell at Clarendon Street and on Clarke's Nursery in Barton Road.

Friday 15 September
11.15 TO 21.50 – SHELLS

In sheer desperation the Germans used everything that would float, from E-boats and R-boats to larger vessels such as trawlers and merchantmen converted to flak ships. The Fleet Air Arm and Coastal Command aircraft attacked them in the moonlight, but in spite of that, few results were observed. As the aircraft made their attacks they had to take avoiding action because of the enemy's concentrated fire from preceding ships. Reconnaissance reports later suggested only three E-boats out of a large force had survived the attack.

Then the shelling started again. There was a high wind blowing at the time and the moon frequently popped out between racing clouds. It was not always possible to connect flashes with explosions. Observers lost count of the number of shells fired. Three had already exploded on the Citadel Barracks in the morning.

The next salvo landed in a trench at Cannon Gate, Dover Castle. There was a delay until about 21.30 when Churchill Street was almost wrecked. Two people were slightly injured. The last two shells damaged the Congregational Church, Victoria Crescent and Beers Yard in Leighton Road, where lorries were damaged.

The American 127th Battalion stood above the town and watched helplessly. There was nothing they could do. Then suddenly air-burst type shells exploded over the positions. Nine of the Americans were killed. Their kitchens were destroyed, two 1-ton trucks, an M9 computer and associated power plant and equipment were all damaged, most of their tented accommodation and personal effects were lost completely.

Allen English, ammunition corporal C Battery, made up the daily record book for his battery. He wrote:

> Shells now come over as they pleased . . . there are no atheists in 'foxholes'. . . . Some never get there, just a reminder. . . . D Battery took a hit . . . a guard was blown . . . four dead . . . one died later in the States . . . five badly wounded . . . of the 17th. . . . March Order . . . we leave Dover . . . its hospitals full . . . new graves . . . no candy or chewing gum . . . next stop Omaha Beach . . . a little late . . . gotta catch up we are only 400 miles behind.

General Sir Frederick A. Pile, General Officer Commanding-in-Chief of the British Anti-Aircraft Command, had written on 11 September thanking General Eisenhower for his generous assistance in providing men and equipment to combat the flying-bomb attack and praising the outstanding performance of both American men and machines. He wrote of American gunners:

> In an astonishingly short time they got to grips with the unfamiliar target, and settled down to some excellent shooting. Indeed, on occasions my men complained to me that your men were knocking down bombs before they themselves had had a proper go at them! The results were brilliant and speak for themselves. From 24 July to 30 August your gunners confirmed claim for flying bombs destroyed to their own guns was 138, while they also participated in the destruction of a further 309.

To Frederick Alfred Pile   Eisenhower
                                                                14 September 1944

Dear General Pile,
During this war I have received no letter that has pleased me more than yours of the 11 September. Not only am I highly gratified that the units and

equipment that we were able to turn over to you proved to be most efficient in action, but I particularly like your letter as a valuable piece of evidence in support of the truism that team-work wins wars. The assistance rendered to you in your problem by S.H.A.E.F. Headquarters and by American Forces was not inspired by mere sentiment – although sentiment alone would have been adequate as long as we could spare the strength involved. The principal motive was a realization that your problem was part of our own; we could not possibly have southern England suffering under unresisted attack without feeling the results in this Command. In planning our land operations, ever since last January, one of the purposes in the back of my mind was the early capture of the Calais area in order to eliminate this threat. Thank you again for your letter, which I shall circulate to my staff and to all our units that operated under your control.

Sincerely,
Eisenhower

★ ★ ★

The *London Gazette*, on Wednesday 20 September, recorded that the MBE had been awarded to Lt. G.W. Holman, RNR, and Lt. V.F. Nichols, RNVR, for bravery, determination and good seamanship in command of the Dover tugs, *Lady Duncannon* and *Lady Brassey*, in fire-fighting on board merchant vessels and towing them to safety. Both officers had been employed by the Dover Harbour Board.

Saturday 23 September
12.50 TO 16.00 – SHELLS

German resistance of Boulogne was less formidable than General Crerar anticipated, and the possession of this vital port had been taken on 20 September. But the German cross-Channel guns east of Boulogne kept up their barrage. Dover citizens were proudly defiant in their isolation.

The first shell of the day demolished 31 Maison Dieu Road, just after midday, before the warning had sounded. Glenfield Road and Green Lane received the remainder of the salvo, then another shell struck the bank just below Constables' Tower at the castle. No. 67 Castle Avenue was hit, then the RAF HQ at Castlemount.

The most serious incident occurred when an armour-piercing shell brought down the Salvation Army Hostel, known locally as the Red Shield Club, in Snargate Street. It was quite impossible to know how many people had been on the premises. It was a popular haunt of service personnel. Rescue squads made prodigious efforts in trying to save those buried beneath the debris. In fact, work went on for 36 hours, non-stop, during which about a hundred tons of

In the foreground is Snargate Street where the Salvation Army's Red Shield Club was flattened by a shell on 23 September 1944, resulting in the death of seven people. Rescue work continued for thirty-six hours non-stop. Top right is Adrian Street, similarly scarred by shell damage

rubble were removed from a very confined space, before the authorities were satisfied there was no one left in the ruins. The death toll was five civilians and two military.

George Chatwin, a gas fitter, broke through a party wall, tunnelled through the rubble in the cellar, to reach and turn off the supply of gas which was escaping from a fractured pipe. He was later awarded the BEM for his courage.

Mutilated bodies were being brought out of the chaos throughout the long vigil. One of the first brought out was that of twenty-three-year-old Ruth Berry, a mobile canteen driver from Devon. Then followed twenty-year-old Betty Bushell, a member of the local FAP, forty-four-year-old Muriel Goldup, forty-seven-year-old Isobella Simpson, a Civil Defence canteen worker, and the last body found was that of Captain William Aspinall, who had been in charge at the hostel for the past two years. Casualties seriously injured were one male and seven female, including Mrs Aspinall, two female children and one serviceman. Six others were slightly injured including one child.

Children, for much of the day, had been confined to caves and shelters and when the ALL CLEAR sounded, they ran out to collect the shrapnel for souvenirs. When the ALERT went off again, it was back to take cover. There, they chatted, read tuppenny books and played with their model tanks, warships and aircraft. They gulped down hastily prepared meals cooked by their mothers at home at some considerable risk. Not one shell hit the town on the following day. They could scarcely believe their luck.

Monday 25 September
11.15 TO 18.30 – SHELLS

The Canadians were closing in to surround the German guns. But the enemy still fired a variety of shells upon Dover, from 15-in to 18-in segmented air-burst types to armour-piercing.

    The first of this penultimate onslaught exploded on the lawn of Victoria House in Union Road, causing two slight casualties and plenty of blast damage.

Due to reopen after a week's closure Dover's Hippodrome Theatre was so severely damaged on 25 September 1944 that it never opened again. The irony of its final demise was that shelling ceased the following day, and the glamorous nudes – Phillis, Dixey, Sheba, Sari, Drina, Andree, Lolita and Denise Vane – were never seen again at Dover

The Canadian Army was closing in to take the last of the German cross-Channel guns. Dover was just hours away from the end of its insufferable ordeal. The Marine Station, Dover, was hit several times on 25 September 1944

Another blew out the rear of 37 Edred Road, where fifty-year-old Elizabeth Wilson lost her life, and two others were injured.

Two MLs in Granville Dock were destroyed, then a shell blasted the Royal Hippodrome. It was due to open after being closed for over two weeks because of the intense shelling. The comedian Sandy Powell had offered to appear as a guest star on Wednesday night. Unfortunately, the theatre was so badly damaged, with a large deep crack appearing in one of the walls, it never opened again.

The Marine Station was the next to suffer damage. Then a shell exploded almost exactly on the already-devastated Salvation Army Hostel site. Houses in Adrian Street nearly toppled into the wreckage. Two more shells arrived just after 13.30, causing considerable damage at the junction of Armourers Walk and Pardoners Way. There was a three-hour lull.

Then at 16.15 a shell buried itself deep in the bowling green, off Maison Dieu Road, before exploding. In the same salvo another shell demolished six houses and two shops opposite 94 London Road. A public house, a tobacconist's, a cooked meat shop and fruiterer's were wrecked. Walking along London Road were twenty-six-year-old Doris Buddle, seven-year-old Patricia Perkins, thirty-year-old Ellen Sydenham and fifty-nine-year-old Mabel Wakefield. They were killed instantly. Seventeen-year-old Ronald Chapman was found seriously hurt and died of his wounds later. There were another seven seriously injured, including one soldier, and a further eight were reported as slightly injured.

Two shells fell on the seafront but the next partially demolished the Griffin public house in Folkestone Road. The Red Cow was also damaged when a crater appeared in the road, ripping up all the underground services. They were not repaired until just before Christmas. Sixty-four-year-old Adeline Busswell was reported missing; she was later found dead beneath rubble in a doorway where she must have sheltered.

Tuesday 26 September
02.04 TO 20.55 – SHELLS

As dawn broke over the French coast the Canadians made their move to secure the cross-channel guns. Dover was just hours away from its own liberation but there would be no rejoicing. Nor would there be until they knew for certain that the Germans had been routed for good from their positions and silenced for ever.

More homes were to topple in the town before the day was out. As the warm sun climbed into a cloudless sky, sentries looked across the Strait at the faintly discernible outlines of Calais. All through the hours of darkness they had seen the gun flashes. The first of over fifty shells had landed just after 02.00, exploding at the rear of Noah's Ark Road. Two others had partially demolished a house called Grantchester in Valley Road, River, and almost wrecked the Coach and Horses in Tower Hamlets Street. Superficial damage occurred at numerous locations. Some shells landed on open ground. One had exploded on an army bungalow at Broadlees Road. One soldier lost his life and three others were seriously injured. In the same salvo two more burst in Victoria Park, at East Cliff, and at the rear of 69 and 71 High Street.

There was a short lull. Then an armour-piercing shell bored its way through 40 feet of chalk, and 9 inches of concrete, before exploding in the entrance of Barwick's Cave, which ran from Durham Hill to Snargate Street. It was here that sixty-three-year-old Patience Ransley lost her life. Five NFS men were slightly injured when a shell fell near the Auto Car Company Garage in Castle Street. At the junction of Barton Road and Beaconsfield Avenue another exploded, and a third burst above Tor House, Castle Avenue.

Policemen, wardens, nurses and the whole paraphernalia of the Civil Defence Services were out visiting incidents. Anyone seen in the streets was immediately persuaded to take cover. Shelters and caves were full to the brim, but many remained at home – stubborn to the last.

The shells kept coming, it was nothing less than ruthless. And yet there was no panic. Courage, fortitude – call it what you will, the townspeople remained patient. If their name was on the next shell – well, so be it.

Shells fell in Mayfield Avenue, St James's Street, Castle Avenue, Green Lane, Queen Street, the Ferry Dock and then Nos 7, 8 and 9 Biggin Street collapsed into the road. Stanhope Road was already severely damaged but suffered more and five casualties occurred. Thirty-five-year-old Leonard Edmund died when an air-burst shell exploded at Military Hill. Salisbury Road came next, then at 19 De Burgh Hill seventy-two-year-old Ethel Cockcroft was found dead in her demolished home.

Just after 15.00, a shell burst in Pencester Road. Large panes of glass, complete with sticky brown paper, blew out of Marks & Spencer's, Vyes Stores, the Oddfellow's Club and the Woolton Restaurant. Twenty minutes later there was an explosion at St Alphege House, Frith Road, formerly the Girls' County School, the headquarters of 961 Balloon Barrage Unit.

WAAF Kathleen McKinlay, a Leading Aircraftwoman, was driving an ambulance and had been out with Flt. Lt. Soden, the medical officer, visiting various incidents. They had just returned to Frith Road. As they got out of the vehicle a shell exploded in the compound. Kathleen recalls:

> There was an almighty bang so we nipped behind a blast wall. He [Flt. Lt. Soden] put his arms round me saying, 'Hold tight!' I was scared to death, then we were showered with bricks, glass and heaven knows what. After a while I realized he wasn't beside me anymore, and I saw him lying on the ground. He was dead. By this time there were yells for an ambulance which helped me to snap out of my stupor. There were a number of injured to be taken to hospital. I don't remember much about the journeys to and from the hospital but I do recall a sergeant who offered to go with me, saying he felt sorry for the poor devils in the back, as I was scaring the life out of him, and wanted to know whose side I was on. I eventually woke up in a hospital bed, having passed out.

Twenty-three-year-old Kathleen had suffered wounds to her hands, feet and thigh, but this did not dissuade her from making several journeys to the casualty hospital in Union Road. Not until the casualties were all removed was she persuaded to have her own injuries attended to. She was later awarded the BEM.

It was fortunate that many shells fell on already-damaged properties which had been evacuated long ago. This happened at Chitty's Mill and Charlton School. The National Provincial Bank in Market Square had the back blown out and Fremlin's Brewery in Dolphin Lane was hit again. When the Mitre public house was blasted in Snargate Street a naval officer lost his life. Two other naval personnel and four civilians were also injured. At 15.00 47 Salisbury Road was partially demolished. Records state that a Mrs Dalley was killed here but she is not mentioned in the Civilian War Graves lists. Sixty-seven-year-old Florence Marsh is listed, however, as having died at No. 41 Salisbury Road.

An unexploded shell fell at Victoria Park Mews. A policeman recorded the number of it – 67857. At 19.15 the last German shell to explode on Dover demolished two unoccupied shops, at the corner of Castle Street and the Market Square, Pickfords, and Hubbard's the umbrella manufacturers.

It was all over. The total destruction for September was the worst experienced in Dover.

In the final assault upon the cross-Channel guns at Cap Griz Nez, 29,945 prisoners were taken at a cost of fewer than 1,500 British and Canadian casualties.

It was over. September 1944 was the worst shelling period experienced in Dover, with over 8,000 buildings either wrecked or destroyed. This tattered postcard depicts the last German shell to hit the town, wrecking two shops on the corner of Castle Street and the Market Square

Wednesday 18 October
ROYAL VISIT TO DOVER

Their Majesties King George VI and Queen Elizabeth arrived by Royal Train, which pulled into Kearsney Station just before noon. During their stay, lasting four hours, which was devoted entirely to non-military matters, they paid a Royal Tribute to Dover's fortitude throughout more than four years of shelling and bombing.

The royal visitors saw the shattered homes and the air-raid shelters and caves which were the only dwellings for so many people. They listened to the grim stories told by the people of the town. There were hundreds of Civil Defence members on parade, the unsung heroes and heroines, whose experiences were soon to fade like the brittle pages of official documents.

Inside the Town Hall Their Majesties shook hands with many people who had steadfastly refused to evacuate and who had just carried on in spite of everything that Hitler could throw at them. They were especially interested in the

Her Majesty Queen Elizabeth, now the Queen Mother, is photographed coming out of the Z4 Warden's Post at Aycliffe, during the king and queen's visit to Dover on 18 October 1944

two Nazi flags which had been captured from the last cross-Channel gun at Cap Griz Nez and a sword belonging to the German Naval Officer who had been taken prisoner. One of the flags had been sent to the Mayor by Sergeant R.J. Duncan of the Canadian Scottish Regiment. He wrote, 'Please accept this flag as a souvenir. After four years of uncertainty of shellfire, that the people of Dover have endured, I think it is a fitting gift. By the example shown us by the people of Dover we were able to do our job of removing the shadow of fear from your city.'

Their Majesties then visited the Z4 Wardens' Post near the Rope Walk, which was always referred to as the nearest Wardens' Post to enemy territory. The motorcade then passed lines of cheering people standing at the kerbside outside their damaged homes. Here and there flags and bunting fluttered from upstairs windows. The royal couple arrived at Winchelsea Caves where the Queen took great interest in the Medical Aid Post below ground. Chatting with residents, many of whom had used the caves almost every night during the past month, the Queen asked of one of them, 'Do you still come down here?' to which she received the reply, 'We have to Ma'am – you see we have no homes to go to.'

The welcome news that the last of the German long-range guns had been captured was not given to the people of Dover until Saturday 30 October when, by means of loudspeakers and one or two mobile loudspeaker vans, the message was relayed. While this was being announced the bells of St Mary's peeled out for the first time since they were silenced in 1940, only to be used in case of an invasion. The Mayor had also just received a message from the Brigadier of the 1st Canadian Brigade, which read: 'Greetings from the Brigade and may you enjoy your pint of beer and stroll on the front in peace from now on. We have all of Jerry's Big Berthas.'

Townspeople took the news calmly as few clearly understood the implications. Occasionally there were some half-hearted cheers. Most people said, 'Thank God' to themselves quietly. A few flags began to appear from buildings, although it was late in the day before bunting of any quantity could be found. After all, it is not easy to find flags and bunting in houses which had suffered so much bombardment.

London newspaper men and cameramen had arrived. They stayed several days, busy arranging and posing their 'shots', but the whole episode was considered by many as artificial. The Mayor, for example, in his robes, was persuaded to climb to the top of the Town Hall tower on Sunday to be taken hoisting the town's flag. On the following Tuesday the Council was filmed in session at their monthly meeting.

Soon, however, the work of repairing damaged properties became a priority. It would have been quite impossible for the town to have survived without the NFS, Army, Navy and the Ministry of Works, the latter using special 'flying squads', in addition to the ordinary extra imported labour from many other counties.

At one period over a thousand men and women had been brought into the town, employed on the essential tasks of making houses weatherproof. Hundreds of tarpaulins were draped from roofs and many thousands of windows were covered in felt. Nor did these helpers stop at this. Some residents, shaken by the constant shelling of the past month in particular, went to find respite outside the town. On their return, a week or so later, they found much of the debris inside their homes cleaned up and even carpets shaken.

No praise was too high for the conduct of the Civil Defence Services, not only during the whole of the war, but more especially during the month of September 1944. In no other part of the country had there been such prolonged and continuous duties performed. The hours of duty put in by some members was no less than phenomenal, with two or three hours' sleep, at the most, in several days being all that they allowed themselves.

Perhaps, too readily, it has been forgotten that while the bulk of the population was under cover these people were out in the streets doing their duty whenever they were needed. Although the police were never regarded as part of the Civil Defence Service they were often the first at a scene of destruction and their work was never less than outstanding.

During the first week of the bad shelling period the warning had lasted for 12 hours, businesses were brought to a standstill and special arrangements were needed to deal with the many problems. The feeding of people kept under cover for many hours was a very real problem in spite of the loudspeaker system advising the population to take food with them to the shelters. Of course, the WVS canteens were in operation and these were often assisted by branches outside the town. In addition there were the Y.M.C.A. mobile canteens which appeared at almost every incident. Nobody can forget the notable work done by the Salvation Army's mobile canteen, especially the sterling efforts of Captain Aspinall and Captain Harvey who, without thought for their own safety, and ably assisted by their female canteen workers, were an accomplished team.

It might have been reasonable to assume that casualties would have been higher with so much damage in the town. The reverse being the case, this was largely due to the discipline of the people who took shelter when directed. The Sub-Controller, Inspector A.J. Fenn, never considered 'off duty' during the war, kept a watchful eye on this aspect.

Despite warnings and appeals asking people not to return to Dover, because of the difficulty in finding suitable accommodation, the population grew alarm-ingly by roughly 400 a week. By the end of October the total stood at almost 20,000. This figure would have been very much higher undoubtably had all those former residents who wished to return been able to do so. But their hous-es were still under repair. A large proportion of residents was classed as homeless. In the event, there were no rooms or boarding residences to accommodate the influx of men and their families working on the buildings.

★ ★ ★

The *London Gazette* on 31 October gave a recommendation for brave conduct in respect of Dr George Walter Hinchliff, MD, B.Ch., medical practitioner, of 1 Cambridge Terrace. The commendation related to an incident on 29 January 1944, when a shell exploded at the entrance to a shelter in which there were WAAFs sleeping. There were twenty-six casualties of which two proved fatal. In order to reach the injured Dr Hinchliff had to crawl through a tunnel in the debris to help those pinned beneath the wreckage.

Dover's Home Guard stood down on Wednesday 1 November 1944, although it was to remain in reserve until officially disbanded. Meanwhile, the King had approved the grant of honorary rank to all officers.

In the first two years of the war much of the Home Guard's duty consisted of enforcement of the Curfew Order, which prevented people being on the seafront after hours. Many servicemen, both officers and men, unable to satisfy a Home Guard sentry as to their identity, found themselves held under arrest until it could be established. Later, when standing guards gave way to patrols, not a few commandos carrying out exercises on the beaches, found them extremely alert. While carrying out nightly patrols and manning defence posts they were given special duties in the defence of the Dover Garrison. The scheme was constantly under review and a great deal of their time was spent on training exercises. These nightly patrols ranged from Archcliffe to the Dock Yard, including Admiralty Pier, harbour installations and pill-boxes, as well as the slopes beneath and around the castle.

The Home Guard was originally armed only with rifles, some acquired from troops returning from Dunkirk. But the range of weapons gradually increased until it finally included Thompson sub-machine guns, Sten guns, Browning automatic rifles, Bren guns, Northover Projectors, Spigot Mortars and one or two Smith guns. The men spent extra hours on duty mastering the various techniques in order to use the weapons efficiently. There was, of course, close contact with Regular Army units stationed in Dover, from which instructors willingly gave every assistance.

Lt. Col. W.R. Brent said, 'After the war, in order to make this old island of ours a better place to live in, you will indeed serve your country well if you carry on in the same unselfish way you have done in wartime.' (Above) Dover's 8th (Cinque Ports) Battalion Home Guard at Crabble Atheletic Ground

When the original LDV was formed in 1940 Dover's men were required to use as a headquarters a few vacant rooms on the seafront. A year later, however, they had obtained headquarters at Mr Thomas's ironmonger's store at 86 London Road. When their numbers increased, due to the introduction of compulsion, whereby all able-bodied men between the ages of sixteen and sixty were required to serve in either the Civil Defence or Home Guard, larger premises were required. In October 1942 the Dover Company moved to the Drill Hall, Liverpool Street, which had recently been repaired after sustaining shell damage.

When Captain Moore, CO of the Dover Company, left Dover at the end of 1940, Major M.G. Lohan took command until he was superseded by Major F.A. Belchamber in March 1941. In September 1942 Major Belchamber had to resign under the age clause, and was succeeded by Major P.A. Mills. Men were, of course, constantly leaving due to many factors, such as call-up to serve in either the Army, Navy or Air Force, and the evacuation of certain industries and building trades. So it was that in late 1944 only sixty originals of the LDV were still serving.

Independent platoons were maintained at the post office, Southern Railway, the gasworks and the electricity works, whose main task was the defence of their own company's buildings. The Dock Yards' platoon was made up of Dover Harbour Board employees, who subsequently manned the coastal guns on Admiralty Pier in 1944, reinforced by sixty men from the main Dover Home Guard.

There was one other line of defence, albeit a kind of suicide force, which came into existence in the autumn of 1940. The C-in-C Home Forces, General Sir Edmund Ironside, brought out Operation Instruction No. 3, about which he said, 'This system will prevent the enemy from running riot and tearing the guts out of the country, as has happened in France.' The result was a 'devil-may-care' unit of civilian volunteers to outwit the German forces.

Colonel McVean Gubbins of Military Intelligence was put in charge. His department, called Section D, was a secret cell within the Foreign Office, where investigative measures were formulated to create subversion and sabotage. These Auxiliary Units were, at government level, known as 201 Battalion Home Guard. They were eventually scattered throughout Kent and Sussex and were largely made up of local people who knew their own areas intimately. Each platoon, acting completely independently of the others, had its own underground bunker from which to operate at night in absolute secrecy. Security was the hallmark of success and few people were aware of their existence, least of all the local Home Guard.

One such unit in the Dover area was the Drellingore Platoon, commanded by Lt. Cecil Lines, with George Marsh, Samuel Osborne, Thomas Holmans, Charles Fayers and Dennis Dewar. The bunker, hewn out of a sloping hillside was beneath a small coppice of ash, hazel and hornbeam, and built by sappers of the Royal Engineers. It was to the west of Dover in the Alkham Valley and far from prying eyes.

Each man was issued with a .38 Smith & Wesson revolver, a Fairbairn Commando knife and a brass knuckleduster. They were to learn the skills of unarmed combat and were taught especially how to kill silently, using either their knife or cheese wire. Other items of equipment included a pair of plimsoles, rubber truncheons, a Thomson sub-machine gun, Springfield .300 rifles, bayonets, grenades, phosphorus bombs, paraffin incendiaries, delay pencil fuses, detonators, gelignite, anti-personnel mines, plastic explosive and spools of trip wire.

The veil of secrecy was thus drawn around the platoon's bunker which held not only the bunk-beds, stove, lamp, water tank, food and sabotage equipment, but also the anonymity of six men who were considered outside the Geneva Convention. They were officially regarded as 'expendable'.

Today, the Drellingore Bunker, along with all the others, has crumbled beyond recognition. Nothing else remains but the concrete entrance shaft, except perhaps the tenuous images of what might have been.

There were over 600 men of the 8th (Cinque Ports) Battalion, Kent Home Guard, attending the 'stand down' parade at Dover on Sunday 3 December 1944. In a steady downpour of rain they assembled on the seafront opposite the Gun Wharf. Buses had brought men from the rural platoons outside the town boundary. Before the battalion was to march off to St Mary's Church, it was addressed by the CO Lt. Col. W.R. Brent, MC, who said that Winston Churchill, the Prime Minister and Lord Warden of the Cinque Ports, had been invited to inspect them on that day, but Mr Churchill, as much as he appreciated the courtesy of the invitation, found that pressure of work would not allow him to accept. Colonel Brent went on:

Although this is a final parade, it is not the end of the Home Guard; you are not disbanded yet, and at any time may be called upon to take up your duties again, and I am quite confident that if the necessity should arise you will do so with the same spirit of self-sacrifice you have shown in the past.

There are a few Home Guardsmen who seem to think that standing down releases them from all further obligations. This is not the case. Now that you are not attending parades, it is difficult for your officers to get instructions out to you, so I am taking this opportunity to remind you of one, at least, of your obligations – to assist in the return of your arms and equipment to stores.

After the war, in order to make this old island of ours a better place to live in, you will, indeed, serve your country well if you carry on in the same unselfish way you have done in war-time, and put consideration for your neighbours and your country before your own personal needs and comfort. There are 60,000 Home Guards in Kent alone, and if they work for the good of the country, their influence will be felt, and we shall have gone a long way towards achieving what we have been fighting for.

We older men may not reap the benefit, but we must see to it that our children do. Little did I think when I signed on as an LDV in May 1940, that I should have the great honour I have today in addressing you as your CO. I will now conclude with my sincere thanks for your loyal support and wish you all the best in the future.

The battalion then marched to church headed by the band of the Royal Marines. After the service they formed up in Biggin Street, and with the band leading them, marched back to the seafront. The salute was taken at Cambridge

Terrace by Colonel W.H.D. Wilson, Home Guard Commander, East Kent. Then, with the battalion formed up in line abreast, Lt. Col. Brent gave the order 'DISMISS' – for the last time.

★ ★ ★

Instructions received from the Ministry of Home Security suggested the relaxation of part-time Civil Defence rota duties at all posts and depots from 9 November. Part-time members were not required to do any duties but they were still required to 'stand by' should there be any incidents due to enemy action. At the same time the reduction in strength of the full-time CD Service was operable but a number of posts and depots were retained. Redundant personnel were given generally one month's notice so as to terminate their services on 31 December.

The year 1944 will be unforgettable to all who lived through it in Dover. After four years of intermittent shelling the attacks increased to such intensity at the end of August and through to September, as to be very like the bombardment of a city under siege. Indeed, at times, owing to enemy action, there was a further similarity for both bread and water were in short supply and on one occasion 5,000 loaves were brought in from Margate owing to the failure of electricity supplies.

Meanwhile, the chief topic of conversation by the Dover Borough Council was on the re-construction and planning of post-war Dover. Plans were first introduced as early as 1942 but attention was promptly diverted by so many dwellings being systematically wrecked. The damage sustained by bomb and shell – especially the September bombardment – was so extensive and widespread that there could be no diversion of attention from the task of getting the damaged houses habitable once again. At least half the houses in Dover were affected in one way or another by the shelling. The shortage of materials and of skilled labour, combined with the stormy weather and the heaviest rainfall for many years, had handicapped the work schedule.

That dour, north-east-countryman 'Jimmy' Cairns, Mayor of Dover for nearly eight years, finally was to relinquish that post in November. Like him or loathe him, he had been privy to many war-time secrets, most of which he had kept to himself. He was awarded the OBE for his services to the town.

CHAPTER SEVEN

1945

'Long Live the Cause of Freedom'

After the Germans had been driven from the Channel coast and their E-boat flotillas based on the French-Belgian coast had been broken up in the late Autumn of 1944, Dover became a busy port of embarkation for reinforcements of men, munitions and the machinery of war. Tanks of various types, landing craft, and amphibious vehicles for crossing the Rhine and the floods of Holland, had been sent from Dover in late October, and continued through to the end of the war.

The seafront, from the one-time Granville Gardens to the embarking jetties built at East Cliff, was often massed with armoured vehicles and lorries, which filled up most of the vacant space on the blitzed areas of Townwall Street and St James's Street. The nights at Dover, which once were noisy in quite another way, were now broken by the long succession of rumbling tanks.

The menace of war, however, was still very strong. The sudden and unexplained disappearance of the Dover-based cable ship *Alert* off the North Foreland one night in February 1945, was just one poignant reminder. Many local men were among her crew but there were no survivors.

German midget submarines operating in the eastern end of the English Channel brought new dangers to our forces. They sometimes laid mines at night. Frequent counter-measures, gun fire and exploding depth-charges, were often heard. On 9 January 1945 a captured midget submarine was hauled up onto the Dover beach opposite New Bridge. The area was soon put out of bounds to the public when a live torpedo was discovered still on board.

In May the Germans surrendered to Field Marshal Bernard Montgomery on Luneberg Heath. The air-raid sirens were also put into official retirement. Barbed-wire entanglements were the first defence obstacles removed on the

In the autumn of 1944 the port of Dover became busy with the embarkation of troops, munitions and the machinery of war. Tanks of various types, and armoured and amphibious vehicles were parked in the blitzed areas of the town before being transported across the Channel in landing craft

beaches and the harbour became busy with troop movements plying between Dover, Calais and Boulogne. While servicemen disembarked from the steamers so Belgian refugees clambered on to return home.

So the day of 8 May 1945 will live for ever in history and in the minds of those who had survived World War II. The day before was fraught with suspense – rumour followed rumour. Every BBC news bulletin was listened to from the first in the morning and each time it was announced that at any hour the Prime Minister was expected to make a statement.

Dover was wide awake early on Tuesday morning. Overnight some flags had appeared on houses and shops and others were added as the day wore on. By midday the main streets became gay with bunting as housewives hurriedly got in their shopping during the few hours the shops were open. A few enterprising street traders wheeled out their barrows with Union Jacks and red, white and blue novelties. The atmosphere grew steadily during the morning and some townspeople enjoyed a few hours' walk along the seafront in the sun. Then at 15.00 when large crowds had gathered in the streets, the loudspeakers – grim

HRH Princess Marina, Duchess of Kent, takes the salute in early 1945 on the playing fields of the Dover Boys' County School. Also present were Dame Vera Laughton-Mathews and Vice-Admiral Dover, Admiral Pridham-Whipple

reminders of Dover's bitter ordeal the year before – relayed the Prime Minister's speech. Churchill said:

> Hostilities will cease at one minute after midnight on Tuesday 8 May, but in the interests of saving life the cease fire will begin the previous day. Advance Britannia! Long live the cause of Freedom! God save the King!

Almost immediately after Churchill's speech, ships in the harbour greeted the official declaration of 'Peace in Europe' by sounding their sirens. It was a deafening noise.

The sirens hooted for more than an hour. The harbour was now a memorable spectacle. There was a big assembly of the now well-known tank landing craft and ships were 'dressed' with every conceivable flag. Dover's pre-war regatta days were no comparison to this sight. Church bells rang louder than ever before. In the streets people thronged and the good-humoured police jostled among the crowds trying to make room for traffic. Buses by this time were also be-flagged, and from the windows people waved flags and anything they could get hold of. Even American jeeps weaved through the cheering crowds with their human cargoes.

The loudspeaker system was now playing dance music and its popularity was tremendous. People danced and sang for hours. There were many impromptu concerts being held in the few remaining undamaged houses and billets where songs were heard in vociferous chorus. Servicemen and women, civilians, young or old, all joined in.

When the King's speech was relayed through the town there must have been thousands in the Market Square and outside the Town Hall. His Majesty was greeted with loud cheers and then everyone fell silent to listen intently.

Public houses had been granted an extension of one hour before closing. Unfortunately many had already sold out before 22.00 that evening, despite the numerous special deliveries made. The dance at the Town Hall was packed to suffocation. It was almost impossible to dance with a floor packed with excited revellers. But no one minded. They shuffled round to the strains of the dance band until late at night. Great rings of people, hand in hand, were swinging around the Market Square until midnight.

So ended Dover's jubilations at Germany's defeat, jubilations thoroughly justified and deserved after years of tolerance.

On the following Sunday a special and moving service was held to remember Admiral Sir Bertram Ramsey, who had been in Command at Dover from 1939 to 1942 and who was tragically killed in an air crash near Paris on 2 January 1945. Throughout the week there had been short five-minute services held in St Mary's.

A week later Dover's Navy Week opened with Admiral Sir Henry Pridham-Wippel, KCB, CVO, giving the address from the steps of the Town Hall. There was an exhibition at the Maison Dieu Hall where model ships, paintings, photographs and naval armament went on display. Then on the Sunday of that week an open-air service was arranged in Pencester Gardens on a Thanksgiving Service to the Navy.

At the end of the celebrations a magnificent march-past of almost every service unit took place with some one thousand people taking part. Admiral Sir Pridham-Whippel presented to the Mayor photographs of the German long-range guns which had, for so long, bombarded the town.

All the schools had closed for a two-day holiday to mark the occasion of Victory in Europe (VE). Children had been trickling back to Dover in small numbers since 1941 but in February the last eighty were returned from Wales. This marked the end of the Government's official evacuation programme.

The day-to-day outlook of the returning evacuees was very different from that of those who had remained behind or had returned earlier. They had not experienced the explosions of bombs and shells and the nightly excursions to the

Although partially deprived through
rationing, Dover's mums, with an
intense confidence in their homely
skills, provided the elementary instincts
of the down-trodden to conjure from
nowhere the ingredients for a 'victory'
street party. This one was in East Cliff

caves and shelters. They also lacked the familiarity with service personnel, the
fascination of observing low-flying aircraft, warships in the harbour, and perhaps
more especially, the fast MTBs and MGBs. But they made up for lost time when
they discovered the delights of playing on bomb-sites, adventure grounds far
superior to anything else. In no time at all, they learned to climb in and out of
skeletal buildings. They began to collect and swap prized pieces of crashed aircraft, shrapnel, bullets, cannon shells, detonators, hand grenades, mortar bombs,
and every conceivable object of war. Cave entrances were blocked up after a
constable found an arsenal of military equipment in one of them.

Teenagers, too old for school but not yet old enough to join the armed services, had seen at first-hand the devastation and chaos left behind after a shell
bombardment. Some had rubbed shoulders with the rescue squads clawing away
debris with their bare hands to reach victims buried beneath. The scenes, especially at night, were so vivid and unforgettable they would remain with them for
the rest of their lives. They could recall clearly the house that collapsed into a

The American Admiral Hart once said, 'Give us strength to accept with serenity the things that cannot be changed. Give us courage to change the things that can and should be changed. And give us wisdom to distinguish one from the other'

deep crater, the smell of escaping gas, the grey air and stench of explosives, the damp brickwork and decaying plaster, but above all, the small, lifeless body of a child, wrapped up in a grubby sheet being carried to an ambulance.

Dover was soon to lose its war-time Naval Command with the collapse of the Axis powers. On the evening of 10 July Admiral Sir Pridham-Wippel finally lowered his flag to be immediately succeeded by Rear-Admiral H.H. Bousfield as Naval Officer-in-Charge of Nore Command. Two months later the Admiralty and the War Office handed back to the Dover Harbour Board those parts of the harbour which were commandeered in 1939.

Dover's Civil Defence Services had declined in numbers since the previous December and were to disband officially in June. The Home Guard and the Fire Watching Parties had already disbanded, and the number of ARP personnel remaining was only a fraction of its original total. Likewise, the NFS was considerably reduced in numbers and had abandoned its temporary stations, many of which had been privately owned properties. This decline continued until the Japanese officially surrendered on board the United States battleship *Missouri* in Tokyo Bay on 2 September. World War II, at last, had come to an end.

VJ (Victory over Japan) Day came on 15 August in Britain. Dover's celebrations were even more prolonged than those held on VE Day. The surrender of Japan was broadcast by wireless at midnight on 14 August by Mr Clement Atlee, the new Prime Minister. Townspeople, most of whom just minutes before had been fast asleep in their beds, suddenly rushed out into the streets. Ships' sirens were heard first, quickly followed by dozens of rockets being fired into the night sky. Searchlights joined in the celebrations, sweeping the sky until, as if by a pre-arranged signal, they joined together in one magnificent cone of luminescence.

A steady stream of people made for the seafront where, on the promenade opposite Waterloo Crescent, they danced and sang. They were joined by lorry-loads of servicemen and women. On the beach there was a huge bonfire. In the madness of these Victory celebrations six of the large public seats on the seafront, which had survived the war, were now burning fiercely. At the water's edge the rusting wreck of HMS *Codrington*, the destroyer leader bombed in the summer of 1940, which had lain beached throughout the war, was set alight. Another bonfire was started between the Dover Club and the Monument. Material for this bonfire was obtained by pulling down blackout boarding from windows of damaged houses in Cambridge Terrace.

The town's official bonfire was erected on Whinless Downs and there was no lack of material for it either. Nothing would satisfy the people of Dover more than to see Dover Castle floodlit once again. It made a striking picture from their high vantage on the downs – it was a symbol of the town's defiance in the face of all that the enemy had thrown at them.

Appendices

ROLL OF HONOUR

A permanent memorial, in honour of those civilians killed as a result of enemy action, was entrusted by Royal Charter on 7 February 1941 to the Imperial War Graves Commission.

The lists of names were submitted to the Commission by the Registrar-Generals from the various counties. These lists formed the basis of several volumes known as the *Roll of Honour*.

On 21 February 1956 the Duke of Gloucester, as President of the Imperial War Graves Commission, handed the *Roll of Honour* to the Dean and Chapter of Westminster Abbey. One volume lies open in a memorial case where a single page is turned each day.

The Municipal Borough of Dover and the Rural District of Dover each has its own *Roll of Honour* and, like those of other boroughs, cities and towns, they are probably and inevitably incomplete. The reasons for this are complex.

The following lists were provided by the Director-General of the Commonwealth War Graves Commission.

MUNICIPAL BOROUGH OF DOVER
Abbott, Alfred, 55, 3 April 1942
Abbott, Martha Annie, 56, 3 April 1942
Abbot, Victor Gordon, 28, 25 October 1940
Amos, Lena Ellen, 20, 11 September 1940
Ashbee, Albert Victor, 57, 20 October 1940
Ashdown, William Richard, 48, 8 October 1940
Aspinall, William Lewis, 45, 23 September 1944
Austen, William Ernest, 57, 23 March 1942
Austen, John, 63, 8 October 1940

Austin, Laura Emily, 40, 5 September 1942
Austin, William James, 51, 13 November 1940
Aylmer, William, 66, 12 November 1940
Bailey, Richard, 45, 12 February 1941
Ball, Lily Elizabeth, 16, 13 November 1940
Banks, Charles William, 54, 23 March 1942
Barker, Helen Jane, 38, 12 August 1940
Benbow, Charles Tyler, 53, 1 September 1944
Berry, Ruth, 23, 23 September 1944
Bexhill, Frederick, 62, 1 October 1941
Botten, Benjamin Maynard, 61, 7 October 1940
Buddle, Doris Elizabeth, 26, 25 September 1944
Burns, Dennis Patrick, 33, 10 December 1942
Burvil, Edith Mary, 39, 10 February 1943
Bushell, Betty Charlotte, 20, 23 September 1944
Bussey, Albert George, 68, 12 September 1944
Buswell, Adaline, 64, 25 September 1944
Cameron, Edith Emily, 62, 26 September 1940
Carberry, Ernest William, 43, 23 December 1941
Carberry, Patrick Joseph, 83, 3 October 1941
Carswell, Percy William, 57, 20 October 1940
Champion, William, 55, 13 September 1944
Chapman, Charles William, 54, 22 May 1943
Chapman, Doris, 17, 22 May 1943
Chapman, Louisa, 53, 22 May 1943
Chapman, Ronald Walter John, 17, 26 September 1944
Cleak, Albert John, 71, 1 November 1940
Cock, Florence Ethel, 57, 12 June 1941
Cock, Frederick Ethelbert, 53, 12 June 1941
Cockcroft, Ethel, 72, 26 September 1944
Cook, Ernest James, 28, 11 September 1940
Cook, William Ernest, 59, 11 September 1940
Cook, William Henry, 67, 1 September 1944
Cooper, Alfred Reginald, 16, 13 November 1940
Court, Alfred James, 50, 2 October 1941
Davis, Elsie Louisa, 58, 21 October 1941
Davis, Sidney, 60, 21 October 1941
Decent, George Henry, 52, 25 October 1940
Deverson, Leonard Douglas, 38, 13 November 1940
Dewell, George William, 37, 8 October 1940

Dive, Edward Henry, 58, 17 September 1941

Dive, Frederick Stephen, 14, 17 September 1941

Dixon, Ella, 17, 23 March 1942

Doherty, Thomas, 52, 13 September 1944

Dowdell, Herbert E., 30, 12 September 1944

Durman, Jesse A., 23 May 1942 (no age given)

Dutnall, William, 66, 30 September 1940

Dyer, Mary Francis, 60, 4 October 1941

Dyer, Sydney James, 58, 12 June 1941

Edmond, Leonard William, 35, 26 September 1944

Eeley, Joseph, 54, 7 May 1941

Field, Frank, 69, 2 October 1941

Finnis, Annie Elizabeth, 65, 3 April 1942

Flynn, Margaret Francis, 3 April 1942 (no age given)

Flynn, Mary Elizabeth, 3 April 1942 (no age given)

Ford, William George, 29, 23 March 1942

Foster, Emily, 54, 4 December 1940

Fussell, Ivy Hannah, 49, 22 May 1943

Garrett, Walter, 34, 28 June 1943

Gatehouse, Henry, 71, 5 October 1942

Godsmark, Thomas, 64, 22 January 1944

Golding, William Alfred, 62, 28 June 1943

Goldup, Muriel Alice, 44, 23 September 1944

Goodbourn, Charles Percy, 47, 9 September 1940

Goodwin, Beatrice Alice, 54, 3 April 1942

Grace, Mary Edith, 58, 18 November 1939 (SS *Simon Bolivar*) She was brought
  ashore when the ship sank, and died in hospital.

Graves, Jack, 49, 23 March 1942

Green, Julie Annette, 61, 13 September 1944

Greer, John, 69, 2 October 1941

Gregory, Dorothy Emily, 50, 24 August 1943

Grey, William Henry, 75, 30 September 1940

Hare, Sheila May, 6, 1 September 1944

Hart, Agnes Flora, 73, 11 September 1944

Harvey, Robert Sydney George, 19, 11 September 1940

Hatton, John, 69, 17 September 1941

Hawkins, Minnie Gladys, 27, 23 March 1942

Hayward, Frederick William Jackson, 63, 11 September 1940

Hemmings, Valerie Ann, 9 months, 21 January 1944

Hill, George, 49, 25 October 1943

Hogben, Frederick James, 55, 23 March 1942
Hogben, Harold Sinclair, 16, 12 September 1944
Hogben, Kathleen Lucy Cassandra, 36, 12 September 1944
Holman, James Robert, 20, 26 September 1940
Horn, William Thomas Bourne, 61, 7 September 1941
Hubbard, Mabel Edith, 54, 1 September 1944
Hutchings, William, 56, 5 September 1944
Jenkins, Alfred, 67, 3 November 1943
Jenkins, Stephen, 72, 7 June 1944
Kerry, George Edgar, 49, 28 June 1943
Keyton, Albert Walter, 80, 17 November 1941
Knights, Cyril, 34, 9 May 1943
Lamkin, George Victor, 18, 8 October 1940
Langley, Alfred, 49, 13 September 1944
Leggatt, George, 62, 13 November 1940
Licence, Margaret, 72, 3 November 1943
Locke, George Clifford, 18, 10 September 1944
Lynch, Robert Magnus, 37, 23 March 1942
Lyus, Arthur Edward, 29, 25 October 1940
McDonald, William, 54, 9 September 1940
McKenzie, Donald, 53, 23 March 1942
MaGuire, Ernest Lionel, 15, 12 September 1944
Marjoram, Alice Violet, 61, 29 August 1944
Marklew, Henry, 59, 14 November 1940
Marsh, Dorothy Georgina, 13, 3 April 1942
Marsh, Emma, 71, 3 April 1942
Marsh, Florence Jane, 67, 26 September 1944
Marsh, William George, 36, 5 October 1942
May, Ethel Nellie, 21, 7 May 1941
Maycock, Mary Alice, 29, 24 August 1940
Maycock, William Charles, 31, 24 August 1940
Mead, Fred Wilshaw, 53, 10 September 1944
Mills, Ellen Kate, 39, 1 September 1944
Mills, Hilda May, 22, 12 June 1941
Mills, Yvonne Mary, 4, 1 September 1944
Mische, Frederick Charles, 45, 23 March 1942
Moore, Doris Winifred Agnes, 16, 12 December 1942
Moore, Frederick Ronald, 10 weeks, 12 June 1941
Moore, Frederick Walter, 33, 12 June 1941
Moore, Ivy Victoria, 26, 12 June 1941

Moore, Minyon Elsie, 4, 12 June 1941
Mullane, John, 64, 7 June 1944
Nicholls, Rosa, 77, 31 March 1941
Norley, William John, 52, 1 November 1941
Odell, Emma, 86, 5 October 1942
Parfitt, John Thomas, 54, 28 June 1943
Payne, Phoebe Sarah, 58, 25 October 1943
Pearson, William, 56, 23 March 1942
Perkins, Patricia May Ann, 7, 25 September 1944
Pilcher, Victor William, 43, 27 March 1942
Playford, Cyril Thomas, 20, 8 October 1940
Pratt, William Ashworth, 50, 13 November 1940
Price, John Arthur, 40, 13 September 1944
Pritchard, Louie Elizabeth, 18, 7 May 1941
Ransley, Patience, 63, 26 September 1944
Reid, Alfred George, 38, 12 August 1940
Revell, Ernest Edwin, 50, 3 April 1942
Revell, Gladys E., 16, 3 April 1942
Revell, Joyce, 13, 3 April 1942
Revell, Queenie Elizabeth, 42, 3 April 1942
Richards, Elma Elisa, 42, 28 November 1940
Richardson, Annie Pendleton, 69, 11 September 1940
Richardson, Grace Mary Luna, 42, 11 September 1940
Richardson, Joan Mary, 17, 11 September 1940
Ricketts, Lydia Ellen, 43, 1 September 1944
Robson, Elsie Agnes, 58, 3 April 1942
Sadler, Marketa, 46, 5 September 1942
Sand, H., 25 July 1940 (no age given)
Seath, Ann Stanner, 64, 3 April 1942
Shearn, Alice Ellen, 38, 25 October 1943
Shearn, Alice Georgina, 15, 25 October 1943
Shearn, Brenda Ann, 3, 25 October 1943
Shearn, Joan Ellen, 13, 25 October 1943
Sherwood, Walter Sidney, 31, 23 March 1942
Silk, Ernest Victor, 53, 25 October 1940
Simpson, Isabella Bonor, 47, 23 September 1944
Skelton, Arthur Edward George, 39, 8 November 1941
Smillie, Donald Drummond, 7, 20 March 1944
Smillie, Maureen Drummond, 5, 20 March 1944
Smith, Doris May, 3, 12 June 1941

Sneller, Percy William, 60, 23 March 1942
Spinner, Frederick Ernest George, 9, 13 September 1944
Stacey, William Edward, 66, 2 October 1941
Stanford, Frederick John Charles, 18, 8 October 1940
Staveley, Rosalyn Elizabeth, 60, 12 September 1944
Streeter, Rubina Georgina, 11, 28 June 1943
Sydenham, Ellen Miriam, 30, 25 September 1944
Talbot, Charles Joseph, 56, 12 June 1941
Talbot, Minnie Jane, 12 June 1941 (no age given)
Tallent, Ruby Winifred Louise, 19, 24 August 1940
Tapsell, Annie Mary, 68, 2 October 1941
Tapsell, James, 68, 2 October 1941
Taylor, Brian, 32, 23 March 1942
Terry, Agnes Annie, 35, 5 October 1942
Terry, Doris Irene, 15, 11 September 1940
Tozer, Cyril Joseph, 62, 8 September 1940
Trinder, Herbert Charles, 36, 18 October 1940
Trow, Sidney Cleveland, 32, 18 October 1940
Turner, Joseph Thomas, 62, 7 September 1941
Turner, Rosa, 65, 7 September 1941
Wade, Christopher, 78, 12 September 1944
Wakefield, Mabel Agnes, 59, 25 September 1944
Walker, John George, 54, 11 September 1940
Warman, Ethel Ann, 53, 3 April 1942
Warman, William Elgar, 58, 3 April 1942
Wells, Basil John, 17, 10 September 1940
Wells, Edith Agnes, 55, 6 June 1940
Wheeler, Robert, 55, 1 September 1944
White, Leonard Wilfred Pearman, 37, 7 September 1942
Whitewood, Henry John, 60, 16 June 1944
Wildey, Sarah Annie, 67, 20 September 1940
Wills, Brian John, 4, 12 June 1941
Wills, Hilda May, 50, 12 June 1941
Wills, Horace Alfred, 25, 12 June 1941
Wills, James, 53, 12 June 1941
Wills, Vera, 16, 12 June 1941
Willson, Elizabeth Ann, 50, 25 September 1944
Wilshire, Ernest Edgar, 47, 9 September 1940
Young, Arthur, 34, 9 October 1940

RURAL DISTRICT OF DOVER
Bennett, William Henry, 52, 2 June 1943
Hall, James, 28, 14 November 1940

AIR-RAID SHELTER ACCOMMODATION IN DOVER

(The figure in brackets denotes maximum capacity)

CAVES
Athol Terrace (725)
Chapel Cave (61 East Cliff) (185)
Trevanion Street (686)
Winchelsea (next to Priory Hill Tunnel) (1,400)
Barwick's Cave (next to Masonic Hall, Snargate Street) (700)
Bonded Store, known as Oil Mill Cave (Limekiln Street) (300)
Laureston Place (75)
Chapel Hill (100)
Lagoon Garage (63 High Street) (400)
Adjoining Regent Cinema (London Road) (200)

TRENCHES
Pencester Gardens (426)
Dover College Playing Field (Elms Vale Road) (426)
Union Road (653)
Connaught Park (423)
Shatterlocks (Heathfield Avenue) (260)
Barton Road (155)

BASEMENT SHELTERS
Leney's Mineral Water Factory (Russel Street) (140)
Fremlin's Brewery (St James's Lane) (314)
St Martin's Church (Church Road) (70)
14 High Street (26)
Messrs Mackeson & Co. Ltd (42 Biggin Street) (150)
Wesleyan Methodist Church (London Road) (125)
Henry Hart & Co. Ltd (11 Cannon Street) (115)
Henry Hart & Co. Ltd (11 Bench Street) (185)
Dover & District Co-Operative Drapery Dept. (16, Biggin Street) (200)
18 Cannon Street (Lately occupied by Messrs Leaonard Bros. Ltd) (144)

John Gale (15–16 London Road) (114)
The Scotch Wool Shop (54 Biggin Street) (68)
Messrs J. & F. Greenstreet (18 Bench Street) (60)
Messrs Bradley (3 New Bridge) (95)
Messrs Woolworth & Co. Ltd (62–3 Biggin Street) (300)
London Outfitters Ltd (64 Biggin Street) (100)

SANDBAG SHELTERS
At rear of No. 51 London Road (40)
Chapel Hill (beside Wesleyan Church) (60)
Biggin Street (beside Maison Dieu Hall) (65)
Tower Hamlets Chalk Pit (88)

OTHER SHELTERS
Old Forts (Archcliffe Road) (18)
Railway Arch (near Buckland Church) (142)
Rear of Co-operative Store (lower River Road) (80)
Railway Arch (Crabble Road) (43)
Castlemount Shelter (165)

SCHOOL SHELTERS
Dover Roman Catholic School (Maison Dieu Road) (100)
Barton Road (Infants) (92)
            (Girls & Infants) (117)
            (Girls) (60)
            (Boys) (78)
Belgrave Road (Infants) (103)
Christ Church (Boys) (56)
Old Laundry (Castle Concrete, Tower Hamlets) (220)
Charlton Girls School (Barton Road) (100)
River Mixed School (65)
St Bartholomew's Boys' School (Widred Road) (104)
St Martin's Schools
  Girls' Area (79)
  Double Shelter Boys' Area (40)
  Single Shelter Boys' Area (56)
  Albany Place (140)

St Mary's Girls & Infants (34)
Old Burial Ground (adjoining St Mary's) (68)
Durham Place (138)

Signed S.R.H. Loxton
Brook House
Dover
22 May 1940

AIR-RAID PRECAUTIONS POSTS

Kearsney, Court Hill House, Whitfield Hill
River, Co-op Stores, Lower Road
Crabble, Ladies Public Convenience, Athletic Ground
The Pines, Old Park Avenue (new post was constructed at Armourers Walk)
Crabble Hill, Buckland Farm Lodge
London Road, Burton's Bakery
Buckland Avenue, No. 150
Union Road, Husk's Yard
Union Road, Public Assistance Institution
No. 51 London Road, ARP Instructional Centre
Tower Hamlets, No. 2 East Street
Priory Hill, entrance to Winchelsea Tunnel
Isolation Hospital, Noah's Ark Road
Woodlands, Bridge Street (ARP Depot)
Frith Road, County Girls School
St Agnes, Castle Avenue
School of Art, Maison Dieu Road
Old Tramway Office, Ladywell
GPO, Priory Street
Christ Church Mission Hall, Folkestone Road
No. 41 Longfield Road
No. 2 Castle Hill Road
Fremlin's Brewery, St James's Lane
Burlington Mansions, Liverpool Street
No. 1a Durham Hill
Limekiln Street
Old Magazine, Archcliffe

FIRST AID POSTS

Pavilion, Crabble Athletic Ground
Victoria Hospital, High Street
Dover Public Assistance Institution, Union Road
Woodlands, Bridge Street
Technical Institute, Ladywell
Christ Church Mission Hall, Folkestone Road
Assembly Hall, St James's Street

SHIPPING IN DOVER HARBOUR 27 MAY–4 JUNE 1940

The list of ships mentioned below either left Dover Harbour or berthed there during the Dunkirk evacuation – 27 May to 4 June 1940. More than a thousand ships took part but the official records reveal that not every ship was entered in the Harbour Master's Log.

Advance	*Doria*	*Grenade*
Anthony	*Duchess of Fife*	*Greyhound*
Archangel	*Eileen Emma*	*Gulzar*
Basilisk	*Elbe*	*Harvester*
Biarritz	*Esk*	*Hebe*
Bideford	*Express*	*Icarus*
Blyskawica	*Fennella*	*Intrepid*
Bouclier	*Foremost 87*	*Isle of Guernsey*
Bourrasque	*Foudroyant*	*Isle of Thanet*
Boy Roy	*Eileen Emma*	*Jaguar*
Branlebas	*Forecast*	*Javelin*
Bullfinch	*Gallant*	*Keith*
Burza	*Gervais Rentoul*	*Kenia*
Calcutter	*Girl Gladys*	*Killarney*
Calvi	*Girl Pamela*	*King George V*
Canterbury	*Gipsy King*	*King Orry*
Canvey Queen	*Golden Eagle*	*Lady Brassey*
Clan McAlister	*Goldeve*	*Lady Duncannon*
Claude	*Golden Gift*	*Lady of Man*
Codrington	*Golden Sunbeam*	*Lochgarry*
Comfort	*Goliath*	*Locust*
Conidaw	*Gondia*	*Lord Howard*
Crested Cock	*Gossamer*	*Lord Howe*
Crested Eagle	*Gracie Fields*	*Lorina*
Cyclone	*Grafton*	*Lydd*

Lydia Suzanne
Mackay
Maid of Orleans
Malcolm
Malines
Manxmaid
Manxman
Marmion
M.A./S.B.10
Mavis
Max
Midas
Minstrel
Mona's Isle
Mona's Queen
Montrose
M.T.B. 102
Nautilus
Netsukis
Niger
Normania
Ocean Cock
Oriole
Pangbourne
Paris
Paxton
Pavon
Persia
Pharailde
Polly Johnson
Prague

Princess Elizabeth
Princess Maud
Queen of the Channel
Queen of England
Roman
Rouen
Royal Daffodil
Royal Scot
Royal Sovereign
Sabre
St Abb's
St Clear's
St David
St Hellier
St Seiriol
Saladin
Salome
Sandown
Sark
Savorgnan De Brazza
Scimitar
Scotia
Shamrock
Semois
Shetland
Shikari
Shipmates
Simla
Siroco
Sun IV
Sun VII

Sun VIII
Sun XI
The Boys
Torbay II
Triumphant
Tynwald
Ut Prosim
Vanquisher
Venetia
Venomous
Verity
Vimiera
Vimy
Vivacious
Vulcan
Waverley
Wessex
Westminster
Whitehall
Whitshed
Wild Swan
Windsor
Wolfhound
Wolsey
Worcester
Worthing
Yewdale
Yorkshire Lass
Young Mun
Zwaluw

RECORD OF DOVER CASUALTIES AND DAMAGE

(PUBLISHED OCTOBER 1944)

Property Wrecked	Dover Borough	910
	Dover Rural	36
Severely Damaged	Dover Borough	2,998
	Dover Rural	141
Slightly Damaged	Dover Borough	7,135
	Dover Rural	1,942

H.E. Bombs	Dover Borough	464
	Dover Rural	389
Incendiary Bombs	Dover Borough	1,500
	Dover Rural	2,380
Shells	Dover Borough	2,226
	Dover rural	—
Parachute Mines	Dover Borough	3
	Dover Rural	—
Flying Bombs	Dover Borough	3
	Dover Rural	21
Civilian Deaths	Dover Borough	199
	Dover Rural	5
Seriously Injured	Dover Borough	307
	Dover Rural	10
Slightly Injured	Dover Borough	420
	Dover Rural	8

ALERTS SOUNDED	3,059
Air raids	2,872
Shell warnings (introduced 13 October 1940)	187

Bibliography

The purpose of this book is to provide a chronology of reference to events which affected Dover during World War II. Further reference to the bibliography will provide the reader with a selection of books which offer any amount of statistical data of a more specialist nature.

Arnold, Major B.E. *Conflict Across the Strait*, Crabwell Publications, Dover, 1982.

Churchill, Winston S., *The Second World War* (6 volumes), Cassell & Co. Ltd, 1954.

Divine, David, *The Nine Days of Dunkirk,* Faber & Faber, London, 1959.

Foster, Reginald, *Dover Front,* Searchlight Reporter Book, Secker & Warburg, 1941.

Langabeer, Ray, *Sunny Corner, England*, A.R. Adams & Sons, Dover, 1982.

Lund, Paul and Ludlam, Harry, *Trawlers Go To War*, W. Foulsham & Co. Ltd, London, 1971.

Ramsey, Winston G., (ed.) *The Battle of Britain – Then and Now*, Plaistow Press, London, 1980.

Ramsey, Winston G. (ed.) *The Blitz – Then and Now*, vols. 1, 2, 3, Plaistow Press, London, 1987, 1988, 1990.

Rootes, Andrew, *Front Line County*, Robert Hale, London, 1980.

Scott, MBE, DSC, RNVR, Peter, Lt. Cdr., *The Battle of the Narrow Seas*, Country Life, London, 1945.

Smith, Peter C., *Hold the Narrow Sea*, Moorland Publishing Co. Ltd, 1984.

Wilmot, Chester, *The Struggle for Europe*, Collins, London, 1952.

NEWSPAPERS
Dover Express and *East Kent News* (complete issues covering World War II.)

Maps

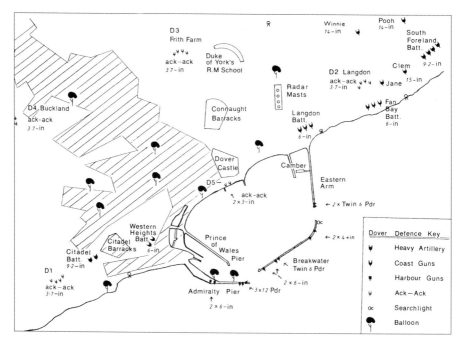

Dover's heavy artillery, coastal guns and heavy ack-ack positions were unchanged throughout World War II. The light ack-ack (40mm) units were usually mobile and regularly changed their positions

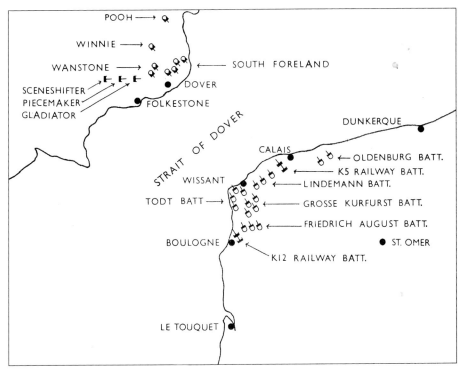

British and German heavy artillery positions

BRITISH HEAVY GUNS

POOH	1 × 14–in (St Margaret's)	Royal Marine Siege Regiment
WINNIE	1 × 14–in (St Margaret's)	Royal Marine Siege Regiment
SCENESHIFTER	1 × 13.5–in (Guston)	Royal Marine Siege Regiment
(Railway Gun)		
PIECEMAKER	1 × 13.5–in (Guston)	Royal Marine Siege Regiment
(Railway Gun)		
GLADIATOR	1× 13.5–in (Guston)	Royal Marine Siege Regiment
(Railway Gun)		
JANE	1 × 15–in (Wanstone)	540 Coast Regiment, RA
CLEM	1 × 15–in (Wanstone)	540 Coast Regiment, RA
SOUTH FORELAND	4 × 9.2–in (St Margaret's)	540 Coast Regiment, RA

GERMAN HEAVY GUNS

OLDENBURG	2 × 240mm (Calais)	244 Naval Coast Battalion
K5 (Rly Gun)	2 × 280mm (Calais)	690 Railway Battery
LINDEMANN	2 × 406mm (Sandgatte)	244 Naval Coast Battalion
GROSSE KURFURST	4 × 280mm (Framzelle)	242 Naval Coast Battalion
TODT	4 × 380mm (Cap Griz Nez)	242 Naval Coast Battalion
FRIEDRICH AUGUST	3 × 305mm (Wimille)	240 Naval Coast Battalion
K12 (Rly Gun)	2 × 280mm (Wimereux)	690 Railway Battery

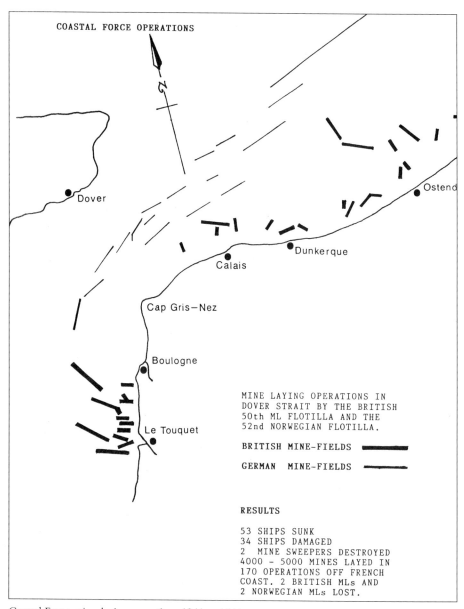

COASTAL FORCE OPERATIONS

Dover

Ostend

Dunkerque

Calais

Cap Gris—Nez

Boulogne

Le Touquet

MINE LAYING OPERATIONS IN
DOVER STRAIT BY THE BRITISH
50th ML FLOTILLA AND THE
52nd NORWEGIAN FLOTILLA.

BRITISH MINE-FIELDS

GERMAN MINE-FIELDS

RESULTS

53 SHIPS SUNK
34 SHIPS DAMAGED
2 MINE SWEEPERS DESTROYED
4000 - 5000 MINES LAYED IN
170 OPERATIONS OFF FRENCH
COAST. 2 BRITISH MLs AND
2 NORWEGIAN MLs LOST.

Coastal Force mine-laying operations 1941 to 1944

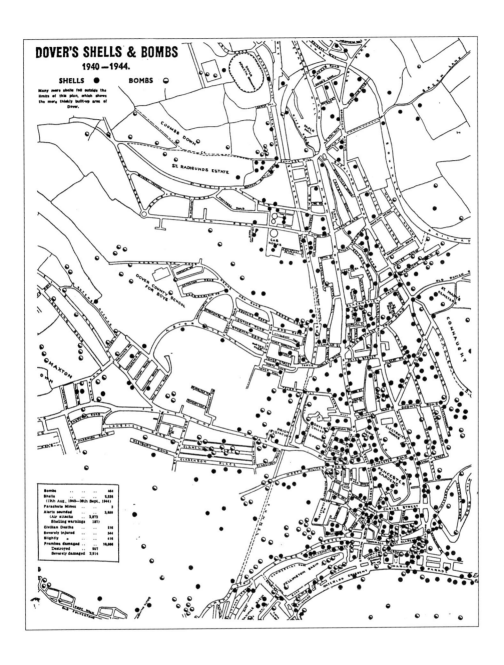

DOVER'S SHELLS & BOMBS
1940 — 1944.

SHELLS ●   BOMBS ○

Many more shells fell outside the
limits of this plan, which shows
the more thickly built-up area of
Dover.

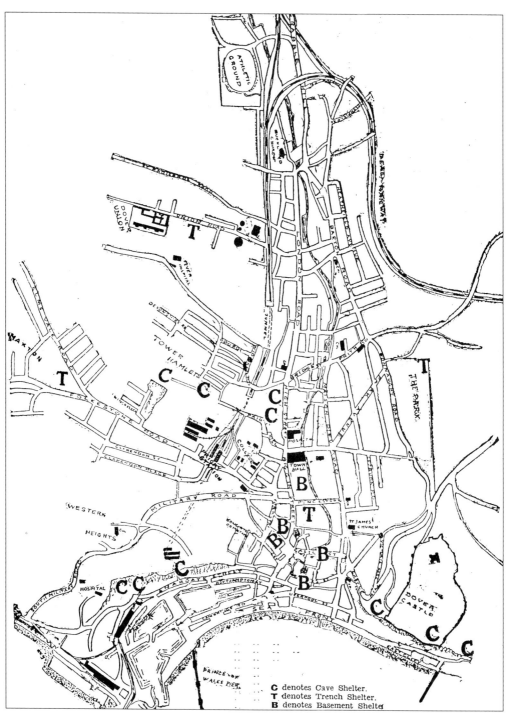

This map showing the location of caves, trenches and basement shelters was published in the
Dover Express in September 1939

Index